ISBN 0-8373-3802-6

C-3802   CAREER EXAMINATION SERIES

This is your
PASSBOOK® for...

Computer
Support
Technician

Test Preparation Study Guide

Questions & Answers

NATIONAL LEARNING CORPORATION

PASSBOOK®

NOTICE

PASSBOOK® SERIES

THE *PASSBOOK® SERIES* has been created to prepare applicants and candidates for the ultimate academic battlefield — the examination room.

At some time in our lives, each and every one of us may be required to take an examination — for validation, matriculation, admission, qualification, registration, certification, or licensure.

Based on the assumption that every applicant or candidate has met the basic formal educational standards, has taken the required number of courses, and read the necessary texts, the *PASSBOOK® SERIES* furnishes the one special preparation which may assure passing with confidence, instead of failing with insecurity. Examination questions — together with answers — are furnished as the basic vehicle for study so that the mysteries of the examination and its compounding difficulties may be eliminated or diminished by a sure method.

This book is meant to help you pass your examination provided that you qualify and are serious in your objective.

The entire field is reviewed through the huge store of content information which is succinctly presented through a provocative and challenging approach — the question-and-answer method.

A climate of success is established by furnishing the correct answers at the end of each test.

You soon learn to recognize types of questions, forms of questions, and patterns of questioning. You may even begin to anticipate expected outcomes.

You perceive that many questions are repeated or adapted so that you can gain acute insights, which may enable you to score many sure points.

You learn how to confront new questions, or types of questions, and to attack them confidently and work out the correct answers.

You note objectives and emphases, and recognize pitfalls and dangers, so that you may make positive educational adjustments.

Moreover, you are kept fully informed in relation to new concepts, methods, practices, and directions in the field.

You discover that you are actually taking the examination all the time: you are preparing for the examination by "taking" an examination, not by reading extraneous and/or supererogatory textbooks.

In short, this PASSBOOK®, used directedly, should be an important factor in helping you to pass your test.

COMPUTER SUPPORT TECHNICIAN

DUTIES

Configures, maintains, and operates personal computers; supports applications and installs them onto personal computers anc1 personal computer local area network (LAN); instructs personal computer users; performs related duties as required.

SUBJECT OF EXAMINATION

The written test will be designed to test for knowledge, skills, and/or abilities in such areas as:

1. Fundamentals of microcomputer systems;
2. Principles of networked communications;
3. Training users of computers;
4. Principles of providing user support; and
5. Understanding and interpreting written material.

HOW TO TAKE A TEST

I. YOU MUST PASS AN EXAMINATION

A. WHAT EVERY CANDIDATE SHOULD KNOW

Examination applicants often ask us for help in preparing for the written test. What can I study in advance? What kinds of questions will be asked? How will the test be given? How will the papers be graded?

As an applicant for a civil service examination, you may be wondering about some of these things. Our purpose here is to suggest effective methods of advance study and to describe civil service examinations.

Your chances for success on this examination can be increased if you know how to prepare. Those "pre-examination jitters" can be reduced if you know what to expect. You can even experience an adventure in good citizenship if you know why civil service exams are given.

B. WHY ARE CIVIL SERVICE EXAMINATIONS GIVEN?

Civil service examinations are important to you in two ways. As a citizen, you want public jobs filled by employees who know how to do their work. As a job seeker, you want a fair chance to compete for that job on an equal footing with other candidates. The best-known means of accomplishing this two-fold goal is the competitive examination.

Exams are widely publicized throughout the nation. They may be administered for jobs in federal, state, city, municipal, town or village governments or agencies.

Any citizen may apply, with some limitations, such as the age or residence of applicants. Your experience and education may be reviewed to see whether you meet the requirements for the particular examination. When these requirements exist, they are reasonable and applied consistently to all applicants. Thus, a competitive examination may cause you some uneasiness now, but it is your privilege and safeguard.

C. HOW ARE CIVIL SERVICE EXAMS DEVELOPED?

Examinations are carefully written by trained technicians who are specialists in the field known as "psychological measurement," in consultation with recognized authorities in the field of work that the test will cover. These experts recommend the subject matter areas or skills to be tested; only those knowledges or skills important to your success on the job are included. The most reliable books and source materials available are used as references. Together, the experts and technicians judge the difficulty level of the questions.

Test technicians know how to phrase questions so that the problem is clearly stated. Their ethics do not permit "trick" or "catch" questions. Questions may have been tried out on sample groups, or subjected to statistical analysis, to determine their usefulness.

Written tests are often used in combination with performance tests, ratings of training and experience, and oral interviews. All of these measures combine to form the best-known means of finding the right person for the right job.

II. HOW TO PASS THE WRITTEN TEST

A. NATURE OF THE EXAMINATION

To prepare intelligently for civil service examinations, you should know how they differ from school examinations you have taken. In school you were assigned certain definite pages to read or subjects to cover. The examination questions were quite detailed and usually emphasized memory. Civil service exams, on the other hand, try to discover your present ability to perform the duties of a position, plus your potentiality to learn these duties. In other words, a civil service exam attempts to predict how successful you will be. Questions cover such a broad area that they cannot be as minute and detailed as school exam questions.

In the public service similar kinds of work, or positions, are grouped together in one "class." This process is known as *position-classification*. All the positions in a class are paid according to the salary range for that class. One class title covers all of these positions, and they are all tested by the same examination.

B. FOUR BASIC STEPS

1) Study the announcement

How, then, can you know what subjects to study? Our best answer is: "Learn as much as possible about the class of positions for which you've applied." The exam will test the knowledge, skills and abilities needed to do the work.

Your most valuable source of information about the position you want is the official exam announcement. This announcement lists the training and experience qualifications. Check these standards and apply only if you come reasonably close to meeting them.

The brief description of the position in the examination announcement offers some clues to the subjects which will be tested. Think about the job itself. Review the duties in your mind. Can you perform them, or are there some in which you are rusty? Fill in the blank spots in your preparation.

Many jurisdictions preview the written test in the exam announcement by including a section called "Knowledge and Abilities Required," "Scope of the Examination," or some similar heading. Here you will find out specifically what fields will be tested.

2) Review your own background

Once you learn in general what the position is all about, and what you need to know to do the work, ask yourself which subjects you already know fairly well and which need improvement. You may wonder whether to concentrate on improving your strong areas or on building some background in your fields of weakness. When the announcement has specified "some knowledge" or "considerable knowledge," or has used adjectives like "beginning principles of…" or "advanced … methods," you can get a clue as to the number and difficulty of questions to be asked in any given field. More questions, and hence broader coverage, would be included for those subjects which are more important in the work. Now weigh your strengths and weaknesses against the job requirements and prepare accordingly.

3) Determine the level of the position

Another way to tell how intensively you should prepare is to understand the level of the job for which you are applying. Is it the entering level? In other words, is this the position in which beginners in a field of work are hired? Or is it an intermediate or advanced level? Sometimes this is indicated by such words as "Junior" or "Senior" in the class title. Other jurisdictions use Roman numerals to designate the level – Clerk I, Clerk II, for example. The word "Supervisor" sometimes appears in the title. If the level is not indicated by the title, check the description of duties. Will you be working under very close supervision, or will you have responsibility for independent decisions in this work?

4) Choose appropriate study materials

Now that you know the subjects to be examined and the relative amount of each subject to be covered, you can choose suitable study materials. For beginning level jobs, or even advanced ones, if you have a pronounced weakness in some aspect of your training, read a modern, standard textbook in that field. Be sure it is up to date and has general coverage. Such books are normally available at your library, and the librarian will be glad to help you locate one. For entry-level positions, questions of appropriate difficulty are chosen – neither highly advanced questions, nor those too simple. Such questions require careful thought but not advanced training.

If the position for which you are applying is technical or advanced, you will read more advanced, specialized material. If you are already familiar with the basic principles of your field, elementary textbooks would waste your time. Concentrate on advanced textbooks and technical periodicals. Think through the concepts and review difficult problems in your field.

These are all general sources. You can get more ideas on your own initiative, following these leads. For example, training manuals and publications of the government agency which employs workers in your field can be useful, particularly for technical and professional positions. A letter or visit to the government department involved may result in more specific study suggestions, and certainly will provide you with a more definite idea of the exact nature of the position you are seeking.

III. KINDS OF TESTS

Tests are used for purposes other than measuring knowledge and ability to perform specified duties. For some positions, it is equally important to test ability to make adjustments to new situations or to profit from training. In others, basic mental abilities not dependent on information are essential. Questions which test these things may not appear as pertinent to the duties of the position as those which test for knowledge and information. Yet they are often highly important parts of a fair examination. For very general questions, it is almost impossible to help you direct your study efforts. What we can do is to point out some of the more common of these general abilities needed in public service positions and describe some typical questions.

1) General information

Broad, general information has been found useful for predicting job success in some kinds of work. This is tested in a variety of ways, from vocabulary lists to questions about current events. Basic background in some field of work, such as sociology or economics, may be sampled in a group of questions. Often these are principles which have become familiar to most persons through exposure rather than through formal training. It is difficult to advise you how to study for these questions; being alert to the world around you is our best suggestion.

2) Verbal ability

An example of an ability needed in many positions is verbal or language ability. Verbal ability is, in brief, the ability to use and understand words. Vocabulary and grammar tests are typical measures of this ability. Reading comprehension or paragraph interpretation questions are common in many kinds of civil service tests. You are given a paragraph of written material and asked to find its central meaning.

3) Numerical ability

Number skills can be tested by the familiar arithmetic problem, by checking paired lists of numbers to see which are alike and which are different, or by interpreting charts and graphs. In the latter test, a graph may be printed in the test booklet which you are asked to use as the basis for answering questions.

4) Observation

A popular test for law-enforcement positions is the observation test. A picture is shown to you for several minutes, then taken away. Questions about the picture test your ability to observe both details and larger elements.

5) Following directions

In many positions in the public service, the employee must be able to carry out written instructions dependably and accurately. You may be given a chart with several columns, each column listing a variety of information. The questions require you to carry out directions involving the information given in the chart.

6) Skills and aptitudes

Performance tests effectively measure some manual skills and aptitudes. When the skill is one in which you are trained, such as typing or shorthand, you can practice. These tests are often very much like those given in business school or high school courses. For many of the other skills and aptitudes, however, no short-time preparation can be made. Skills and abilities natural to you or that you have developed throughout your lifetime are being tested.

Many of the general questions just described provide all the data needed to answer the questions and ask you to use your reasoning ability to find the answers. Your best preparation for these tests, as well as for tests of facts and ideas, is to be at your physical and mental best. You, no doubt, have your own methods of getting into an exam-taking mood and keeping "in shape." The next section lists some ideas on this subject.

IV. KINDS OF QUESTIONS

Only rarely is the "essay" question, which you answer in narrative form, used in civil service tests. Civil service tests are usually of the short-answer type. Full instructions for answering these questions will be given to you at the examination. But in case this is your first experience with short-answer questions and separate answer sheets, here is what you need to know:

1) Multiple-choice Questions

Most popular of the short-answer questions is the "multiple choice" or "best answer" question. It can be used, for example, to test for factual knowledge, ability to solve problems or judgment in meeting situations found at work.

A multiple-choice question is normally one of three types—

- It can begin with an incomplete statement followed by several possible endings. You are to find the one ending which *best* completes the statement, although some of the others may not be entirely wrong.
- It can also be a complete statement in the form of a question which is answered by choosing one of the statements listed.

- It can be in the form of a problem – again you select the best answer.

Here is an example of a multiple-choice question with a discussion which should give you some clues as to the method for choosing the right answer:

When an employee has a complaint about his assignment, the action which will *best* help him overcome his difficulty is to
   A. discuss his difficulty with his coworkers
   B. take the problem to the head of the organization
   C. take the problem to the person who gave him the assignment
   D. say nothing to anyone about his complaint

In answering this question, you should study each of the choices to find which is best. Consider choice "A" – Certainly an employee may discuss his complaint with fellow employees, but no change or improvement can result, and the complaint remains unresolved. Choice "B" is a poor choice since the head of the organization probably does not know what assignment you have been given, and taking your problem to him is known as "going over the head" of the supervisor. The supervisor, or person who made the assignment, is the person who can clarify it or correct any injustice. Choice "C" is, therefore, correct. To say nothing, as in choice "D," is unwise. Supervisors have and interest in knowing the problems employees are facing, and the employee is seeking a solution to his problem.

2) True/False Questions

The "true/false" or "right/wrong" form of question is sometimes used. Here a complete statement is given. Your job is to decide whether the statement is right or wrong.

SAMPLE: A roaming cell-phone call to a nearby city costs less than a non-roaming call to a distant city.

This statement is wrong, or false, since roaming calls are more expensive.

This is not a complete list of all possible question forms, although most of the others are variations of these common types. You will always get complete directions for answering questions. Be sure you understand *how* to mark your answers – ask questions until you do.

V. RECORDING YOUR ANSWERS

Computer terminals are used more and more today for many different kinds of exams.

For an examination with very few applicants, you may be told to record your answers in the test booklet itself. Separate answer sheets are much more common. If this separate answer sheet is to be scored by machine – and this is often the case – it is highly important that you mark your answers correctly in order to get credit.

An electronic scoring machine is often used in civil service offices because of the speed with which papers can be scored. Machine-scored answer sheets must be marked with a pencil, which will be given to you. This pencil has a high graphite content which responds to the electronic scoring machine. As a matter of fact, stray dots may register as answers, so do not let your pencil rest on the answer sheet while you are pondering the correct answer. Also, if your pencil lead breaks or is otherwise defective, ask for another.

Since the answer sheet will be dropped in a slot in the scoring machine, be careful not to bend the corners or get the paper crumpled.

The answer sheet normally has five vertical columns of numbers, with 30 numbers to a column. These numbers correspond to the question numbers in your test booklet. After each number, going across the page are four or five pairs of dotted lines. These short dotted lines have small letters or numbers above them. The first two pairs may also have a "T" or "F" above the letters. This indicates that the first two pairs only are to be used if the questions are of the true-false type. If the questions are multiple choice, disregard the "T" and "F" and pay attention only to the small letters or numbers.

Answer your questions in the manner of the sample that follows:

32. The largest city in the United States is
    A. Washington, D.C.
    B. New York City
    C. Chicago
    D. Detroit
    E. San Francisco

1) Choose the answer you think is best. (New York City is the largest, so "B" is correct.)
2) Find the row of dotted lines numbered the same as the question you are answering. (Find row number 32)
3) Find the pair of dotted lines corresponding to the answer. (Find the pair of lines under the mark "B.")
4) Make a solid black mark between the dotted lines.

VI. BEFORE THE TEST

Common sense will help you find procedures to follow to get ready for an examination. Too many of us, however, overlook these sensible measures. Indeed, nervousness and fatigue have been found to be the most serious reasons why applicants fail to do their best on civil service tests. Here is a list of reminders:

- Begin your preparation early – Don't wait until the last minute to go scurrying around for books and materials or to find out what the position is all about.
- Prepare continuously – An hour a night for a week is better than an all-night cram session. This has been definitely established. What is more, a night a week for a month will return better dividends than crowding your study into a shorter period of time.
- Locate the place of the exam – You have been sent a notice telling you when and where to report for the examination. If the location is in a different town or otherwise unfamiliar to you, it would be well to inquire the best route and learn something about the building.
- Relax the night before the test – Allow your mind to rest. Do not study at all that night. Plan some mild recreation or diversion; then go to bed early and get a good night's sleep.
- Get up early enough to make a leisurely trip to the place for the test – This way unforeseen events, traffic snarls, unfamiliar buildings, etc. will not upset you.
- Dress comfortably – A written test is not a fashion show. You will be known by number and not by name, so wear something comfortable.

6

- Leave excess paraphernalia at home – Shopping bags and odd bundles will get in your way. You need bring only the items mentioned in the official notice you received; usually everything you need is provided. Do not bring reference books to the exam. They will only confuse those last minutes and be taken away from you when in the test room.
- Arrive somewhat ahead of time – If because of transportation schedules you must get there very early, bring a newspaper or magazine to take your mind off yourself while waiting.
- Locate the examination room – When you have found the proper room, you will be directed to the seat or part of the room where you will sit. Sometimes you are given a sheet of instructions to read while you are waiting. Do not fill out any forms until you are told to do so; just read them and be prepared.
- Relax and prepare to listen to the instructions
- If you have any physical problem that may keep you from doing your best, be sure to tell the test administrator. If you are sick or in poor health, you really cannot do your best on the exam. You can come back and take the test some other time.

VII. AT THE TEST

The day of the test is here and you have the test booklet in your hand. The temptation to get going is very strong. Caution! There is more to success than knowing the right answers. You must know how to identify your papers and understand variations in the type of short-answer question used in this particular examination. Follow these suggestions for maximum results from your efforts:

1) Cooperate with the monitor
The test administrator has a duty to create a situation in which you can be as much at ease as possible. He will give instructions, tell you when to begin, check to see that you are marking your answer sheet correctly, and so on. He is not there to guard you, although he will see that your competitors do not take unfair advantage. He wants to help you do your best.

2) Listen to all instructions
Don't jump the gun! Wait until you understand all directions. In most civil service tests you get more time than you need to answer the questions. So don't be in a hurry. Read each word of instructions until you clearly understand the meaning. Study the examples, listen to all announcements and follow directions. Ask questions if you do not understand what to do.

3) Identify your papers
Civil service exams are usually identified by number only. You will be assigned a number; you must not put your name on your test papers. Be sure to copy your number correctly. Since more than one exam may be given, copy your exact examination title.

4) Plan your time
Unless you are told that a test is a "speed" or "rate of work" test, speed itself is usually not important. Time enough to answer all the questions will be provided, but this does not mean that you have all day. An overall time limit has been set. Divide the total time (in minutes) by the number of questions to determine the approximate time you have for each question.

5) Do not linger over difficult questions

If you come across a difficult question, mark it with a paper clip (useful to have along) and come back to it when you have been through the booklet. One caution if you do this – be sure to skip a number on your answer sheet as well. Check often to be sure that you have not lost your place and that you are marking in the row numbered the same as the question you are answering.

6) Read the questions

Be sure you know what the question asks! Many capable people are unsuccessful because they failed to *read* the questions correctly.

7) Answer all questions

Unless you have been instructed that a penalty will be deducted for incorrect answers, it is better to guess than to omit a question.

8) Speed tests

It is often better NOT to guess on speed tests. It has been found that on timed tests people are tempted to spend the last few seconds before time is called in marking answers at random – without even reading them – in the hope of picking up a few extra points. To discourage this practice, the instructions may warn you that your score will be "corrected" for guessing. That is, a penalty will be applied. The incorrect answers will be deducted from the correct ones, or some other penalty formula will be used.

9) Review your answers

If you finish before time is called, go back to the questions you guessed or omitted to give them further thought. Review other answers if you have time.

10) Return your test materials

If you are ready to leave before others have finished or time is called, take ALL your materials to the monitor and leave quietly. Never take any test material with you. The monitor can discover whose papers are not complete, and taking a test booklet may be grounds for disqualification.

VIII. EXAMINATION TECHNIQUES

1) Read the general instructions carefully. These are usually printed on the first page of the exam booklet. As a rule, these instructions refer to the timing of the examination; the fact that you should not start work until the signal and must stop work at a signal, etc. If there are any *special* instructions, such as a choice of questions to be answered, make sure that you note this instruction carefully.

2) When you are ready to start work on the examination, that is as soon as the signal has been given, read the instructions to each question booklet, underline any key words or phrases, such as *least, best, outline, describe* and the like. In this way you will tend to answer as requested rather than discover on reviewing your paper that you *listed without describing*, that you selected the *worst* choice rather than the *best* choice, etc.

3) If the examination is of the objective or multiple-choice type – that is, each question will also give a series of possible answers: A, B, C or D, and you are called upon to select the best answer and write the letter next to that answer on your answer paper – it is advisable to start answering each question in turn. There may be anywhere from 50 to 100 such questions in the three or four hours allotted and you can see how much time would be taken if you read through all the questions before beginning to answer any. Furthermore, if you come across a question or group of questions which you know would be difficult to answer, it would undoubtedly affect your handling of all the other questions.

4) If the examination is of the essay type and contains but a few questions, it is a moot point as to whether you should read all the questions before starting to answer any one. Of course, if you are given a choice – say five out of seven and the like – then it is essential to read all the questions so you can eliminate the two that are most difficult. If, however, you are asked to answer all the questions, there may be danger in trying to answer the easiest one first because you may find that you will spend too much time on it. The best technique is to answer the first question, then proceed to the second, etc.

5) Time your answers. Before the exam begins, write down the time it started, then add the time allowed for the examination and write down the time it must be completed, then divide the time available somewhat as follows:
    - If 3-1/2 hours are allowed, that would be 210 minutes. If you have 80 objective-type questions, that would be an average of 2-1/2 minutes per question. Allow yourself no more than 2 minutes per question, or a total of 160 minutes, which will permit about 50 minutes to review.
    - If for the time allotment of 210 minutes there are 7 essay questions to answer, that would average about 30 minutes a question. Give yourself only 25 minutes per question so that you have about 35 minutes to review.

6) The most important instruction is to *read each question* and make sure you know what is wanted. The second most important instruction is to *time yourself properly* so that you answer every question. The third most important instruction is to *answer every question*. Guess if you have to but include something for each question. Remember that you will receive no credit for a blank and will probably receive some credit if you write something in answer to an essay question. If you guess a letter – say "B" for a multiple-choice question – you may have guessed right. If you leave a blank as an answer to a multiple-choice question, the examiners may respect your feelings but it will not add a point to your score. Some exams may penalize you for wrong answers, so in such cases *only*, you may not want to guess unless you have some basis for your answer.

7) Suggestions
    a. Objective-type questions
        1. Examine the question booklet for proper sequence of pages and questions
        2. Read all instructions carefully
        3. Skip any question which seems too difficult; return to it after all other questions have been answered
        4. Apportion your time properly; do not spend too much time on any single question or group of questions

5. Note and underline key words – *all, most, fewest, least, best, worst, same, opposite,* etc.
6. Pay particular attention to negatives
7. Note unusual option, e.g., unduly long, short, complex, different or similar in content to the body of the question
8. Observe the use of "hedging" words – *probably, may, most likely,* etc.
9. Make sure that your answer is put next to the same number as the question
10. Do not second-guess unless you have good reason to believe the second answer is definitely more correct
11. Cross out original answer if you decide another answer is more accurate; do not erase until you are ready to hand your paper in
12. Answer all questions; guess unless instructed otherwise
13. Leave time for review

b. Essay questions
1. Read each question carefully
2. Determine exactly what is wanted. Underline key words or phrases.
3. Decide on outline or paragraph answer
4. Include many different points and elements unless asked to develop any one or two points or elements
5. Show impartiality by giving pros and cons unless directed to select one side only
6. Make and write down any assumptions you find necessary to answer the questions
7. Watch your English, grammar, punctuation and choice of words
8. Time your answers; don't crowd material

8) Answering the essay question

Most essay questions can be answered by framing the specific response around several key words or ideas. Here are a few such key words or ideas:

M's: manpower, materials, methods, money, management
P's: purpose, program, policy, plan, procedure, practice, problems, pitfalls, personnel, public relations
a. Six basic steps in handling problems:
1. Preliminary plan and background development
2. Collect information, data and facts
3. Analyze and interpret information, data and facts
4. Analyze and develop solutions as well as make recommendations
5. Prepare report and sell recommendations
6. Install recommendations and follow up effectiveness

b. Pitfalls to avoid
1. *Taking things for granted* – A statement of the situation does not necessarily imply that each of the elements is necessarily true; for example, a complaint may be invalid and biased so that all that can be taken for granted is that a complaint has been registered

2. *Considering only one side of a situation* – Wherever possible, indicate several alternatives and then point out the reasons you selected the best one
3. *Failing to indicate follow up* – Whenever your answer indicates action on your part, make certain that you will take proper follow-up action to see how successful your recommendations, procedures or actions turn out to be
4. *Taking too long in answering any single question* – Remember to time your answers properly

IX. AFTER THE TEST

Scoring procedures differ in detail among civil service jurisdictions although the general principles are the same. Whether the papers are hand-scored or graded by machine we have described, they are nearly always graded by number. That is, the person who marks the paper knows only the number – never the name – of the applicant. Not until all the papers have been graded will they be matched with names. If other tests, such as training and experience or oral interview ratings have been given, scores will be combined. Different parts of the examination usually have different weights. For example, the written test might count 60 percent of the final grade, and a rating of training and experience 40 percent. In many jurisdictions, veterans will have a certain number of points added to their grades.

After the final grade has been determined, the names are placed in grade order and an eligible list is established. There are various methods for resolving ties between those who get the same final grade – probably the most common is to place first the name of the person whose application was received first. Job offers are made from the eligible list in the order the names appear on it. You will be notified of your grade and your rank as soon as all these computations have been made. This will be done as rapidly as possible.

People who are found to meet the requirements in the announcement are called "eligibles." Their names are put on a list of eligible candidates. An eligible's chances of getting a job depend on how high he stands on this list and how fast agencies are filling jobs from the list.

When a job is to be filled from a list of eligibles, the agency asks for the names of people on the list of eligibles for that job. When the civil service commission receives this request, it sends to the agency the names of the three people highest on this list. Or, if the job to be filled has specialized requirements, the office sends the agency the names of the top three persons who meet these requirements from the general list.

The appointing officer makes a choice from among the three people whose names were sent to him. If the selected person accepts the appointment, the names of the others are put back on the list to be considered for future openings.

That is the rule in hiring from all kinds of eligible lists, whether they are for typist, carpenter, chemist, or something else. For every vacancy, the appointing officer has his choice of any one of the top three eligibles on the list. This explains why the person whose name is on top of the list sometimes does not get an appointment when some of the persons lower on the list do. If the appointing officer chooses the second or third eligible, the No. 1 eligible does not get a job at once, but stays on the list until he is appointed or the list is terminated.

X. HOW TO PASS THE INTERVIEW TEST

The examination for which you applied requires an oral interview test. You have already taken the written test and you are now being called for the interview test – the final part of the formal examination.

You may think that it is not possible to prepare for an interview test and that there are no procedures to follow during an interview. Our purpose is to point out some things you can do in advance that will help you and some good rules to follow and pitfalls to avoid while you are being interviewed.

What is an interview supposed to test?

The written examination is designed to test the technical knowledge and competence of the candidate; the oral is designed to evaluate intangible qualities, not readily measured otherwise, and to establish a list showing the relative fitness of each candidate – as measured against his competitors – for the position sought. Scoring is not on the basis of "right" and "wrong," but on a sliding scale of values ranging from "not passable" to "outstanding." As a matter of fact, it is possible to achieve a relatively low score without a single "incorrect" answer because of evident weakness in the qualities being measured.

Occasionally, an examination may consist entirely of an oral test – either an individual or a group oral. In such cases, information is sought concerning the technical knowledges and abilities of the candidate, since there has been no written examination for this purpose. More commonly, however, an oral test is used to supplement a written examination.

Who conducts interviews?

The composition of oral boards varies among different jurisdictions. In nearly all, a representative of the personnel department serves as chairman. One of the members of the board may be a representative of the department in which the candidate would work. In some cases, "outside experts" are used, and, frequently, a businessman or some other representative of the general public is asked to serve. Labor and management or other special groups may be represented. The aim is to secure the services of experts in the appropriate field.

However the board is composed, it is a good idea (and not at all improper or unethical) to ascertain in advance of the interview who the members are and what groups they represent. When you are introduced to them, you will have some idea of their backgrounds and interests, and at least you will not stutter and stammer over their names.

What should be done before the interview?

While knowledge about the board members is useful and takes some of the surprise element out of the interview, there is other preparation which is more substantive. It *is* possible to prepare for an oral interview – in several ways:

1) Keep a copy of your application and review it carefully before the interview

This may be the only document before the oral board, and the starting point of the interview. Know what education and experience you have listed there, and the sequence and dates of all of it. Sometimes the board will ask you to review the highlights of your experience for them; you should not have to hem and haw doing it.

2) Study the class specification and the examination announcement

Usually, the oral board has one or both of these to guide them. The qualities, characteristics or knowledges required by the position sought are stated in these documents. They offer valuable clues as to the nature of the oral interview. For example, if the job involves supervisory responsibilities, the announcement will usually indicate that knowledge of modern supervisory methods and the qualifications of the candidate as a supervisor will be tested. If so, you can expect such questions, frequently in the form of a hypothetical situation which you are expected to solve. NEVER go into an oral without knowledge of the duties and responsibilities of the job you seek.

3) Think through each qualification required

Try to visualize the kind of questions you would ask if you were a board member. How well could you answer them? Try especially to appraise your own knowledge and background in each area, *measured against the job sought*, and identify any areas in which you are weak. Be critical and realistic – do not flatter yourself.

4) Do some general reading in areas in which you feel you may be weak

For example, if the job involves supervision and your past experience has NOT, some general reading in supervisory methods and practices, particularly in the field of human relations, might be useful. Do NOT study agency procedures or detailed manuals. The oral board will be testing your understanding and capacity, not your memory.

5) Get a good night's sleep and watch your general health and mental attitude

You will want a clear head at the interview. Take care of a cold or any other minor ailment, and of course, no hangovers.

What should be done on the day of the interview?

Now comes the day of the interview itself. Give yourself plenty of time to get there. Plan to arrive somewhat ahead of the scheduled time, particularly if your appointment is in the fore part of the day. If a previous candidate fails to appear, the board might be ready for you a bit early. By early afternoon an oral board is almost invariably behind schedule if there are many candidates, and you may have to wait. Take along a book or magazine to read, or your application to review, but leave any extraneous material in the waiting room when you go in for your interview. In any event, relax and compose yourself.

The matter of dress is important. The board is forming impressions about you – from your experience, your manners, your attitude, and your appearance. Give your personal appearance careful attention. Dress your best, but not your flashiest. Choose conservative, appropriate clothing, and be sure it is immaculate. This is a business interview, and your appearance should indicate that you regard it as such. Besides, being well groomed and properly dressed will help boost your confidence.

Sooner or later, someone will call your name and escort you into the interview room. *This is it.* From here on you are on your own. It is too late for any more preparation. But remember, you asked for this opportunity to prove your fitness, and you are here because your request was granted.

What happens when you go in?

The usual sequence of events will be as follows: The clerk (who is often the board stenographer) will introduce you to the chairman of the oral board, who will introduce you to the other members of the board. Acknowledge the introductions before you sit down. Do not be surprised if you find a microphone facing you or a stenotypist sitting by. Oral interviews are usually recorded in the event of an appeal or other review.

Usually the chairman of the board will open the interview by reviewing the highlights of your education and work experience from your application – primarily for the benefit of the other members of the board, as well as to get the material into the record. Do not interrupt or comment unless there is an error or significant misinterpretation; if that is the case, do not hesitate. But do not quibble about insignificant matters. Also, he will usually ask you some question about your education, experience or your present job – partly to get you to start talking and to establish the interviewing "rapport." He may start the actual questioning, or turn it over to one of the other members. Frequently, each member undertakes the questioning on a particular area, one in which he is perhaps most competent, so you can expect each member to participate in the examination. Because time is limited, you may also expect some rather abrupt switches in the direction the questioning takes, so do not be upset by it. Normally, a board member will not pursue a single line of questioning unless he discovers a particular strength or weakness.

After each member has participated, the chairman will usually ask whether any member has any further questions, then will ask you if you have anything you wish to add. Unless you are expecting this question, it may floor you. Worse, it may start you off on an extended, extemporaneous speech. The board is not usually seeking more information. The question is principally to offer you a last opportunity to present further qualifications or to indicate that you have nothing to add. So, if you feel that a significant qualification or characteristic has been overlooked, it is proper to point it out in a sentence or so. Do not compliment the board on the thoroughness of their examination – they have been sketchy, and you know it. If you wish, merely say, "No thank you, I have nothing further to add." This is a point where you can "talk yourself out" of a good impression or fail to present an important bit of information. Remember, *you close the interview yourself.*

The chairman will then say, "That is all, Mr. _____, thank you." Do not be startled; the interview is over, and quicker than you think. Thank him, gather your belongings and take your leave. Save your sigh of relief for the other side of the door.

How to put your best foot forward
Throughout this entire process, you may feel that the board individually and collectively is trying to pierce your defenses, seek out your hidden weaknesses and embarrass and confuse you. Actually, this is not true. They are obliged to make an appraisal of your qualifications for the job you are seeking, and they want to see you in your best light. Remember, they must interview all candidates and a non-cooperative candidate may become a failure in spite of their best efforts to bring out his qualifications. Here are 15 suggestions that will help you:

1) Be natural – Keep your attitude confident, not cocky
If you are not confident that you can do the job, do not expect the board to be. Do not apologize for your weaknesses, try to bring out your strong points. The board is interested in a positive, not negative, presentation. Cockiness will antagonize any board member and make him wonder if you are covering up a weakness by a false show of strength.

2) Get comfortable, but don't lounge or sprawl
Sit erectly but not stiffly. A careless posture may lead the board to conclude that you are careless in other things, or at least that you are not impressed by the importance of the occasion. Either conclusion is natural, even if incorrect. Do not fuss with your clothing, a pencil or an ashtray. Your hands may occasionally be useful to emphasize a point; do not let them become a point of distraction.

3) Do not wisecrack or make small talk
This is a serious situation, and your attitude should show that you consider it as such. Further, the time of the board is limited – they do not want to waste it, and neither should you.

14) Do not be afraid to admit an error in judgment if you are shown to be wrong

The board knows that you are forced to reply without any opportunity for careful consideration. Your answer may be demonstrably wrong. If so, admit it and get on with the interview.

15) Do not dwell at length on your present job

The opening question may relate to your present assignment. Answer the question but do not go into an extended discussion. You are being examined for a *new* job, not your present one. As a matter of fact, try to phrase ALL your answers in terms of the job for which you are being examined.

Basis of Rating

Probably you will forget most of these "do's" and "don'ts" when you walk into the oral interview room. Even remembering them all will not ensure you a passing grade. Perhaps you did not have the qualifications in the first place. But remembering them will help you to put your best foot forward, without treading on the toes of the board members.

Rumor and popular opinion to the contrary notwithstanding, an oral board wants you to make the best appearance possible. They know you are under pressure – but they also want to see how you respond to it as a guide to what your reaction would be under the pressures of the job you seek. They will be influenced by the degree of poise you display, the personal traits you show and the manner in which you respond.

ABOUT THIS BOOK

This book contains tests, divided into Examination Sections. Go through each test, answering every question in the margin. We have also attached a sample answer sheet at the back of the book that can be removed and used. At the end of each test look at the answer key and check your answers. On the ones you got wrong, look at the right answer choice and learn. Do not fill in the answers first. Do not memorize the questions and answers, but understand the answer and principles involved. On your test, the questions will likely be different from the samples. Questions are changed and new ones added. If you understand these past questions you should have success with any changes that arise. Tests may consist of several types of questions. We have additional books on each subject should more study be advisable or necessary for you. Finally, the more you study, the better prepared you will be. This book is intended to be the last thing you study before you walk into the examination room. Prior study of relevant texts is also recommended. NLC publishes some of these in our Fundamental Series. Knowledge and good sense are important factors in passing your exam. Good luck also helps. So now study this Passbook, absorb the material contained within and take that knowledge into the examination. Then do your best to pass that exam.

———

EXAMINATION SECTION

EXAMINATION SECTION

TEST 1

DIRECTIONS: Each question or incomplete statement is followed by several suggested answers or completions. Select the one that BEST answers the question or completes the statement. *PRINT THE LETTER OF THE CORRECT ANSWER IN THE SPACE AT THE RIGHT.*

1. Which one of the following is considered a word processor program?
   A. Microsoft Word
   B. Microsoft Works
   C. Notepad
   D. Both A and B

   1.____

2. Default headings are available under the _____ tab.
   A. Insert
   B. Home
   C. File
   D. View

   2.____

3. _____ deals with font, alignment and margins.
   A. Selecting
   B. Formatting
   C. Composing
   D. Pattern

   3.____

4. Which one of the following is the BEST format for storing bit-mapped images on the computer?
   A. .JPG
   B. .PNG
   C. .GIF
   D. .TIF

   4.____

5. A header specifies an area in the _____ margins of every page.
   A. top
   B. bottom
   C. left
   D. right

   5.____

6. When an Excel file is inserted into a Word document, the data is
   A. hyperlinked
   B. placed in a Word table
   C. linked
   D. embedded

   6.____

7. A workbook in Excel is defined as a file that
   A. holds text and data
   B. can be modified
   C. can contain many sheets, chart sheets and worksheets
   D. both A and B

   7.____

8. Excel can produce chart types that include
   A. only line graphs
   B. bar charts, line graphs and pie charts
   C. line graphs and pie charts only
   D. bar charts and line graphs only

   8.____

9. In PowerPoint, the motion path is a
   A. method of moving items on the slide
   B. method of advancing slides
   C. indentation
   D. type of animation

   9.____

10. _____ replaces similar words in a document.

    A. Word Count   B. Thesaurus   C. Wrap Text   D. Format Printer

10.____

11. The MOST simple description of the Internet is
    A. a single network
    B. a huge collection of different networks
    C. collection of LAN
    D. single WAN

11.____

12. How can a computer be connected to the Internet?
    A. Through internet service provider   B. Internet society
    C. Internet architecture board   D. Local area network

12.____

13. A software program that is used to view web pages is known as a(n)
    A. Internet browser   B. interpreter
    C. operating system   D. website

13.____

14. Which of the following is used to search anything on the Internet?
    A. Search engines   B. Routers
    C. Social networks   D. Websites

14.____

15. When a website is accessed, its main page is called
    A. home page   B. back end page
    C. dead end   D. both A and B

15.____

16. Google Docs provides _____, which is a salient feature of Google Doc.
    A. image processing   B. synchronization
    C. both A and B   D. installation

16.____

17. Documents in Google Drive could be accessed from
    A. only a personal computer
    B. any computer that has Internet connection
    C. only that computer that has Google drive on hard disk
    D. both B and C

17.____

18. In an email address, for example test@gmail.com, "gmail" is known as
    A. domain
    B. host computer in commercial domain
    C. internet service provider
    D. URL

18.____

19. Which of the following is NOT a well-known domain?
    A. .edu   B. .com   C. .org   D. .army

19.____

20. Cyberspace is an alternative name used for
    A. Internet   B. information   C. virtual space   D. data space

20.____

21. Which one of the following is NOT an Internet browser?
    A. Chrome   B. Firefly   C. Firefox   D. Safari

21.____

22. Which of the following is NOT a past or current search engine?　　22.____
　　　A. Apple　　　　　B. Lycos　　　　C. Bing　　　　D. Google

23. Document scanning could be done through　　23.____
　　　A. OCR　　　　　　　　　　　B. OMR
　　　C. both A and B　　　　　　　D. dot-matrix printer

24. _____ are used to fill out empty fields in scanned images of data.　　24.____
　　　A. Computerized optical scanners　　B. OCR software
　　　C. Scanners　　　　　　　　　　　　D. Laser printers

25. All of the following are examples of hardware for standard home use EXCEPT　　25.____
　　　A. flash drives　　　　　　　　B. inkjet printers
　　　C. servers　　　　　　　　　　D. laser printers

KEY (CORRECT ANSWERS)

1.	D		11.	B
2.	B		12.	A
3.	B		13.	A
4.	D		14.	A
5.	A		15.	A
6.	B		16.	B
7.	C		17.	B
8.	B		18.	B
9.	A		19.	D
10.	B		20.	A

21.	B
22.	A
23.	C
24.	A
25.	C

TEST 2

DIRECTIONS: Each question or incomplete statement is followed by several suggested answers or completions. Select the one that BEST answers the question or completes the statement. *PRINT THE LETTER OF THE CORRECT ANSWER IN THE SPACE AT THE RIGHT.*

1. In a spreadsheet, data is organized in the form of
   A. lines and spaces
   B. rows and columns
   C. layers and planes
   D. height and width

   1.____

2. Which one of the following menus is used to protect a worksheet?
   A. Edit   B. Format   C. Data   D. Tools

   2.____

3. _____ corrects spelling mistakes automatically.
   A. Word wrap
   B. AutoCorrect
   C. Spell checker
   D. Thesaurus

   3.____

4. Which function is used to automatically align text?
   A. Justification
   B. Indentation
   C. Both A and B
   D. None of the above

   4.____

5. Orientation is the property of the _____ function.
   A. Print
   B. Design
   C. Image
   D. Both A and B

   5.____

6. Special effects that are used to present slides in a presentation are known as
   A. effects
   B. custom animation
   C. transition
   D. present animation

   6.____

7. Page setup and print functions can typically be found in the ____ menu.
   A. tools   B. format   C. file   D. edit

   7.____

8. Which one of the following is considered removable storage media?
   A. Scanner
   B. Flash drive
   C. External hard drive
   D. Both B and C

   8.____

9. Which component of the computer is called the brain of the computer?
   A. ALU   B. Memory   C. Control Unit   D. CPU

   9.____

10. .txt is a file that is named for _____ files.
    A. Notepad   B. Word   C. Paint   D. Excel

    10.____

11. Software programs that are automatically downloaded and work within a browser are known as
    A. plug-in   B. utilities   C. widgets   D. add-on

    11.____

12. _____ is a computer that requests data from other computers on the Internet.   12.____
    A. Client   B. Server
    C. Super computer   D. Personal computer

13. A wizard is considered as a _____ file with prompt display.   13.____
    A. system   B. program   C. help   D. application

14. E-mails from unknown senders go into the _____ folder.   14.____
    A. Spam   B. Trash   C. Drafts   D. Inbox

15. LAN is an abbreviation for _____ area network.   15.____
    A. line   B. local   C. large   D. limited

16. Which of the following is NOT an extension for an image file?   16.____
    A. .bmp   B. .jpg   C. .png   D. .xls

17. In the e-mail address *test@gmail.com*, "test" is the _____ name.   17.____
    A. domain   B. user   C. server   D. ISP

18. To e-mail multiple recipients while hiding the recipients from view, use the ___ function.   18.____
    A. BCC   B. CC   C. send   D. hide

19. The system that translates an IP address into a simple form that is easy to   19.____
    remember is
    A. domain name system   B. domain
    C. domain numbering system   D. server domain

20. Which one of the following is the CORRECT method to send a file through   20.____
    e-mail?
    A. CC   B. Attachment
    C. Embed through HTML   D. Both A and B

21. Inkjet printers are categorized as a(n) _____ printer.   21.____
    A. character   B. ink   C. line   D. band

22. Which one of the following is a storage medium that has a shape of a   22.____
    circular plate?
    A. Disk   B. CPU   C. ALU   D. Printer

23. Ctrl+P activates the _____ function.   23.____
    A. reboot   B. save   C. print   D. paint

24. The file extension .exe represents an _____ file.   24.____
    A. examination   B. extra   C. executable   D. extension

25. Which of the following is NOT considered an input device? 25.____
    A. OCR   B. Optical scanner
    C. Printer   D. Keyboard

KEY (CORRECT ANSWERS)

1.	B		11.	B
2.	D		12.	A
3.	B		13.	C
4.	A		14.	A
5.	A		15.	B
6.	C		16.	D
7.	C		17.	B
8.	D		18.	A
9.	D		19.	A
10.	A		20.	B

21.	C
22.	A
23.	C
24.	C
25.	C

TEST 3

DIRECTIONS: Each question or incomplete statement is followed by several suggested answers or completions. Select the one that BEST answers the question or completes the statement. *PRINT THE LETTER OF THE CORRECT ANSWER IN THE SPACE AT THE RIGHT.*

1. Excel is a _____ program.
   A. graphics
   B. word processor
   C. spreadsheet
   D. typewriter

   1.____

2. Basically, a word processor program like Microsoft Word is a replacement for
   A. manual work
   B. typewriters
   C. both A and B
   D. graphical programs

   2.____

3. Which one of the following could be added as a sound effect to a PowerPoint presentation?
   A. .wav files and.mid files
   B. .wav files and .gif files
   C. .wave files and .jpg files
   D. .jpg files and.gif files

   3.____

4. Google Drive is an example of _____ software.
   A. system
   B. application
   C. database
   D. firmware

   4.____

5. PDF stands for _____ document format.
   A. portable
   B. picture
   C. plain
   D. private

   5.____

6. Which one of the following is an example of internal memory of a computer?
   A. Disks
   B. Pen drive
   C. RAM
   D. CDs

   6.____

7. A keyboard is an example of a(n) _____ device.
   A. input
   B. output
   C. word processor
   D. printing

   7.____

8. Clip art is a collection of _____ that can be inserted into a document.
   A. text files
   B. image files
   C. templates
   D. audio files

   8.____

9. _____ is a distinctive part of memory which holds the contents temporarily during cut or copy functions.
   A. Clipboard
   B. Macro
   C. Template
   D. Clip art

   9.____

10. _____ is a process to store files on a computer from the Internet.
    A. Uploading
    B. Downloading
    C. Pulling
    D. Transferring

    10.____

11. "Cut and paste" refers to
    A. deleting and moving text
    B. restoring and updating software
    C. cleaning images
    D. replacing images

    11.____

12. Which one of the following is a compressed format for images?   12._____
    A. GIF   B. JPGE   C. PNG   D. JPG

13. A computer stores information and data inside the   13._____
    A. hard drive   B. CPU   C. CD   D. monitor

14. WWW is an abbreviation of   14._____
    A. world wide web   B. wide world web
    C. web worldwide   D. world wide website

15. A _____ computer holds more than one processor.   15._____
    A. multithread   B. multi-unit
    C. multiprocessor   D. multiprogramming

16. Landscape and portrait are properties of   16._____
    A. page layout   B. design   C. formatting   D. text

17. _____ includes the company's name, address, phone number and e-mail   17._____
address.
    A. Letterhead   B. Template   C. Visiting Card   D. Brochure

18. _____ Server provides database services for other computers.   18._____
    A. Application   B. Web   C. Database   D. FTP

19. Which one of the following is responsible for storing movies, images and   19._____
pictures?
    A. File server   B. Web server
    C. Database server   D. Application server

20. GUI stands for graphical   20._____
    A. user interface   B. unified instrument
    C. unified interface   D. user instrument

21. Scanner is an example of a(n) _____ device.   21._____
    A. output   B. input   C. printing   D. both A and B

22. Which one of the following is NOT an example of computer hardware?   22._____
    A. Printer   B. Scanner   C. Mouse   D. Antivirus

23. Which one of the following provides the BEST quality reproduction of   23._____
graphics?
    A. Laser printer   B. Inkjet printer
    C. Dot-matrix printer   D. Plotter

24. If an e-mail sender is unknown, then do not download the _____ because   24._____
it might contain a virus.
    A. attachment   B. email
    C. spam   D. both A and B

25. The BEST way to send identical emails to more than one person is to   25.____
     A. use the CC option   B. add email ID to address
     C. forward   D. both A and B

_____

KEY (CORRECT ANSWERS)

1.	C		11.	A
2.	B		12.	A
3.	A		13.	A
4.	B		14.	A
5.	A		15.	C
6.	C		16.	A
7.	A		17.	A
8.	B		18.	C
9.	A		19.	A
10.	B		20.	A

21.	B
22.	D
23.	D
24.	A
25.	A

_____

TEST 4

DIRECTIONS: Each question or incomplete statement is followed by several suggested answers or completions. Select the one that BEST answers the question or completes the statement. *PRINT THE LETTER OF THE CORRECT ANSWER IN THE SPACE AT THE RIGHT.*

1. A keyboard shortcut for saving files is   1.____
    A. Alt+S   B. Ctrl+S   C. Ctrl+SV   D. S+Enter

2. Which of the following is NOT a term relevant to Excel?   2.____
    A. slide   B. cell
    C. formula   D. column

3. A _____ background is a grainy and non-smooth surface.   3.____
    A. texture   B. gradient   C. solid   D. pattern

4. Word wrap forces all text to fit within the defined   4.____
    A. margin   B. indent   C. block   D. box

5. In Microsoft Word, overview of the prepared document could be better seen through   5.____
    A. Preview   B. Print Preview
    C. Review   D. both A and B

6. The amount of vertical space between text line in a document is known as   6.____
    A. double space   B. line spacing
    C. single space   D. vertical spacing

7. Which one of the following devices is required for Internet connection?   7.____
    A. Joy stick   B. Modem   C. NIC card   D. Optical drive

8. IBM is a short form used for   8.____
    A. Internal Business Management
    B. International Business Management
    C. Internal Business Machines
    D. International Business Machines

9. Which one of the following is static and non-volatile memory?   9.____
    A. RAM   B. ROM   C. BIOS   D. Cache

10. One disadvantage of Google Docs is   10.____
    A. less storage   B. compatibility
    C. needs connectivity to Internet   D. synchronization

11. WAN is an abbreviation of _____ area network.   11.____
    A. wide   B. wired   C. whole   D. while

12. Bibliography can be created through the _____ tab.   12.____
    A. References   B. Design   C. Review   D. Insert

13. The _____ is MOST likely shared in a computer network.   13.____
    A. keyboard   B. speaker   C. printer   D. scanner

14. A normal computer is not able to boot if it does not have a(n)   14.____
    A. operating system   B. complier
    C. loader   D. assembler

15. _____ is another name for junk e-mails.   15.____
    A. Spam   B. Spoof   C. Spool   D. Sniffer scripts

16. A table of contents can be created automatically by using an option in   16.____
    A. Page Layout   B. Insert   C. References   D. View

17. ALU stands for   17.____
    A. arithmetic logic unit   B. array logic unit
    C. application logic unit   D. both A and B

18. Orientation is concerned with the _____ set-up of the page.   18.____
    A. horizontal   B. vertical   C. both A and B D. spacing

19. _____ is a form of written communication within the same company which   19.____
    comprises guide words as heading.
    A. Memorandum   B. Letterhead
    C. Template   D. None of the above

20. Which one of the following is NOT a web browser?   20.____
    A. Chrome   B. Opera   C. Firefox   D. Drupal

21. .net domain is specifically used for   21.____
    A. international organization
    B. internet infrastructure and service providers
    C. educational institutes
    D. commercial business

22. A modem is not required when the Internet is connected through   22.____
    A. Wi-Fi   B. LAN
    C. dial-up phone   D. cable

23. Mail Merge uses _____ to create separate copies of a document for   23.____
    multiple people in Microsoft Word.
    A. primary document   B. data document
    C. both A and B   D. web page

24. Linus is an example of   24.____
    A. operating system   B. malware
    C. firmware   D. application program

25. Which one of the following is a CORRECT format for a website address?　　　　25.____
    A. www@com　　　　　　　　　　B. www.test.com
    C. www.test25A@com　　　　　　　D. www#TeST.com

_____

KEY (CORRECT ANSWERS)

1.	B	11.	A
2.	A	12.	A
3.	B	13.	C
4.	A	14.	A
5.	B	15.	A
6.	B	16.	C
7.	B	17.	A
8.	D	18.	C
9.	B	19.	A
10.	C	20.	D

21.	B
22.	A
23.	C
24.	A
25.	B

_____

EXAMINATION SECTION

TEST 1

DIRECTIONS: Each question or incomplete statement is followed by several suggested answers or completions. Select the one that BEST answers the question or completes the statement. *PRINT THE LETTER OF THE CORRECT ANSWER IN THE SPACE AT THE RIGHT.*

1. Physical components of computers are known as
   A. software   B. hardware   C. firmware   D. human ware

   1.____

2. A touchscreen is considered a(n) _____ device.
   A. input   B. output   C. display   D. both A and B

   2.____

3. Keyboards and microphones are examples of computer
   A. peripherals   B. software   C. add-ons   D. uploads

   3.____

4. Unauthorized access to a computer is prevented through the use of
   A. passwords   B. user logins
   C. access control software   D. computer keys

   4.____

5. In order to establish an Internet connection, a modem is always connected to a
   A. keyboard   B. monitor
   C. telephone line   D. printer

   5.____

6. _____ does NOT hold data permanently.
   A. RAM   B. ROM   C. Hard drive   D. Flash drive

   6.____

7. Identification of a user who comes back to the same website is done through the use of
   A. scripts   B. plug-in   C. cookies   D. both A and B

   7.____

8. File _____ is the process of moving a file from one computer to another computer across the network.
   A. encryption   B. transfer   C. copying   D. updating

   8.____

9. _____ is a type of software that controls specific hardware.
   A. Driver   B. Browser   C. Plug-in   D. Control panel

   9.____

10. _____ is a downloadable program that is used for Internet surfing.
    A. Messenger   B. Firefox
    C. Windows Explorer   D. Internet

    10.____

11. In Microsoft Word, _____ is NOT a font style.
    A. Bold   B. Regular   C. Superscript   D. Italic

    11.____

12. Which of the following is NOT associated with page margins in a Word document?   12.____
    A. Top   B. Center   C. Left   D. Right

13. Microsoft Office is a type of _____ software.   13.____
    A. application   B. system   C. Internet   D. website

14. A function that is inside another function is known as a(n) _____ function.   14.____
    A. round   B. nested   C. sum   D. average

15. To write a formula in Microsoft Excel, a user would start by typing   15.____
    A. %   B. =   C. #   D. @

16. The individual boxes used for data entry in an Excel file are known as   16.____
    A. cells   B. data points
    C. formulas   D. squares

17. In PowerPoint, _____ do NOT show with the slide layout.   17.____
    A. titles   B. animations   C. lists   D. charts

18. _____ is a basic option when looking for colorful images or graphics to publish   18.____
in a PowerPoint presentation.
    A. Clip art   B. Online search
    C. MS Paint   D. Drawing

19. In a web browser, the addresses of Internet pages are known as   19.____
    A. web pages   B. URLs   C. scripts   D. plug-in

20. A company that provides Internet services is called a(n)   20.____
    A. ISP   B. IBM   C. LAN   D. Both A and B

21. _____ is the process of copying a file from personal computer to a remote   21.____
computer.
    A. Downloading   B. Uploading
    C. Updating   D. Modification

22. _____ is a text that opens another page when clicked.   22.____
    A. Link   B. Hyperlink
    C. Both A and B   D. Web page

23. Dots per inch is the measure of printing   23.____
    A. quality   B. type   C. time   D. layout

24. _____ is the collection of computers connected with each other.   24.____
    A. Group   B. Team   C. Network   D. Meeting

25. Which one of the following is considered a high-end printer?   25.____
    A. Dot matrix printer   B. Inkjet printer
    C. Laser   D. Thermal

KEY (CORRECT ANSWERS)

1.	B		11.	C
2.	D		12.	B
3.	A		13.	A
4.	A		14.	B
5.	C		15.	B
6.	A		16.	A
7.	C		17.	B
8.	B		18.	A
9.	A		19.	B
10.	B		20.	A

21. B
22. C
23. A
24. C
25. C

TEST 2

DIRECTIONS: Each question or incomplete statement is followed by several suggested answers or completions. Select the one that BEST answers the question or completes the statement. *PRINT THE LETTER OF THE CORRECT ANSWER IN THE SPACE AT THE RIGHT.*

1. Which one of the following is a storage device?
   A. Printer   B. Hard drive
   C. Scanner   D. Motherboard   1._____

2. DVD is an example of a(n) _____ disk.
   A. hard   B. optical   C. magnetic   D. floppy   2._____

3. _____ computers provide resources to other computers across the network.
   A. Server   B. Client   C. Framework   D. Digital   3._____

4. Random access memory is considered _____ computer memory.
   A. non-volatile   B. volatile   C. cache   D. permanent   4._____

5. Which one of the following is NOT an operating system?
   A. Windows   B. IOS   C. Android   D. MS Office   5._____

6. A(n) _____ is a person who gets illegal access to a computer system and steals information.
   A. administrator   B. computer operator
   C. hacker   D. programmer   6._____

7. Which one of the following is NOT application software?
   A. MS Word   B. Media player
   C. Linux   D. MS Power Point   7._____

8. Which one of the following represents a domain name?
   A. .com   B. www   C. URL   D. HTTP   8._____

9. _____ is NOT an example of an Internet browser.
   A. Opera   B. Google
   C. Mozilla   D. Internet Explorer   9._____

10. Which one of the following is NOT a search engine?
    A. Altavista   B. Bing
    C. Yahoo   D. Facebook   10._____

11. E-mail is an abbreviation of
    A. electronic mail   B. easy mail
    C. electric email   D. both A and B   11._____

12. A(n) _____ is a person who takes care of websites for large companies.   12.____
  A. administrator   B. webmaster
  C. programmer   D. hacker

13. _____ connect web pages with each other.   13.____
  A. Connecters   B. Links   C. Hyperlinks   D. Browsers

14. _____ is a program that is harmful for computers.   14.____
  A. Spam   B. Virus
  C. Operating system   D. Plug-in

15. CC is an abbreviation of _____ in emails.   15.____
  A. core copy   B. copycat
  C. carbon copy   D. copy copy

16. Software most commonly used for basic personal computing is   16.____
  A. Excel   B. SPSS   C. Illustrator   D. Dreamweaver

17. _____ is an option to send the same letter to different persons.   17.____
  A. Template   B. Macros   C. Mail Merge   D. Layout

18. Which one of the following is a file extension for MS Word?   18.____
  A. .doc   B. .txt   C. .bmp   D. .pdf

19. _____ displays the number of words in a document.   19.____
  A. Character Count   B. Word Count   C. Word Wrap   D. Thesaurus

20. In an Excel sheet, an active cell is specified with   20.____
  A. dotted border   B. dark wide border
  C. italic text   D. a dotted border

21. A(n) _____ is a file that contains rows and columns.   21.____
  A. database   B. spreadsheet
  C. word   D. drawing

22. _____ are objects on the slides that hold text in a PowerPoint presentation.   22.____
  A. Placeholders   B. Text holders
  C. Auto layouts   D. Object holders

23. Which one of the following brings up the first slide in a PowerPoint presentation? 23.____
  A. Ctrl+End   B. Ctrl+Home
  C. Page up   D. Next slide button

24. Which one of the following sends printing commands to a printer?   24.____
  A. F5   B. Ctrl+P   C. Ctrl+S   D. F12

25. Scanners are used to capture _____ copy of documents.   25.____
  A. soft   B. hard   C. single   D. first

KEY (CORRECT ANSWERS)

1.	B		11.	A
2.	B		12.	B
3.	A		13.	C
4.	B		14.	B
5.	D		15.	C
6.	C		16.	A
7.	C		17.	C
8.	A		18.	A
9.	B		19.	B
10.	D		20.	B

21.	B
22.	A
23.	B
24.	B
25.	B

TEST 3

DIRECTIONS: Each question or incomplete statement is followed by several suggested answers or completions. Select the one that BEST answers the question or completes the statement. *PRINT THE LETTER OF THE CORRECT ANSWER IN THE SPACE AT THE RIGHT.*

1. Which one of the following is the MOST appropriate operation to move a text block in MS Word?
   A. Cut
   C. Cut and Paste
   B. Save As
   D. Copy and Paste

   1.____

2. The Navigation pane opens under the _____ tab.
   A. View
   B. Review
   C. Page Layout
   D. Mailings

   2.____

3. Ctrl+B makes selected test
   A. italic
   B. bold
   C. bigger
   D. uppercase

   3.____

4. _____ is NOT an acceptable formula in Excel.
   A. 10+50
   B. =10+50
   C. =B7+B8
   D. =B7*B8

   4.____

5. A worksheet usually contains _____ columns.
   A. 128
   B. 256
   C. 512
   D. 320

   5.____

6. _____ is the process of getting data from the cell that is located in different worksheets.
   A. Accessing
   B. Referencing
   C. Updating
   D. Functioning

   6.____

7. The shortcut _____ selects all PowerPoint slides at once.
   A. Ctrl+Home
   B. Ctrl+A
   C. Alt+Home
   D. Shift+A

   7.____

8. By pressing Ctrl+V in a Word document, the user
   A. pastes text
   C. adds a video box
   B. cuts and pastes text
   D. deletes a page

   8.____

9. Transitions are applicable only on
   A. Excel worksheets
   C. image files
   B. PowerPoint slides
   D. Word document

   9.____

10. In MS Word, the _____ tab has options for margin, orientation and spacing.
    A. Design
    B. Review
    C. Page Layout
    D. Insert

    10.____

11. Which one of the following is graphic software?
    A. MS Office
    C. Firefox
    B. Adobe Photoshop
    D. Notepad

    11.____

12. Which one of the following is a social networking website?
    A. Facebook
    B. Yahoo
    C. Google
    D. ASK

    12.____

13. A computer monitor is referred to as a(n) _____ device.   13.____
    A. output   B. input   C. sound   D. printing

14. _____ memory is another name for the main memory of the computer.   14.____
    A. Primary   B. Direct   C. Simple   D. Quick

15. An operating system is _____ software.   15.____
    A. application   B. system   C. editing   D. both A and C

16. Which one of the following pieces of equipment is necessary for video calls?   16.____
    A. Webcam   B. Mouse   C. Scanner   D. Printer

17. _____ is a primary input device that is used to enter text and numbers.   17.____
    A. Mouse   B. Keyboard   C. Joystick   D. Microphone

18. Of the following, which is NOT an example of a web browser?   18.____
    A. Firefox   B. Opera   C. Chrome   D. Google Talk

19. A _____ is a collection of many web pages that are related to each other.   19.____
    A. web browser   B. website
    C. search engine   D. Firefox

20. Which one of the following is considered a personal journal used for posts?   20.____
    A. Blog   B. E-mail   C. Chat   D. Messengers

21. Windows _____ provides security against external threats.   21.____
    A. antivirus   B. spyware   C. firmware   D. firewall

22. Desktop and laptop computers are different from each other in terms of _____ and cost.   22.____
    A. operating system   B. functions
    C. physical structure   D. application software

23. _____ is a process of stealing confidential information without permission of the user.   23.____
    A. Forwarding   B. Hacking   C. Searching   D. Complaining

24. RAM is located in the _____ board.   24.____
    A. extension   B. external   C. mother   D. chip

25. All files on the computer are stored in   25.____
    A. hard drive   B. RAM
    C. cache   D. associative memory

KEY (CORRECT ANSWERS)

1.	C		11.	B
2.	A		12.	A
3.	B		13.	A
4.	A		14.	A
5.	B		15.	B
6.	B		16.	A
7.	B		17.	B
8.	A		18.	D
9.	B		19.	B
10.	C		20.	A

21.	D
22.	C
23.	B
24.	C
25.	A

TEST 4

DIRECTIONS: Each question or incomplete statement is followed by several suggested answers or completions. Select the one that BEST answers the question or completes the statement. *PRINT THE LETTER OF THE CORRECT ANSWER IN THE SPACE AT THE RIGHT.*

1. Which one of the following functions are performed by RAM?   1.____
   A. Read and Write   B. Read
   C. Write   D. Update

2. _____ is an example of secondary storage.   2.____
   A. Diode   B. Hard disk   C. RAM   D. ROM

3. USB is a type of _____ storage.   3.____
   A. primary   B. secondary   C. tertiary   D. temporary

4. MPG file extension is used for _____ files.   4.____
   A. video   B. audio   C. image   D. flash

5. .exe is an extension for _____ files.   5.____
   A. saved   B. executable   C. system   D. software

6. Which one of the following is NOT a type of printer?   6.____
   A. Inkjet   B. Dot matrix   C. Laser   D. CRT

7. _____ sends digital data across a phone line.   7.____
   A. Flash   B. Modem   C. NIC card   D. Keyboard

8. _____ is a wireless technology used to transfer data among devices over   8.____
   short distances.
   A. USB   B. Modem   C. Wi-Fi   D. Bluetooth

9. A user is listening to a song on his computer's music player. He is most likely   9.____
   listening to a(n) _____ file.
   A. .exe   B. .mus   C. .wav   D. .mp3

10. PNG is an extension used for _____ files.   10.____
    A. audio   B. video   C. text   D. image

11. Cache memory is located in the   11.____
    A. monitor   B. CPU   C. DVD   D. hard drive

12. Computer resolution determines the number of   12.____
    A. colors   B. pixels   C. images   D. icons

13. _____ is an extension used for images.   13.____
    A. GIF   B. MP3   C. MPG   D. PPT

14. Which one of the following is NOT an e-mail server?   14.____
    A. Gmail   B. Yahoo   C. Chrome   D. Hotmail

15. _____ is an operating system developed by Apple.   15.____
    A. Mac IOS   B. Linux   C. Android   D. Windows

16. "What You See Is What You Get" (WYSIWYG) refers to   16.____
    A. editing text and graphics for web design
    B. buying a computer at a set price that can't be negotiated
    C. purchasing products as is on websites like Amazon and eBay
    D. printing web pages exactly as they appear on the screen

17. Which one of the following is the BEST option to add a new slide in an   17.____
    existing PowerPoint presentation?
    A. File, add a new slide   B. File, open
    C. Insert, new slide   D. File, new

18. _____ is the default setup for page orientation in PowerPoint.   18.____
    A. Horizontal   B. Vertical   C. Landscape   D. Portrait

19. Items in a list are typically shown by using   19.____
    A. graphics   B. bullets   C. icons   D. markers

20. In PowerPoint, _____ displays only text.   20.____
    A. outline view   B. slide show
    C. print view   D. slider sorter view

21. In Excel, a cell can be edited by use of   21.____
    A. a single click   B. a double click
    C. the format menu   D. formulas

22. Formulas are important features of Microsoft   22.____
    A. Word   B. PowerPoint   C. Excel   D. Publisher

23. In MS Word, which one of the following is used to underline a text?   23.____
    A. Ctrl+I   B. Ctrl+B   C. Ctrl+U   D. Ctrl+P

24. Page color option can be found under the _____ tab.   24.____
    A. Page Layout   B. Design   C. Insert   D. View

25. The F1 key typically displays a program's ____ menu.   25.____
    A. print   B. help
    C. tools   D. task manager

KEY (CORRECT ANSWERS)

1.	A		11.	B
2.	B		12.	B
3.	C		13.	A
4.	A		14.	C
5.	B		15.	A
6.	D		16.	A
7.	B		17.	C
8.	D		18.	C
9.	D		19.	B
10.	D		20.	A

21.	A
22.	C
23.	C
24.	B
25.	B

EXAMINATION SECTION

TEST 1

DIRECTIONS: Each question or incomplete statement is followed by several suggested answers or completions. Select the one that BEST answers the question or completes the statement. *PRINT THE LETTER OF THE CORRECT ANSWER IN THE SPACE AT THE RIGHT.*

1. What is VGA?   1._____
   A. Video Graphics Array   B. Video Graphics Adapter
   C. Visual Graphics Array   D. None of the above

2. IBM 1401 was a   2._____
   A. fourth generation computer   B. second generation computer
   C. third generation computer   D. none of the above

3. A micro program is a collection of   3._____
   A. large scale operations   B. DMA
   C. registers   D. microinstructions

4. The time a CPU takes to recognize an interrupt request is called   4._____
   A. interrupt latency   B. timer delay
   B. response deadline   D. throughput

5. A _____ regulates the arrangement of the flow of microinstructions. 5._____
   A. multiplexer   B. micro program controller
   C. DMA controller   D. virtual memory

6. Which of the following techniques will not be used when CPU exchanges 6._____
   data with a peripheral device?
   A. Interrupt driven I/O   B. Direct Memory Access (DMA)
   C. Programmed I/O   D. Virtual memory

7. If a prior received character is not read by CPU and overwritten by new 7._____
   character received, the error will be called a _____ error.
   A. framing   B. parity   C. overrun   D. under-run

8. Which of the following networks needs manual routing?   8._____
   A. Fiber optic   B. Bus   C. T-switched   D. Ring

9. Which layer of TCP/IP responds to the OSI models to three layers?   9._____
   A. Application   B. Presentation C. Session   D. Transport

10. _____ transport layer protocols is connectionless.   10._____
    A. UDP   B. TCP   C. FTP   D. NVT

11. _____ applications permit a user to approach and modify/change remote files without physical transfer.   11._____
    A. DNS   B. FTP   C. NFS   D. Telnet

12. Which of the following is a non-impact and quiet printer?   12._____
    A. Inkjet   B. Laser   C. Thermal   D. Dot matrix

13. Which of the following are high-end printers?   13._____
    A. Inkjet   B. Laser   C. Thermal   D. Dot matrix

14. For the purpose of plotting designs and graphs on papers, _____ is/are used.   14._____
    A. trackball   B. joystick   C. light pen   D. plotters

15. What is a Snowbol?   15._____
    A. Operating system   B. HLL
    C. Software   D. Search engine

16. Which of the following connects to a modem?   16._____
    A. Telephone line   B. Keyboard   C. Printer   D. Monitor

17. In automated organizations, _____ processing is used by large transaction processing systems.   17._____
    A. online   B. batch   C. once-a-day   D. end-of-day

18. What should a technician do after addition of a new cable segment to the network?   18._____
    A. Revise the disaster recovery plan
    B. Update the changes in document
    C. Update the wiring schematics
    D. None of the above

19. For the purpose of breaking up a broadcast domain, a _____ can be used.   19._____
    A. bridge   B. router
    C. DHCP server   D. printer

20. The secure way of transferring files between two devices is   20._____
    A. SFTP   B. SNMPv3   C. TFTP   D. FTP

21. An administrator networking closet (with all the networking and communication equipment) is on the second floor of a building and the communications lines are installed on the first floor. A _____ will be extended to connect communication lines to the networking closet.   21._____
    A. smart jack   B. demarcation point
    C. patch panel   D. router

22. To provide access to a VPN, _____ is used.   22._____
    A. IGP   B. PPTP   C. PPP   D. RAS

23. Two users are directly linked via RJ-45 and CAT5e cables and are communicating through IP. If the first user transmits data out of the RJ-45 on pins 1 and 2, the client should expect to receive a response on pins

    A. 1 and 2   B. 2 and 4   C. 3 and 6   D. 4 and 6

23.____

24. Examination of physical hardware addresses is done in _____ network access security method.

    A. IP filtering   B. L2TP   C. MAC filtering D. RAS

24.____

25. Wireless standards give the direct advantage of

    A. increased use of wireless spectrum
    B. greater device security
    C. interoperability between devices
    D. increased number of protocols can be used

25.____

KEY (CORRECT ANSWERS)

1.	A		11.	C
2.	B		12.	A
3.	D		13.	B
4.	A		14.	D
5.	B		15.	D
6.	D		16.	A
7.	C		17.	B
8.	C		18.	C
9.	A		19.	B
10.	A		20.	A

21.	C
22.	B
23.	C
24.	C
25.	C

TEST 2

DIRECTIONS: Each question or incomplete statement is followed by several suggested answers or completions. Select the one that BEST answers the question or completes the statement. *PRINT THE LETTER OF THE CORRECT ANSWER IN THE SPACE AT THE RIGHT.*

1. What is an ALU?   1._____
   A. Arithmetic Logic Unit   B. Array Logic Unit
   C. Application Logic Unit   D. None of the above

2. In a client-server system, which type of computers are usually client   2._____
   computers?
   A. Mainframe   B. Mini computer
   C. Micro computer   D. PDA

3. A(n) _____ is necessary for a computer to *boot*.   3._____
   A. compiler   B. loader
   C. operating system   D. assembler

4. In the present technology age, computers are typically   4._____
   A. digital   B. analog   C. hybrid   D. complex

5. What is the physical structure of a computer called?   5._____
   A. CPU   B. Hardware   C. Software   D. All of the above

6. Data is represented in the form of discrete signals in a(n) _____ computer.   6._____
   A. analog   B. digital   C. both A and B D. hybrid

7. _____ is now available in the form of PC.   7._____
   A. Mainframe   B. Micro computer
   C. Mini computer   D. Both B and C

8. Which of the following is larger than a portable computer but is a small   8._____
   general function micro computer?
   A. Hybrid   B. Digital
   C. Desktop   D. None of the above

9. Most of the processing in a computer takes place in   9._____
   A. memory   B. RAM   C. both A and B D. CPU

10. What does LAN stand for?   10._____
    A. Limited Area Network   B. Logical Area Network
    C. Local Area Network   D. Large Area Network

11. Which of the following defines the rules and procedures for regulating data   11._____
    transmission over the internet?
    A. IP address   B. Domains   C. Protocol   D. Gateway

12. Which of the following protocol is used by the intranets, extranets and internet?   12.____
    A. TCP/IP   B. Protocol
    C. Open system   D. Internet work processor

13. On which ring does the data travel in FDDI?   13.____
    A. The primary   B. The secondary
    C. Both rings   D. None of the above

14. _____ is the logical topology.   14.____
    A. Bus   B. Tree   C. Star   D. Both A and C

15. The main drawback of ring topology is that   15.____
    A. if one computer fails, it affects the whole network
    B. adding/removing computers affects the network activity
    C. failure of the central hub makes the whole network unable to work
    D. both A and B

16. _____ is NOT anti-virus software.   16.____
    A. NAV   B. F-Prot   C. Oracle   D. McAfee

17. DMA stands for   17.____
    A. Direct Memory Allocation   B. Direct Memory Access
    C. Direct Module Access   D. none of the above

18. Which of the following is a storage device?   18.____
    A. Tape   B. Hard disk
    C. Floppy disk   D. All of the above

19. Which of the following are determined by user needs?   19.____
    A. System software   B. Application software
    C. Assemblers   D. Compilers

20. Which tools are available with system analysis?   20.____
    A. Review of procedure and conducting interviews
    B. Review of documentation and observation of the situation
    C. Conducting interviews and questionnaire administration
    D. Both B and C

21. Programs used to catch errors and their causes are called   21.____
    A. operating system extensions   B. cookies
    C. diagnostic software   D. boot diskettes

22. A virus which reproduces itself by using the computer host is called   22.____
    A. time bomb   B. worm
    C. Melissa virus   D. macro virus

23. The best practice for implementing a basic wireless network is
    A. disabling ESSID broadcast
    B. adding two access points per area of service
    C. not configuring the ESSID point
    D. none of the above

24. For connecting a single network node to a switch, _____ wiring standards will usually be used.
    A. loopback   B. straight   C. rollover   D. crossover

25. Before having a db loss, a CAT5 cable can run a maximum distance of
    A. 106 feet (31 meters)   B. 203 feet (60 meters)
    C. 328 feet (100 meters)   D. none of the above

KEY (CORRECT ANSWERS)

1.	A		11.	C
2.	C		12.	A
3.	C		13.	A
4.	A		14.	C
5.	B		15.	D
6.	B		16.	C
7.	B		17.	B
8.	C		18.	D
9.	D		19.	A
10.	C		20.	D

21.	C
22.	B
23.	A
24.	B
25.	C

10. Which of the following can combine transmissions from different input/output devices into one line?
    A. Concentrator communication device
    B. Modifier
    C. Multiplexer
    D. Full duplex line

10._____

11. For the analysis of retinal scans, fingerprints, etc. in security access systems, which of the following techniques is used?
    A. Biometrics   B. Bio measurement
    C. Computer security   D. Smart weapon machinery

11._____

12. _____ guards a computer against unauthorized access to a network.
    A. Hacker-proof antivirus   B. Firewall
    C. Encryption safe wall   D. All of the above

12._____

13. What is scrambling of code called?
    A. Encryption   B. Firewall
    C. Scrambling   D. Password proofing

13._____

14. What should be used to prevent data loss due to power failure?
    A. Encryption program   B. Surge protector
    C. Firewall   D. UPS

14._____

15. If an administrator wants to install a device which can detect and control peer-to-peer traffic, a _____ device type will be installed.
    A. bandwidth shaper   B. intrusion detection
    C. proxy server   D. load balancer

15._____

16. If a technician needs to troubleshoot an unfamiliar network, the first step taken to diagnose the problem would be to
    A. report the problem to administrative technician
    B. make use of a port analyzer to analyze the network topology
    C. analyze symptoms and draw a network diagram
    D. all of the above

16._____

17. To discover MAC address of a connecting router, _____ commands can be used.
    A. ARP   B. trace route   C. ping   D. ping sweep

17._____

18. E-mails sent to users with malicious website links are an example of
    A. viruses   B. phishing
    C. rogue access points   D. man-in-the-middle

18._____

19. To analyze that a RJ-45 jack in a cubicle responds to a specific RJ-45 jack in a patch panel, an administrator will use a
    A. punch-down tool   B. spectrum analyzer
    C. toner probe   D. multi-meter

19._____

20. _____ network types are suitable for a 10 gigabyte core network using 33 feet (10 meter) fiber runs.
    A. 10Base-FX
    B. 10GBase-SR
    C. 10GBase-SW
    D. None of the above
    20.____

21. When an administrator troubleshoots network connectivity and wants to view which packets are going through from workstation X to server 1, he will use _____ command line tools.
    A. view route
    B. route
    C. trace route
    D. ping
    21.____

22. For the purpose of updating physical network diagrams, revising _____ is the most appropriate policy.
    A. whenever a connection is changed
    B. before regularly scheduled network audits
    C. after new personnel are hired
    D. after weekly network support team review
    22.____

23. When a firewall accepts a request packet on port 80, it allows the reply packet to pass through automatically. This behavior of firewall is best described as
    A. stateful inspection
    B. intrusion detection
    C. content filtering
    D. passive fingerprinting
    23.____

24. A network technician can face _____ connectivity issues as a result of bundling network cables tightly together.
    A. collision
    B. attenuation
    C. crosstalk
    D. open circuit
    24.____

25. On a wireless network, a _____ mechanism uses a separate network authentication server.
    A. Kerberos
    B. TKIP
    C. RADIUS
    D. WEP
    25.____

KEY (CORRECT ANSWERS)

1. C	11. A
2. B	12. B
3. A	13. A
4. C	14. D
5. D	15. A
6. D	16. C
7. B	17. A
8. D	18. B
9. B	19. D
10. C	20. B

21. C
22. A
23. A
24. C
25. C

─────────

TEST 4

DIRECTIONS: Each question or incomplete statement is followed by several suggested answers or completions. Select the one that BEST answers the question or completes the statement. *PRINT THE LETTER OF THE CORRECT ANSWER IN THE SPACE AT THE RIGHT.*

1. The electrical pathway through which the processor communicates with peripheral devices is called the
   A. computer bus   B. hazard   C. memory   D. disk

   1.____

2. If a 0 is transmitted instead of a stop bit, a(n) _____ error will be the serial communication error condition.
   A. framing   B. parity   C. overrun   D. under-run

   2.____

3. An interrupt can be defined as a process where
   A. an external device can speed up the working of the microprocessor
   B. input devices can take over the working of the microprocessor
   C. an external device gets the attention of the microprocessor
   D. none of the above

   3.____

4. What controls the sequence of the flow of microinstructions?
   A. Multiplexer   B. Micro program controller
   C. DMA controller   D. Virtual memory

   4.____

5. What is MSI?
   A. Medium Scale Integrated Circuits
   B. Medium System Intelligence
   C. Medium Scale Intelligent Circuit
   D. None of the above

   5.____

6. If a network has N number of devices and every device has N-1 ports for cables, this topology is known as
   A. mesh   B. star   C. bus   D. ring

   6.____

7. Usenet is also known as
   A. Gopher   B. Newsgroups   C. Browser   D. CERN

   7.____

8. Junk e-mail is also known as
   A. spam   B. spoof   C. sniffer script   D. spool

   8.____

9. Geographical scattered office LANS can be connected by
   A. VAN   B. LAN   C. DAN   D. WAN

   9.____

10. _____ gathers information of the user and sends it to someone over the internet.
    A. A virus   B. Spybot
    C. Logic bomb   D. Security patch

    10.____

11. A worm virus is terminated eventually due to the lack of   11._____
    A. memory or disk space   B. time
    C. CD drive space   D. CD-RW

12. Instructions of a computer are executed by direct involvement of the   12._____
    A. scanner   B. main storage
    C. secondary storage   D. processor

13. Most processing of a computer takes place in   13._____
    A. memory   B. RAM   C. motherboard   D. CPU

14. Which of the following is NOT a storage medium?   14._____
    A. Hard disk   B. Flash drive   C. DVD   D. Scanner

15. Suppose a user calls you for network support and says that his e-mail is not   15._____
working. What will you do first?
    A. Inquire about the operation performed by the user and what was the
        expected and actual result
    B. Restart the hub the user was connected to
    C. Send a test e-mail message to see if it's sent
    D. None of the above

16. Suppose two networks in different departments are using DHCP set up for   16._____
192.168.0.0/24 and after consolidation of the officer's network we have run out
of IP addresses. The BEST cost-effective solution for this will be
    A. adding a router to connect both networks
    B. switching to static IP addressing
    C. changing the subnet mask to 255.255.254.0
    D. none of the above

17. Suppose that packets to an IP address are getting lost over the internet.   17._____
Which tools will an administrator use to find out the responsible hop?
    A. Ping   B. nslookup   C. Trace route   D. netstat

18. What should a technician check if a workstation on the network is able to   18._____
ping hosts on the network but it is not able to ping any addresses on the
internet?
    A. The DNS server entries   B. The network card
    C. The default gateway   D. The host's file

19. To find out the status of all established TCP connections by port 80, the   19._____
administrator will use the _____ command.
    A. netstat –at   B. netstat –r   C. netstat –v   D. netstat -p tcp

20. To evaluate the network traffic, which of the following tools will be used? 20._____
    A. OTDR   B. Protocol analyzer
    C. Certifier   D. Toner probe

21. Which port is usually used for FTP traffic?   21.____
    A. 20   B. 22   C. 23   D. 25

22. _____ can function as a router, support VLANs and connect multiple   22.____
    workstations.
    A. Repeater   B. Switch
    C. Hub   D. Multilayer switch

23. 208.177.23.1 belongs to class   23.____
    A. A   B. B   C. C   D. D

24. If 25 clients on the same network want to see a video, _____ should be   24.____
    configured on the user's computer to reduce network traffic.
    A. class C addresses   B. class A addresses
    C. broadcast   D. multicast

25. Suppose we have installed a new LAN switch on fiber ports. In order to   25.____
    allow compatibility to the existing fiber network, what will a technician need on
    the new switch?
    A. Router   B. Repeater
    C. Media converter   D. Hub

KEY (CORRECT ANSWERS)

1.	A		11.	A
2.	A		12.	D
3.	C		13.	D
4.	B		14.	D
5.	A		15.	A
6.	A		16.	C
7.	B		17.	C
8.	A		18.	C
9.	D		19.	D
10.	B		20.	B

21.	A
22.	D
23.	C
24.	D
25.	C

EXAMINATION SECTION
TEST 1

DIRECTIONS: Each question or incomplete statement is followed by several suggested answers or completions. Select the one that BEST answers the question or completes the statement. *PRINT THE LETTER OF THE CORRECT ANSWER IN THE SPACE AT THE RIGHT.*

1. A microprocessor includes media for each of the following EXCEPT   1._____

   A. secondary storage   B. control
   C. logic   D. memory

2. Which of the following protocols is LEAST likely to be used in a wide–area network (WAN)?   2._____

   A. SNA   B. Token passing
   C. TCP/IP   D. DEC DNA

3. In an expert system, the rule base is sometimes searched using a strategy that begins with a hypothesis and seeks out more information until the hypothesis is either proved or disproved. This strategy is known as   3._____

   A. backward chaining
   B. key fielding
   C. indexed sequential access
   D. process specification

4. The meaning of signs, symbols, messages or systems are involved in a body of inquiry known as   4._____

   A. linguistics   B. semantics
   C. communications   D. syntactics

5. Which of the following is a query language?   5._____

   A. Nomad   B. Ideal   C. Systat   D. RPG–III

6. Which of the following is the typical unit of measurement used by systems designers to estimate the length of time needed to complete a project?   6._____

   A. Data–week   B. Man–hour
   C. File–hour   D. Man–month

7. Which of the following is the oldest professional computer society in the United States?   7._____

   A. Data Processing Management Association (DPMA)
   B. Institute for Certification of Computer Professionals (ICP)
   C. Association of Computing Machinery (ACM)
   D. Information Technology Association of America (ITAA)

8. Which of the following terms is commonly used to describe the interaction of people and machines in the work environment, especially in terms of job design and health issues?   8._____

   A. Connectivity   B. Ergonomics
   C. Feasibility   D. Interface

9. Which of the following is a likely application of the sensitivity analysis models of a decision–support system?

    A. Forecasting sales
    B. Determining the proper product mix within a given market
    C. Predicting the actions of competitors
    D. Goal seeking

9.___

10. What is the term for the temporary storage location in a control unit where small amounts of data or instructions reside for thousandths of a second just before use?

    A. Cache   B. Register   C. Sector   D. Buffer

10.___

11. Systems whose behavior includes options without specification of probabilities within the system are described as

    A. runaway   B. possibilistic
    C. stochastic   D. probabilistic

11.___

12. The physical devices and software that link various hardware components and transfer data from one physical location to another are known collectively as

    A. cyberspace
    B. wide–area networks
    C. telecommunications technology
    D. semantic networks

12.___

13. Which of the following is a tangible benefit associated with organizational information systems?

    A. Streamlined operations   B. Higher asset utilization
    C. Inventory reduction   D. Improved planning

13.___

14. Which of the following is NOT generally considered to be a physical component of an MIS?

    A. Personnel   B. Information
    C. Procedures   D. Software

14.___

15. Any undesired information in a communication channel which is not part of the intended message is typically referred to as

    A. resistance   B. noise
    C. data error   D. cross–talk

15.___

16. Which of the following is the ASCII 8–bit binary code for the number 1?

    A. 0001 0001   B. 0101 0001
    C. 0000 1000   D. 1001 0001

16.___

17. Which of the following is a method of organizing expert system knowledge into chunks in which relationships are based on shared characteristics determined by the user?

    A. Indexing   B. GUI
    C. Batch processing   D. Frames

17.___

18. Which of the following is a telecommunications requirement that is particular to the task   18.____
of on–line data entry?

    A. High–capacity video and data capabilities
    B. Infrequent, high–volume bursts of information
    C. Instant response
    D. Direct response

19. What is the term for the technology which breaks blocks of text into small fixed bundles of   19.____
data and routes them in an economical way through an available communications channel?

    A. Optical character recognition
    B. Frame relay
    C. Packet switching
    D. Branch exchange

20. A transaction processing system rejects a transaction on the basis that it includes a   20.____
Social Security number which contains an alphabetic character. This is an example of
a(n) _____ check.

    A. reasonableness   B. format
    C. dependency   D. existence

21. The smallest unit of data for defining an image in a computer is the   21.____

    A. byte   B. pixel   C. quark   D. bit

22. In a microcomputer, which of the following transmits signals specifying whether to read or   22.____
write data from a given primary storage address, input device, or output device?

    A. Control bus   B. Address bus
    C. Data bus   D. CPU

23. Which of the following stages occurs the LATEST in the traditional systems life cycle   23.____
model?

    A. Systems study   B. Programming
    C. Design   D. Project definition

24. The fastest and most expensive memory used in a microcomputer is located in the   24.____

    A. cache   B. register   C. hard disk   D. RAM

25. Which of the following is an optical disk system that allows users to record data only   25.____
once, but to read the data indefinitely?

    A. WORM   B. EPROM   C. RAM   D. TQM

KEY (CORRECT ANSWERS)

1.	A	11.	B
2.	B	12.	C
3.	A	13.	C
4.	B	14.	B
5.	D	15.	B
6.	D	16.	B
7.	C	17.	D
8.	B	18.	D
9.	D	19.	C
10.	B	20.	B

21.	B
22.	A
23.	B
24.	B
25.	A

TEST 2

DIRECTIONS: Each question or incomplete statement is followed by several suggested answers or completions. Select the one that BEST answers the question or completes the statement. *PRINT THE LETTER OF THE CORRECT ANSWER IN THE SPACE AT THE RIGHT.*

1. Which of the following styles of systems development is most often used for information systems at the individual level?

    A. End–user computing
    B. Commercial software packages
    C. Prototyping
    D. Traditional life cycle

1.____

2. Which of the following is a programming language that was developed in 1956 for scientific and mathematical applications?

    A. COBOL   B. BASIC   C. Pascal   D. FORTRAN

2.____

3. Which of the following personnel would be considered a *technical specialist* in an MIS department?

    A. Education specialist   B. Database administrator
    C. Applications programmer   D. Systems analyst

3.____

4. Which of the following is NOT a characteristic of a fault–tolerant system?

    A. The use of special software routines to detect hardware failures
    B. Extra memory chips, processors, and disk storage
    C. Continuous detection of bugs or program defects
    D. Hardware parts that can be removed without system disruption

4.____

5. Defining a system program in such a way that it may call itself is an example of

    A. eudemony   B. recursion
    C. redundancy   D. artificial intelligence

5.____

6. What is the term used to enumerate the number of bits that can be processed at one time by a computer?

    A. Data bus width   B. Word length
    C. RAM capacity   D. Bandwidth

6.

7. Which of the following is another term for a field, or a grouping of characters into a word, group of words, or complete number?

    A. Code   B. Byte
    C. Data element   D. File

7.____

8. A person in a multi–user system sends a message using the OSI model to another user at a different location. At the messenger's end of the system, after passing through the *session* layer of the model, the message will then enter the _____ layer.

    A. transport   B. network
    C. presentation   D. data link

8.____

9. Which of the following is NOT a disadvantage associated with the traditional life cycle model of systems development?

9.___

    A. Time consumption
    B. Oversimplification
    C. Cost
    D. Inflexibility

10. Transmission speeds that would fall within the expected range of coaxial cable are _____ per second.

10.___

    A. 400 bits
    B. 50 megabits
    C. 300 megabits
    D. 7 gigabits

11. Which of the following is a telecommunications computer that collects and temporarily stores messages from terminals for batch transmission to the host computer?

11.___

    A. Assembler
    B. Concentrator
    C. Buffer
    D. Compiler

12. Which of the following is an advantage associated with the centralized or teleprocessing model of multi–user systems?

12.___

    A. Local computing
    B. Scaleability
    C. Low start–up costs
    D. Low technical risk

13. Software systems that can operate on different hardware platforms are referred to as _____ systems.

13.___

    A. open
    B. interoperable
    C. branched
    D. transmigrational

14. What is the term for the process by which the properties of a collection (i.e., of data) are described in terms of the sums of the properties of the units contained in the collection?

14.___

    A. Unity
    B. Autarky
    C. Chunking
    D. Aggregation

15. In systems terminology, what is the term for output that is returned to the appropriate members of an organization to help them evaluate or correct input?

15.___

    A. Exit data
    B. Feedback
    C. Assessor
    D. Valuation

16. The years 1957 to 1963 are generally considered to have been the _____ generation in the evolution of computer hardware technology.

16.___

    A. first
    B. second
    C. third
    D. fourth

17. A conversion approach in which the new system completely replaces the old one on an appointed day is known as

17.___

    A. focused differentiation
    B. direct cutover
    C. allied distribution
    D. batch processing

18. Of the following types of business network redesign, the one that can be said to be most highly coupled is/are
    18.____

    A. interenterprise system access
    B. knowledge networks
    C. EDI
    D. interenterprise process integration

19. Which of the following terms is used to describe the shape or configuration of a telecommunications network?
    19.____

    A. Duplex
    B. Topology
    C. Protocol
    D. Transmissivity

20. Which of the following is/are recognized differences between microcomputers and workstations?
    20.____

    I.   Microcomputers have more powerful mathematical processing capabilities.
    II. Microcomputers are more useful for computer–aided design (CAD).
    III. Workstations are more widely used by knowledge workers.
    IV. Workstations can more easily perform multiple tasks simultaneously.

The CORRECT answer is:

    A. I, II
    B. II, III
    C. III, IV
    D. II, IV

21. Which of the following signifies a tool for retrieving and transferring files from a remote computer?
    21.____

    A. EDI
    B. CPU
    C. TCP/IP
    D. FTP

22. Which of the following is a federal privacy law that applies to private institutions?
    22.____

    A. Freedom of Information Act of 1968 (as amended)
    B. Privacy Act of 1974 (as amended)
    C. Privacy Protection Act of 1980
    D. Computer Matching and Privacy Protection Act of 1988

23. The main contribution of end–user systems development typically occurs in the area of
    23.____

    A. productivity enhancement
    B. improved updating functions
    C. increased technical complexity
    D. improved efficiency in transaction processing

24. In cooperative processing, a mainframe and a microcomputer generally share tasks. The mainframe, however, is generally best at performing
    24.____

    A. screen presentation
    B. error processing
    C. data field editing
    D. file input and output

25. In a systems development process, users are made active members of development 25.___
    project teams, and some users are placed in charge of system training and installation.
    In this case, management has made use of _____ tools.

    A. external integration   B. internal integration
    C. formal planning   D. formal control

———————

KEY (CORRECT ANSWERS)

1.	C	11.	B
2.	D	12.	D
3.	B	13.	A
4.	C	14.	D
5.	B	15.	B
6.	B	16.	B
7.	C	17.	B
8.	A	18.	B
9.	B	19.	B
10.	B	20.	C

21.	D
22.	C
23.	A
24.	D
25.	A

———————

TEST 3

DIRECTIONS: Each question or incomplete statement is followed by several suggested answers or completions. Select the one that BEST answers the question or completes the statement. *PRINT THE LETTER OF THE CORRECT ANSWER IN THE SPACE AT THE RIGHT.*

1. As a general rule, the development of a system that will be used by others can be expected to take_____ as long as the development of an individual system that will be used only by the developer.

    A. half
    C. three times
    B. twice
    D. five times

1._____

2. In LANs, the token ring configuration is most useful for

    A. broadcasting messages to the entire network through a single circuit
    B. multidirectional transmissions between microcomputers or between micros and a larger computer
    C. transmissions between microcomputers and a larger computer that require a degree of traffic control
    D. transmitting large volumes of data between microcomputers

2._____

3. Which of the following statements about expert systems is generally TRUE? They

    A. function best in lower–level clerical functions
    B. require minimal development resources
    C. are highly adaptable over time
    D. are capable of representing a wide range of causal models

3._____

4. A middle–range machine with a RAM capacity that measures from about 10 megabytes to over 1 gigabyte is known as a

    A. microcomputer
    C. desktop computer
    B. minicomputer
    D. mainframe

4._____

5. Which of the following media uses the sector method for storing data?

    A. Cache
    C. Hard disk
    B. Floppy disk
    D. CD–ROM

5._____

6. When mechanisms of functional subsystems are connected causally to influence each other, they are said to be

    A. aggregated
    C. synchronous
    B. coupled
    D. constrained

6._____

7. Which of the following storage media generally has the largest capacity?

    A. Cache
    C. Optical disk
    B. Magnetic disk
    D. Magnetic tape

7._____

8. In terms of information ethics, the mechanisms for assessing responsibility for decisions and actions are referred to as

    A. liability
    C. creditability
    B. capacity
    D. accountability

8._____

9. Which of the following signifies the central switching system that handles a firm's voice and digital communications?

9.___

   A. OSI   B. DSS   C. PBX   D. LAN

10. What is the term for the LAN channel technology that provides a single path for transmitting text, graphics, voice, or video data at one time?

10.___

   A. Bus   B. Baseband
   C. Firewall   D. Broadband

11. The stage in a system's life cycle in which testing, training, and conversion occur is termed

11.___

   A. evaluation   B. design
   C. installation   D. documentation

12. Which of the following is NOT a type of processor used in telecommunications systems?

12.___

   A. Coaxial cable   B. Controller
   C. Modem   D. Multiplexer

13. A database that is stored in more than one physical location is described as

13.___

   A. sequential   B. wide–area
   C. distributed   D. indexed

14. An organization decides to redesign its information system using only the components that are already available to it. In the language of systems theory, the resulting system would be described as a(n)

14.___

   A. ensemble   B. creod   C. kluge   D. cyborg

15. What is the term for an integrated circuit made by printing thousands or millions of transistors on a small silicon chip?

15.___

   A. Cache   B. Semiconductor
   C. Control unit   D. Microprocessor

16. Computer programming includes a logic pattern that allows for the repetition of certain actions while a specified condition occurs or until a certain conditions exists. This pattern is known as the

16.___

   A. object linkage   B. selection construct
   C. key field   D. iteration construct

17. Which of the following is the standard or reference model for allowing e–mail systems operating on different hardware to communicate?

17.___

   A. X.400   B. X.25   C. X.12   D. FDDI

18. Which of the following terms is used to denote circular tracks on the same vertical line within a disk pack?

18.___

   A. Track   B. Spindle   C. Sector   D. Cylinder

19. A system that is capable of listing the descriptions of each of a certain set of alternatives is described as   19.____

    A. generative   B. contingency–based
    C. smart   D. stochastic

20. Which of the following is an operating cost associated with an information system?   20.____

    A. Database establishment   B. Facilities
    C. Personnel training   D. Hardware acquisition

21. As a collaboration tool, the World Wide Web involves   21.____

    A. data that undergoes frequent updating
    B. documents predominantly authored by a single user
    C. applications with data at multiple sites
    D. applications with high security requirements

22. A mathematical formula used to translate a record's key field directly into its storage location is known as a(n) _____ algorithm.   22.____

    A. synchronous   B. genetic
    C. asynchronous   D. transform

23. Which of the following is a common DISADVANTAGE associated with outsourcing the systems development process?   23.____

    A. Loss of control over system function
    B. Increased costs
    C. Generally slow progress
    D. Increased paperwork requirements

24. Which of the following is a network topology in which all computers and other devices are connected to a central host computer?   24.____

    A. LAN   B. Star   C. Ring   D. Bus

25. In terms of information systems, *processing* means the   25.____

    A. assignment of data to certain categories for later use
    B. calculation or computation of data to arrive at a solution or conclusion
    C. conversion, manipulation, and analysis of raw input into a meaningful form
    D. collection or capture of raw data for use in an information system

KEY (CORRECT ANSWERS)

1.	C		11.	C
2.	D		12.	A
3.	A		13.	C
4.	B		14.	C
5.	B		15.	B
6.	B		16.	D
7.	C		17.	A
8.	D		18.	D
9.	C		19.	A
10.	B		20.	B

21.	B
22.	D
23.	A
24.	B
25.	C

———————

EXAMINATION SECTION
TEST 1

DIRECTIONS: Each question or incomplete statement is followed by several suggested answers or completions. Select the one that BEST answers the question or completes the statement. *PRINT THE LETTER OF THE CORRECT ANSWER IN THE SPACE AT THE RIGHT.*

1. When deciding the means by which training is to be delivered, the designer of instruction should FIRST select the

   A. type of delivery system technology
   B. trainer
   C. necessary instructional properties
   D. delivery system

   1.____

2. _____ does NOT directly involve instruction, but offers the power to make learning more efficient.

   A. Computer-managed instruction (CMI)
   B. Computer-based training (CBT)
   C. Technical training function (TTF)
   D. Computer-assisted instruction (CAI)

   2.____

3. The use of case studies as a means of instructional delivery should be avoided when

   A. training involves management or supervisory personnel
   B. instructional goals include critical thinking
   C. there is unhealthy competition among trainees
   D. time constraints on preparation exist

   3.____

4. Each of the following is a function of audience response systems (ARS) software EXCEPT

   A. analyzing group responses to items
   B. performing demographic analyses
   C. storing scores for later analysis
   D. administering progressive evaluations during instruction

   4.____

5. Which of the following is a step typically involved in the design phase of instructional design?

   A. Pilot instruction
   B. Developing instructional materials
   C. Analyzing job tasks
   D. Developing testing strategies

   5.____

6. Which of the following is NOT a typical component of a performance support system (PSS)?

   A. Expert system
   C. Text retrieval
   B. Printed job aids
   D. Computer-aided instruction

   6.____

7. An expert system includes knowledge structured for capturing regularly occurring cir-
cumstances. This structured knowledge is known as

    A. logic
    B. frames
    C. neural network processing
    D. rules

7.___

8. In a training situation, a(n) _____ is MOST likely to be held liable for misrepresentation.

    A. employer
    B. outside contractors/vendors
    C. owner/employer
    D. trainer

8.___

9. A good computer-assisted instruction delivery system will use

    A. norming
    B. scrolling
    C. page-turning
    D. branching

9.___

10. Each of the following is usually considered to be a characteristic of effective instructional
design EXCEPT

    A. rule-based design
    B. holistic self-evaluation
    C. interconnected tasks
    D. systematic approach

10.___

11. Instructional media are typically used to

    A. direct learning activities
    B. predict the best method of instructional delivery
    C. support learning activities
    D. evaluate trainee performance

11.___

12. Which of the following instructional delivery techniques typically involves the LOWEST
development cost?

    A. Audiotape
    B. Multimedia computer
    C. Lecture
    D. Live video

12.___

13. Computer-aided instruction is often designed so that only the precise knowledge needed
at that point in the activity is taught.
This is referred to as _____ CAI.

    A. secular
    B. granular
    C. partitioned
    D. modular

13.___

14. Each of the following is an advantage associated with the use of vendors as trainers
EXCEPT

    A. no additional strain on training budget
    B. initiation of function that can later be turned over to in-house trainer
    C. usual offering of continued support
    D. proficiency in using new equipment or machines

14.___

15. Which of the following is a mode of computer-supported learning resources?   15.____

    A. Evaluation   B. Tutorial
    C. Instructional games   D. Hypermedia

16. Which of the following conditions does NOT typically indicate the use of performance   16.____
support devices?

    A. Regulation requirements
    B. Frequently changing tasks
    C. Infrequently performed tasks
    D. Cost of mistakes is relatively low

17. Which of the following performance support devices can MOST accurately be described   17.____
as *procedural?*

    A. Printed job aids
    B. Computer-based references (CBR)
    C. Hypertext
    D. Computer help systems

18. If a typical instructor-led training delivery system requires ten hours of instructional time,   18.____
a textual computer-based training approach will typically require about _____ instructional hours.

    A. 40   B. 100   C. 200   D. 400

19. Which of the following is an advantage associated with the use of performance observa-   19.____
tion as a means of gathering data during instructional design?

    A. Immediate response availability
    B. Minimal disturbance in work routines
    C. Generation of motivational information
    D. Low relative cost

20. Each of the following is a mode of computer-managed instruction EXCEPT   20.____

    A. record keeping   B. simulation
    C. prescription generation   D. testing

21. Which of the following is typically addressed in the evaluation strategy produced during   21.____
instructional design?

    A. Balance of activities encompassed by the design
    B. Development of instructional materials
    C. Outcomes required to satisfy each performance criterion
    D. Provision of learner reinforcement

22. As a means of instructional delivery, role playing is useful under each of the following   22.____
conditions EXCEPT when

    A. training involves the application of content knowledge
    B. technical or psychomotor skills are the focus
    C. training involves management or supervisory personnel
    D. instructional objectives are concerned with interpersonal relations

23. _____ is NOT a step typically involved in the analysis phase of instructional design.   23.___

    A. Writing instructional objectives
    B. Selecting tasks for training
    C. Determining instructional prerequisites
    D. Assessing learning requirements

24. Instruction delivered to new employees before they begin regular work is called_____   24.___
training.

    A. OJT   B. vestibule
    C. independent study   D. apprenticeship

25. If a company decides to contract out to an external training provider, each of the following   25.___
elements must be included in a request for proposal EXCEPT

    A. project background   B. outputs and deliverables
    C. delivery strategy   D. project procedures

KEY (CORRECT ANSWERS)

1.	C	11.	C
2.	A	12.	C
3.	D	13.	B
4.	D	14.	B
5.	D	15.	D
6.	B	16.	D
7.	B	17.	A
8.	B	18.	C
9.	D	19.	B
10.	B	20.	B

21.	C
22.	B
23.	C
24.	B
25.	C

TEST 2

DIRECTIONS: Each question or incomplete statement is followed by several suggested answers or completions. Select the one that BEST answers the question or completes the statement. *PRINT THE LETTER OF THE CORRECT ANSWER IN THE SPACE AT THE RIGHT.*

1. It is a good idea to use lecturing as a method of instructional delivery when   1.____

   A. complex processes need to be explained
   B. introducing training provided by other methods or media
   C. the trainer is unfamiliar with the audience
   D. instructional goals deal with affective or psycho-motor skills

2. Typically, the LARGEST part of all training costs is   2.____

   A. job aids
   B. vendor contracts
   C. travel expense associated with off-site training
   D. trainee salary during training

3. The systemic approach to training evaluation is typically divided into four parts. Which of the following is NOT one of these parts?   3.____

   A. Identification of trainee prerequisites
   B. Identification of training goals
   C. Production of learning outcomes
   D. Support performance development

4. During the instructional design process, an analysis document is produced which includes specifications for each of the following EXCEPT   4.____

   A. measurement factors
   B. target audience characteristics
   C. instructional media
   D. program management

5. Each of the following is a disadvantage associated with the use of employee-trainers EXCEPT   5.____

   A. least economical for recurrent training needs
   B. increased head count in labor budget
   C. less likely to have knowledge of adult learning techniques
   D. lack of knowledge of new-hire trainers

6. Which of the following is NOT among the modes of computer-assisted instruction?   6.____

   A. Problem solving   B. Calculation
   C. Modeling   D. Drill and practice

7. Which of the following performance support devices offers the GREATEST availability to trainees?   7.____

   A. Printed job aids   B. Expert systems
   C. Hypertext   D. Computer help systems

8. Demonstrations might be used as a method of instructional delivery when 8._

    A. instructional goals involve cognitive or affective domains
    B. dealing with especially large groups of trainees
    C. tasks require manual dexterity or are difficult for learners to understand
    D. when materials and equipment are scarce

9. Which of the following is typically addressed during the implementation phase of instructional design? 9._

    A. Revision of instructional materials
    B. Selection of tasks for training
    C. Creation of design syllabus
    D. Creation of delivery strategy

10. The psychomotor domain of learning progresses in four discrete stages. Which of the following stages is typically the LAST to be accomplished? 10._

    A. Manipulation   B. Articulation
    C. Imitation   D. Precision

11. A well-written instructional objective should include three key components. Which of the following is NOT one of these? 11._

    A. Conditions   B. Performance
    C. Media   D. Criteria

12. If a job requires high technical knowledge but low manual skill, which of the following learning methods would be BEST suited for job training? 12._

    A. Self-study and lab
    B. Classroom and on-the-job training with mentor
    C. Classroom and lab
    D. Classroom and self-practice

13. The computer- _____ component of technology-based training does NOT actually teach or manage instruction, but serves to make learning easier and more appropriate. 13._

    A. managed instruction (CMI)
    B. based training (CBT)
    C. supported learning resource (CSLR)
    D. assisted instruction (CAI)

14. _____ simulation is used in information systems training. 14._

    A. Manual   B. Hybrid
    C. Sequential   D. Computer

15. In order for trainees to move nonsequentially through a computerized training document, will need to be installed. 15._

    A. an expert system   B. hypertext
    C. an authoring system   D. a hierarchy

16. If a job requires high technical knowledge and manual skill, which of the following learn-   16.____
ing methods would be BEST suited for job training?

    A. Self-study and lab
    B. Classroom and on-the-job training with mentor
    C. Classroom and lab
    D. Classroom and self-practice

17. Which of the following is typically addressed in the design syllabus created during   17.____
instructional design?

    A. Sequence in which content is presented
    B. Evaluation of training objectives
    C. Means of administering precourse assessment
    D. Evaluation of prerequisite skills

18. The use of peer tutoring as a method of instructional delivery will usually have all of the   18.____
following benefits EXCEPT

    A. facilitating pacing of instruction in groups with heterogeneous abilities
    B. encouraging competition among trainees
    C. easing trainer"s workload
    D. increasing trainee's satisfaction with instruction

19. Which of the following instructional delivery techniques typically offers the GREATEST   19.____
opportunity for self-pacing?

    A. Audiotape   B. Multimedia computer
    C. Lecture   D. Live video

20. In the development of technology-based training, the logical starting point is computer-   20.____

    A. managed instruction (CMI)
    B. based training (CBT)
    C. supported learning resources (CSLR)
    D. assisted instruction (CAI)

21. As a means of instructional delivery, case studies are MOST useful for   21.____

    A. very large groups of trainees
    B. bridging theory and practice
    C. shaping attitudinal objectives
    D. drill and practice of psychomotor skills

22. An advantage commonly associated with the use of consultants as trainers is   22.____

    A. employees may be able to earn college credit for training course
    B. no increase in labor budget
    C. availability for modular training
    D. *one-shot* training

23. Discussion should be avoided as a method of instructional delivery when   23.____

    A. dealing with a group of trainees that is forty or larger
    B. content is rigid and restricted to facts
    C. there are strict time constraints on instruction
    D. instructional goals deal with attitudes or critical thinking skills

24. The component of technology-based learning that actually teaches is 24.___

    A. computer-managed instruction (CMI)
    B. computer-based training (CBT)
    C. technical training function (TTF)
    D. computer-assisted instruction (CAI)

25. Which of the following instructional delivery approaches would typically require the FEW- 25.___
EST number of development hours?

    A. Textual computer-based training
    B. Workbook
    C. Videotape
    D. Instructor-led

KEY (CORRECT ANSWERS)

1.	B		11.	C
2.	D		12.	D
3.	A		13.	C
4.	C		14.	D
5.	A		15.	B
6.	B		16.	B
7.	A		17.	A
8.	C		18.	B
9.	A		19.	B
10.	B		20.	A

21.	B
22.	B
23.	C
24.	D
25.	D

EXAMINATION SECTION

TEST 1

DIRECTIONS: Each question or incomplete statement is followed by several suggested answers or completions. Select the one that BEST answers the question or completes the statement. *PRINT THE LETTER OF THE CORRECT ANSWER IN THE SPACE AT THE RIGHT.*

1. The primary storage is
    A. used by processor
    C. both A and B
    B. used by RAM
    D. none of the above

    1._____

2. Clock speed is measured in
    A. hertz
    C. gigahertz
    B. megahertz
    D. none of the above

    2._____

3. Which of the following temperatures can cause component failure?
    A. 180 degrees   B. 185 degrees   C. 190 degrees   D. 205 degrees

    3._____

4. A motherboard has _____ connections to the power supply.
    A. one or more
    C. two
    B. just one
    D. none of the above

    4._____

5. CMOS setup is used
    A. to change motherboard settings
    C. both A and B
    B. for basic input/output
    D. none of the above

    5._____

6. ROM chips that can be overwritten are known as
    A. flash ROM
    C. BIOS
    B. micro ROM
    D. none of the above

    6._____

7. A secure way of transferring files from one device to another is
    A. FTP
    C. SFTP
    B. TFTP
    D. none of the above

    7._____

8. A method to provide access to a VPN is
    A. RAS   B. PPP   C. PPTP   D. IGP

    8._____

9. A big advantage of having a wireless standard is
    A. interoperability between devices   B. greater device security
    C. both A and B
    D. none of the above

    9._____

10. When you are implementing a basic wireless network,
    A. disable ESSID broadcast
    C. both A and B
    B. don't configure the ESSID point
    D. none of the above

    10._____

11. You are installing a device that can throttle and detect peer-to-peer traffic.   11._____
This device belongs to the device type
    A. load balancer   B. bandwidth shaper
    C. proxy server   D. none of the above

12. The first step involved in troubleshooting after arriving on the site is   12._____
    A. identifying the symptoms and drawing a network diagram
    B. comparing wiring schematics to the industry standards
    C. both A and B
    D. none of the above

13. _____ describes an email that has web links to direct users to malicious   13._____
websites.
    A. Phishing   B. Viruses
    C. Both A and B   D. None of the above

14. You are troubleshooting network connectivity and want to see the path that   14._____
the packets are taking from a workstation to the server. The _____ command
line tool will be used for this.
    A. ping   B. traceroute   C. route   D. nslookup

15. The process or steps required to be applied to develop an information system   15._____
is
    A. system development life cycle   B. program specification
    C. design cycle   D. analytical code

16. Project plan is a document   16._____
    A. describing how the project team will develop the proposed system
    B. that outlines the technical feasibility of the proposed system
    C. both A and B
    D. none of the above

17. The primary goal of a system analyst is to   17._____
    A. create value for the organization   B. create a wonderful system
    C. acquire a working tool   D. none of the above

18. Understanding the purpose of the information system to be built and finding   18._____
out how the project team is to accomplish making it is part of the _____ phase
of the SDLC.
    A. analysis   B. system request
    C. planning   D. none of the above

19. Examining the economic, technical and organizational advantages and   19._____
disadvantages of developing a new system is known as
    A. feasibility analysis   B. committee approval
    C. risk analysis   D. system request

20. The calculation measuring the amount of money an organization is going to get in return for the money it has spent is known as
    A. cash flow
    B. return on investment
    C. tangible costs
    D. none of the above

20.____

21. New users should be encouraged to use software by taking help first from
    A. tutorial software
    B. training software
    C. both A and B
    D. none of the above

21.____

22. A wizard is
    A. a person who can do magic
    B. software that helps and walks user through a complex process
    C. hardware that speeds up performance
    D. all of the above

22.____

23. How can you determine the level of a trainee's knowledge?
    A. By watching them type
    B. By taking a test
    C. By asking them questions
    D. Both B and C

23.____

24. Which of the following is the most important step when giving training users?
    A. Make them want to learn
    B. Push them until they master the task
    C. Leave learning or not learning up to them; just provide the training
    D. None of the above

24.____

25. It is important that while training, the trainees are shown the
    A. training agenda
    B. results of previous training sessions
    C. trainer's achievements
    D. none of the above

25.____

KEY (CORRECT ANSWERS)

1.	C	11.	B
2.	A	12.	A
3.	B	13.	A
4.	A	14.	B
5.	A	15.	A
6.	A	16.	A
7.	C	17.	A
8.	C	18.	C
9.	A	19.	A
10.	A	20.	B

21.	C
22.	B
23.	C
24.	A
25.	A

––––––––––

TEST 2

DIRECTIONS: Each question or incomplete statement is followed by several suggested answers or completions. Select the one that BEST answers the question or completes the statement. *PRINT THE LETTER OF THE CORRECT ANSWER IN THE SPACE AT THE RIGHT.*

1. _____ makes it possible for the system to power up with the help of a keyboard.   1.____
    A. ACPI   B. APM
    C. Both A and B   D. None of the above

2. Which of the following are data path sizes?   2.____
    A. 8, 16   B. 32, 64   C. 128   D. All of the above

3. The lines that carry the data in a bus is known as   3.____
    A. data bus   B. memory bus
    C. micro bus   D. none of the above

4. Which of the following can be used to boot, recover or reinstall the Windows operating system?   4.____
    A. Recovery CD   B. Windows CD
    C. Memory CD   D. None of the above

5. Which of the following explains the proper handling of substances like chemical solvents?   5.____
    A. Material safety data sheet   B. POST
    C. Memory data sheet   D. None of the above

6. A _____ tests a USB, networks, serial or other port.   6.____
    A. loop back plug   B. three-head plug
    C. both A and B   D. none of the above

7. Bundling network cables can cause   7.____
    A. crosstalk   B. attenuation
    C. collision   D. none of the above

8. The greatest concern while using an orbital satellite WAN link is   8.____
    A. cable length   B. duplex   C. latency   D. collision

9. If packets to an IP address are dropping over the Internet, _____ will be used to determine the responsible hop.   9.____
    A. netstat   B. traceroute
    C. ping   D. none of the above

10. _____ ports can be used for FTP traffic.   10.____
    A. 25   B. 24   C. 23   D. 20

11. The _____ connects multiple workstations, functions as a router and supports
    VLANs.
      A. hub   B. multilayer switch
      C. switch   D. repeater
         11._____

12. To provide VoIP phones with power but without having to arrange independent
    power supplies for them, the switches on the network should have
      A. spanning tree   B. PoE
      C. PPPoE   D. VLAN tagging
         12._____

13. _____ has the same functionality as Telnet but operates more securely.
      A. SSH   B. RSH   C. TFTP   D. SNAT
         13._____

14. You use a logical network diagram to determine the number of
      A. cables in the network
      B. broadcast domains on the network
      C. users on the network
      D. none of the above
         14._____

15. Planning and controlling the system development within a deadline at the
    lowest cost and with the right functionality is called
      A. project management   B. task identification
      C. task   D. none of the above
         15._____

16. One way of calculating project completion time is to apply industry standard
    factors for each phase of the project. In this method, the planning phase takes
    almost 15% of the total time. If a project takes three months for planning, then
    the remaining project will need approximately
      A. 20 months   B. 15 months
      C. 3 months   D. none of the above
         16._____

17. Fourteen factors impact the complexity of a project when we are using a
    function point estimation worksheet. _____ are included in these factors.
      A. Data communications, end user efficiency and reusability
      B. Data communications, estimated effort and time tradeoffs
      C. Both A and B
      D. None of the above
         17._____

18. In determining the tasks for a work plan, you can
      A. list the four phases of SDLC and steps occurring in each phase
      B. control and direct the project
      C. establish a possible reporting structure
      D. none of the above
         18._____

19. If someone is examining existing paperwork so that he can better understand
    the As-Is system, this is
      A. observation   B. JAD
      C. document analysis   D. none of the above
         19._____

20. _____ is an information-gathering technique that helps an analyst to find out facts and opinions from a large number of geographically dispersed people.   20.____
    A. Questionnaire
    B. Document analysis
    C. JAD session
    D. None of the above

21. All of the following are examples of privacy and security risks EXCEPT   21.____
    A. viruses
    B. spam
    C. hackers
    D. Trojan horses

22. _____ can recover a deleted/damaged file of a computer.   22.____
    A. Robotics
    B. Simulation
    C. Both A and B
    D. None of the above

23. _____ language is used by the computer to process data.   23.____
    A. Binary
    B. Processing
    C. Both A and B
    D. None of the above

24. The operating system   24.____
    A. enables drawing of a flowchart
    B. provides user-friendly interface
    C. both A and B
    D. none of the above

25. _____ is not an application software package.   25.____
    A. Microsoft Office
    B. Redhat Linux
    C. Adobe PageMaker
    D. Microsoft PowerPoint

KEY (CORRECT ANSWERS)

1.	A		11.	B
2.	D		12.	B
3.	A		13.	A
4.	A		14.	B
5.	A		15.	A
6.	A		16.	A
7.	A		17.	A
8.	C		18.	A
9.	B		19.	C
10.	D		20.	A

21.	B
22.	D
23.	A
24.	B
25.	B

TEST 3

DIRECTIONS: Each question or incomplete statement is followed by several suggested answers or completions. Select the one that BEST answers the question or completes the statement. *PRINT THE LETTER OF THE CORRECT ANSWER IN THE SPACE AT THE RIGHT.*

1.   The character repeat rate can be adjusted in   1.____
   A. Control Panel > Keyboard   B. My Computer
   C. Recycle Bin   D. none of the above

2.   There are _____ means of using a wireless mouse.   2.____
   A. 1   B. 2
   C. 3   D. none of the above

3.   _____ is used for creating and manipulating sound.   3.____
   A. MIDI   B. SIDI
   C. MODO   D. None of the above

4.   Picture quality is expressed in   4.____
   A. megapixels   B. hexapixels
   C. both of the above   D. none of the above

5.   The microphone port is located on the   5.____
   A. sound card   B. motherboard
   C. driver   D. none of the above

6.   The _____ is the peripheral device that transfers the audio from the PC.   6.____
   A. headphones   B. microphone
   C. camera   D. all of the above

7.   _____ is a secure connection.   7.____
   A. HTTP   B. TELNET   C. HTTPs   D. RCP

8.   A computer can be a client and a server to other computers in a _____   8.____
   network.
   A. bus   B. VPN   C. ring   D. peer-to-peer

9.   A _____ is used to send a signal at one end of a cable and found at the other   9.____
   end of the cable.
   A. cable tester   B. toner probe
   C. multimeter   D. none of the above

10. A company's ISP uses _____ to troubleshoot network issues.   10.____
   A. Smart Jack   B. 110 Block   C. 66 Block   D. Demarc

11. A firewall has not blocked a remote web server. To verify this, a _____ can be used.   11.____
    A. port scanner   B. toner probe
    C. both A and B   D. none of the above

12. _____ should be enabled to prevent broadcast storms.   12.____
    A. Bonding   B. Spanning tree
    C. Port mirroring   D. DHCP

13. A _____ network is least likely to collide.   13.____
    A. bus   B. star   C. ring   D. mesh

14. _____ tests the operation of NIC.   14.____
    A. Crossover   B. Rollover   C. 568B   D. Loopback

15. Planning includes   15.____
    A. conducting preliminary investigation
    B. conducting feasibility study
    C. identifying constraints
    D. all of the above

16. Feasibility study types include   16.____
    A. technical   B. economic return
    C. non-economic return   D. all of the above

17. Analysis includes   17.____
    A. gathering competent team members
    B. sending instructions to users
    C. documenting the existing system
    D. all of the above

18. The design phase includes determining   18.____
    A. technical systems configuration   B. data structure
    C. make or buy decision   D. all of the above

19. Which one of the following is a type of documentation?   19.____
    A. System documentation   B. Document feeder
    C. Audio coding   D. None of the above

20. The implementation phase includes   20.____
    A. conducting cutover   B. training users
    C. managing change   D. all of the above

21. Processing takes place at the   21.____
    A. box   B. CPU   C. system unit   D. motherboard

22. Memory is of _____ type(s).   22.____
    A. one   B. two   C. three   D. four

23. The _____ card is used while playing a video game.   23.____
    A. sound   B. graphic
    C. modem   D. network information

24. To do a specific task, a set of instructions is given to the computer. This   24.____
most closely describes
    A. software   B. hardware
    C. Internet browsing   D. none of the above

25. A user is allowed to analyze and maintain a computer by a program called   25.____
    A. Utility   B. Windows XP
    C. MS Office   D. Device Driver

KEY (CORRECT ANSWERS)

1.	A		11.	A
2.	B		12.	B
3.	A		13.	C
4.	A		14.	D
5.	A		15.	D
6.	A		16.	D
7.	C		17.	C
8.	D		18.	D
9.	A		19.	A
10.	A		20.	D

21.	C
22.	B
23.	A
24.	A
25.	A

TEST 4

DIRECTIONS: Each question or incomplete statement is followed by several suggested answers or completions. Select the one that BEST answers the question or completes the statement. *PRINT THE LETTER OF THE CORRECT ANSWER IN THE SPACE AT THE RIGHT.*

1. A(n) _____ is a device resembling a hypodermic needle.
    A. extractor
    B. detracter
    C. loop back plug
    D. none of the above

1.____

2. Which of the following are components of the microcomputer?
    A. Memory, Unit System
    B. Input device
    C. Output device
    D. All of the above

2.____

3. _____ is a common type of keyboard.
    A. USB
    B. PS/2
    C. Both A and B
    D. None of the above

3.____

4. How can we differentiate between a mouse's and keyboard's port?
    A. Keyboard is purple and mouse is green
    B. Keyboard is green and mouse is purple
    C. Keyboard is blue and mouse is green
    D. None of the above

4.____

5. If you reboot your computer and receive an error message of BIOS keyboard,
    A. the mouse is plugged into the keyboard input
    B. the keyboard is plugged into the mouse input
    C. both A and B
    D. none of the above

5.____

6. The mouse settings can be adjusted in
    A. Control Panel
    B. DOS
    C. My Computer
    D. none of the above

6.____

7. _____ prevents the propagating of different departments network broadcasts if they are located on the same switch.
    A. Hub
    B. VLAN
    C. Firewall
    D. Trunk

7.____

8. The most secure protocol for transferring network device configuration is
    A. TFTP
    B. RCP
    C. SCP
    D. none of the above

8.____

9. _____ Internet devices operate the OSI layer.
    A. One
    B. Two
    C. Three
    D. Four

9.____

10. You need to determine which buildings have multimode or single mode fiber. You will use the

    A. security policy   B. physical network diagram

    C. baseline configuration   D. none of the above

10.____

11. Many users are complaining about network issues. Of the following steps, which will you take FIRST?

    A. Collect information about the symptoms

    B. Make a plan of action and a solution

    C. Document the solution

    D. None of the above

11.____

12. Employees utilizing wireless laptops outdoors at the office are experiencing new connectivity problems. _____ is/are most likely causing the problems.

    A. Signal bounce   B. Antenna distance

    C. Environment factors   D. None of the above

12.____

13. The _____ contain(s) information about unlabeled data center connections.

    A. wiring schematics   B. emergency call list

    C. procedures manual   D. none of the above

13.____

14. If you have to install a phone that needs only one wire for both data and power to be supplied, _____ must be supported by the switch.

    A. PoE   B. spanning tree

    C. VLAN   D. none of the above

14.____

15. During the analysis phase, _____ is the type of prototype.

    A. discovery   B. evolving

    C. functioning   D. none of the above

15.____

16. _____ is a review technique that checks the validity of the documents produced during system analysis.

    A. Structured walkthrough   B. Prototyping

    C. Joint application   D. None of the above

16.____

17. Implementation classes

    A. describe the user interface   B. show implementation rules

    C. describe database interactions   D. none of the above

17.____

18. Databases and file definition are prepared in the _____ phase.

    A. implementation   B. design

    C. analysis   D. none of the above

18.____

19. _____ is requirements analysis deliverables.

    A. Requirement specification   B. User manual

    C. Design specification   D. All of the above

19.____

20. _____ can help an analyst to work with users to find out system usage.   20.____
    A. Use case   B. Class
    C. Actor   D. None of the above

21. _____ is a data-transfer technique.   21.____
    A. DMA   B. CAD
    C. Both A and B   D. None of the above

22. _____ devices are designed under electromechanical principle.   22.____
    A. Input   B. Output
    C. Storage   D. All of the above

23. A monitor consists of   23.____
    A. BRT   B. ARU
    C. CRT   D. none of the above

24. Exception is also known as   24.____
    A. interrupt   B. traps
    C. system calls   D. none of the above

25. _____ is a mutually exclusive operation.   25.____
    A. Signal instruction   B. Wait instruction
    C. Both A and B   D. None of the above

_____

KEY (CORRECT ANSWERS)

1.	A		11.	A
2.	D		12.	C
3.	C		13.	A
4.	A		14.	A
5.	C		15.	A
6.	A		16.	A
7.	B		17.	A
8.	C		18.	A
9.	C		19.	A
10.	B		20.	A

21.	A
22.	A
23.	C
24.	C
25.	C

_____

EXAMINATION SECTION

TEST 1

DIRECTIONS: Each question or incomplete statement is followed by several suggested answers or completions. Select the one that BEST answers the question or completes the statement. *PRINT THE LETTER OF THE CORRECT ANSWER IN THE SPACE AT THE RIGHT.*

1. During troubleshooting, you want to see the number of connections which are open on the user machine. The _____ command will be used to see these connections.
   A. Arp   B. Netstat   C. NsLookup   D. Netgear

   1.____

2. Two users want their PCs to be connected for file sharing. A _____ cable would be used to connect their PCs.
   A. crossover
   C. straight
   B. loopback
   D. none of the above

   2.____

3. A remote user complains that he is not able to connect to the office via VPN, though he has established Internet connectivity. What step should you take next to troubleshoot this situation?
   A. Find out if the user is using a valid VPN address and password
   B. Power cycle the VPN concentrator
   C. Reinstall the VPN client
   D. None of the above

   3.____

4. A _____ server limits the availability of types of websites that LAN users have access to.
   A. DHCP   B. DC   C. proxy   D. DNS

   4.____

5. If you are asked by the head of the company to block certain websites for the employees, what should you configure on the workstation to do so?
   A. Port scanner
   C. Network-based firewall
   B. Antivirus service
   D. Host-based firewall

   5.____

6. While troubleshooting a user's problems connecting to their network shares, you find out that the problem lies in the network cabling between the workstation and the switch. If all the other users are able to connect to the network, _____ will probably be the cause.
   A. crosstalk and interference occurring
   B. cable has been damaged or cut within the wall
   C. cable is not punched down properly at the punch panel
   D. none of the above

   6.____

7. Users are reporting that on a Windows network they are not able to   7.____
   access any network resources. The users can ping the IP address and use it
   to connect to the network resources. The cause of the problem may be
   A. the file server is offline
   B. the DNS server is not resolving properly
   C. the domain controller is not responding
   D. none of the above

8. If you have to give access to 64 servers on a network, which subnet of the   8.____
   following will provide the required access while conserving the IP address?
   A. 192.168.1.0.23   B. 192.168.1.0.24
   C. 192.168.1.0.25   D. 192.168.1.0.26

9. You are called by a user due to connection issues. You should start troubleshooting   9.____
   by
   A. resetting the router   B. installing a new NIC
   C. reinstalling the OS   D. checking the LEDs on NIC

10. You are called to extend the data circuit to the other side of the office.   10.____
    _____ would be set up at the new location.
    A. ESD   B. IDF   C. MDF   D. EMI

11. If a connection is punched down and noise is coming across the cable,   11.____
    which of the following tools would be used to identify the problem?
    A. Protocol analyzer   B. Cable tester
    C. Multimeter   D. None of the above

12. You have tested a cable and determined that it can successfully receive and   12.____
    send signals. A _____ can be used to determine the speed and condition of
    the signal.
    A. TDR   B. toner probe
    C. voltage event recorder   D. protocol analyzer

13. A network has many network printers with server-hosted queues. A client   13.____
    reports that they are not printing. It is verified that all tasks sent from the users'
    computers to the network printers fail. What should be your next step to
    troubleshoot this situation?
    A. Replace the printer   B. Reboot the print server
    C. Power cycle the switch   D. Try the printer from another PC

14. A visitor is insisting that he wants to use the company's wireless network on   14.____
    his laptop. DHCP is configured perfectly and a temporary WEP key is
    assigned to him, but his laptop is still not able to connect to the network
    because
    A. MAC filtering is enabled of the WAP
    B. the network is out of wireless connections
    C. the DNS server is not working properly
    D. none of the above

15. An accounting department employee's workstation needs to be connected
to the accounting server but is only able to connect to the Internet. The _____
setting should be verified in this case.
    A. VPN   B. WINS   C. DNS   D. VLAN

15.____

16. If you discover that the phone company has not installed the smart jack in
the right location and it needs to be moved 23 meters to the computer room, a
_____ should be requested.
    A. demark extension   B. 66 block extension
    C. replacement smart jack   D. none of the above

16.____

17. Remote users complain of not being able to access files from the file
server. You should first check the
    A. connectivity   B. access rights
    C. network resources   D. user accounts

17.____

18. You can successfully remote into the company's server but you cannot
connect to any other server's directories from the server itself; however, you
can ping them via the IP address. What is the problem?
    A. DHCP is not properly configured
    B. DNS is not properly configured
    C. Server is on a different VLAN
    D. None of the above

18.____

19. A _____ will be used to relocate a T1 nearer to the switch for connectivity.
    A. patch panel   B. smart jack
    C. 25 pair cable   D. none of the above

19.____

20. Your organization has 2,500 users, and they have exhausted their Internet
bandwidth. You discover that 96% of the traffic is comprised of web browsing.
A _____ network device will be added to reduce the amount of Internet
bandwidth.
    A. proxy server   B. load balancer
    C. content switch   D. none of the above

20.____

21. Which document will you reference to discover a rogue WAP?
    A. Policies   B. Baseline
    C. Wiring schematics   D. None of the above

21.____

22. _____ can allow you to restrict communication between network devices.
    A. ACL   B. CIDR   C. NAT   D. DHCP

22.____

23. Your company has a number of traveling sales employees who need secure
access to the company's resources from no trusted devices. A _____ VPN
solution will be the MOST appropriate for this.
    A. L2TP   B. IPSec   C. PPTP   D. SSL

23.____

24. You are troubleshooting a switch and have determined the symptoms.   24.____
    What should you do next?
    A. Implement and test solution   B. Find out the scope of the problem
    C. Escalate the issue   D. None of the above

25. In order to find out a physical interface problem, which of the following cables   25.____
    would you use?
    A. Loopback   B. Console   C. Rollover   D. Serial

_____

KEY (CORRECT ANSWERS)

1.	B		11.	B
2.	A		12.	A
3.	A		13.	D
4.	C		14.	A
5.	D		15.	D
6.	A		16.	A
7.	B		17.	A
8.	C		18.	B
9.	D		19.	B
10.	B		20.	A

21.	B
22.	A
23.	D
24.	B
25.	A

_____

TEST 2

DIRECTIONS: Each question or incomplete statement is followed by several suggested answers or completions. Select the one that BEST answers the question or completes the statement. *PRINT THE LETTER OF THE CORRECT ANSWER IN THE SPACE AT THE RIGHT.*

1.   You are asked to implement a separate network for the visitors. What   1._____
     would be the MOST cost-effective solution?
     A. Installing a firewall   B. Creating a VLAN
     C. Installing a VPN   D. None of the above

2.   A user complains that he is not able to send an email to his fellow user   2._____
     at the company and you believe that it is a DNS-related issue. After typing
     nslookup, the _____ command will allow finding out the IP address of the
     company's mail server.
     A. set type=ptr   B. set type=mx
     C. set type=soa   D, none of the above

3.   The _____ command will allow you to find out the DNS servers configured   3._____
     on a computer.
     A. nslookup   B. nbtstat
     C. netstat   D. none of the above

4.   A multiple devices network has to be set with a smaller broadcast domain while   4._____
     remaining on a small budget. The best solution is to
     A. create VLANs   B. implement more switches
     C. implement more hubs   D. none of the above

5.   If users at your company are not able to connect to servers using the   5._____
     FQDN, the likely cause of this issue would be the _____ is not enabled.
     A. DHCP   B. DNS
     C. WINS   D. none of the above

6.   If you need to extend the range of the wireless network in your office without   6._____
     running wires throughout the office, which of the following should you implement?
     A. At the end of the office install a repeater
     B. In the middle of the office install a WAP
     C. Both A and B
     D. None of the above

7.   You are troubleshooting a network error using a laptop as a network sniffer   7._____
     and are able to see all the communications on the network. What network
     device is the laptop plugged into?
     A. Router   B. Gateway
     C. Hub   D. None of the above

8. To provide the users with better network performance for accessing Internet websites, you should install 8.____
   A. traffic shaping
   B. load balancing
   C. caching engine
   D. none of the above

9. After gathering information about a client's network issue and determining the affected area, you will 9.____
   A. test the best solution
   B. check for any recent changes in the network
   C. none of the above
   D. both A and B

10. Some users complain that they are not able to access the network. The computers that are not able to access the network carry an IP address of 169.254.0.1. The _____ network service should be checked for troubleshooting. 10.____
    A. TFTP
    B. DNS
    C. BOOTP
    D. DHCP

11. You are in charge of several remote servers in the United States. Users call and complain that they are not able to connect to the company's resources that are located on those servers. Which command would you use to verify whether the servers are running? 11.____
    A. Ping
    B. Nbstat
    C. Netstat
    D. Telnet

12. A user's star network connected workstation is not able to connect to the network resources. You should first check the 12.____
    A. installed network drivers
    B. link lights on the switch
    C. link lights on the network card
    D. none of the above

13. You should be aware of _____ while installing a wireless network in a multiple-floor building. 13.____
    A. SSID naming
    B. channel overlap
    C. frequency configuration
    D. none of the above

14. You are contacted by a user. According to him, his system is not able to connect to a file server. After troubleshooting and successfully resolving the issue, you should 14.____
    A. create an action plan
    B. document the solution
    C. reboot the server
    D. none of the above

15. A user's computer is affected with an automated application without the user interaction. You should tell the user that this issue is referred to as a 15.____
    A. trojan
    B. worm
    C. smurf attack
    D. none of the above

16. You are troubleshooting an application that is frequently terminating. What can be used to determine the problem? 16.____
    A. History log
    B. DNS log
    C. Port scanner
    D. Application log

17. A network issue has just been reported to you. Which of the following steps   17.____
should you take first to troubleshoot the issue?
    A. Ask the user to explain the symptoms in detail
    B. Ask the user about what documentation they had in the past
    C. Record the solution in appropriate logs
    D. None of the above

18. A user complains that after his transfer from the accounting team to HR team   18.____
he can only print to the accounting team printer and not the HR team printer.
What is the cause of this problem?
    A. Wrong DNS   B. Wrong gateway
    C. Wrong host file   D. Wrong VLAN

19. If five computers are connected to a single server for file and printing and   19.____
one computer is not able to connect to the network while the others work
properly, this could be caused by
    A. failure of the switch
    B. failure of the server
    C. failure of the NIC
    D. the computer's OS needing to be updated

20. _____ is commonly used to test the fiber connectivity.   20.____
    A. Multimeter   B. Butt set
    C. Toner probe   D. OTDR

21. A user demands a fault-tolerant server. To provide him with this in a most   21.____
cost-effective way, you should install
    A. a single router   B. a single fiber NIC
    C. two NICs for teaming   D. none of the above

22. A user is having issues accessing the shared resources on the file server.   22.____
You should first
    A. test the results   B. identify the symptoms
    C. document the problem   D. none of the above

23. A user complains that her wireless connection has decreased signal   23.____
strength, whereas the network configuration has not been changed. The
MOST likely cause of the decreased signals is
    A. standards mismatch   B. incorrect SSID
    C. environmental factors   D. incorrect encryption

24. A user complains that his wireless 802.11g Internet connection is disrupted.   24.____
What might be the cause of the problem?
    A. Cell phone   B. Incandescent light
    C. Cordless phone   D. Infrared printer

25. You have been asked to retrieve device statistics, errors and information. Which of the following should you use?

    A. SNMP   B. SMTP

    C. Packet sniffer   D. TFTP

25.____

———

KEY (CORRECT ANSWERS)

1.	B		11.	A
2.	B		12.	C
3.	A		13.	B
4.	A		14.	B
5.	B		15.	B
6.	B		16.	D
7.	C		17.	A
8.	C		18.	D
9.	B		19.	C
10.	D		20.	D

21.	C
22.	B
23.	C
24.	C
25.	A

———

TEST 3

DIRECTIONS: Each question or incomplete statement is followed by several suggested answers or completions. Select the one that BEST answers the question or completes the statement. *PRINT THE LETTER OF THE CORRECT ANSWER IN THE SPACE AT THE RIGHT.*

1. A user is reporting slow network response in his class. The class needs many students to be able to access the same website every day. According to you, which of the following is the BEST remedy for this problem?
   A. Firewall
   B. Caching engine
   C. Fault tolerance
   D. Jitter correction

1.____

2. A user complains that he has moved a VoIP phone to a new location. The phone does not start now when it is plugged into the network. The reason for this is that
   A. the phone requires a fiber port
   B. Qos is not enabled on the switch
   C. the switch does not support PoE
   D. none of the above

2.____

3. A port scanner is used to
   A. secure switches and routers
   B. find routers with weak passwords
   C. find open ports on network hosts
   D. none of the above

3.____

4. A remote web server is not blocked by a firewall. To verify that, a _____ should be used.
   A. port scanner
   B. toner probe
   C. packet injector
   D. none of the above

4.____

5. For the purpose of providing redundant paths to network resources, if a link fails, _____ switch features will be needed by you to accomplish the task.
   A. trunking
   B. PoE
   C. VLAN
   D. spanning tree

5.____

6. To connect a user to a WPA-encrypted network, you will require a
   A. pre-shared key
   B. PIN
   C. SSID
   D. none of the above

6.____

7. Network-based _____ is the most cost-effective technology for protecting a large amount of networked workstations from external attacks.
   A. firewall
   B. IDS
   C. IPS
   D. none of the above

7.____

8. After installing and testing a new wireless network for your client and turning wireless access on, you should
   A. document the physical layout
   B. configure wireless adapters
   C. configure the DHCP server
   D. none of the above

8.____

9.   A ping _____ command would check the loopback adapter of an internal NIC.   9._____
     A. 127.1.1.1   B. 127.0.0.1
     C. 127.127.0.0   D. none of the above

10. To prevent broadcast storms for your client, you should enable   10._____
     A. DHCP   B. port mirroring
     C. bonding   D. spanning tree

11. You are configuring a router for SOHO network. You have disabled DHCP   11._____
     service and replaced the IP address scheme on the router. Now you have to
     establish the connection while keeping the router's current configuration state.
     What would be the BEST solution?
     A. Assign a static IP address so the PC matches the router
     B. Use APIPA to connect the PC to the router
     C. Both A and B
     D. None of the above

12. When you are configuring a wireless access point, select the channel   12._____
     A. frequency range least used in a given area
     B. closest to that configured on neighboring access points
     C. that is the same channel configured on the neighboring access points
     D. none of the above

13. A client has accidentally unplugged the network cable of their computer   13._____
     (in a wired bus topology environment). Which of the following is TRUE?
     A. It will not function until the wires are reconnected
     B. It will function with minimal downtime
     C. It will function with no downtime
     D. None of the above

14. A user complains that he can access the network shares and his email but   14._____
     cannot access any website. Which command tools will you use to begin
     troubleshooting?
     A. Trace route to any website to determine where the disconnection is
         happening
     B. Use route add command
     C. Use ping command
     D. None of the above

15. Users at a branch office complain that access to static web content is very   15._____
     slow from their location. Which of the following will improve WAN utilization?
     A. A traffic shaper
     B. An application level firewall
     C. A caching proxy server at the branch
     D. None of the above

16. Your head asks you to verify the available phone numbers at your company. 16.____
Which of the following should you use to verify the available numbers?
    A. Multimeter   B. Toner probe
    C. Punch down tool   D. Butt set

17. You need to run a network for your company, which should be able to handle 17.____
30 Mbps data-transfer speeds while keeping the installation cost of the network
down. Which cable types would you prefer?
    A. CAT3   B. CAT6   C. CAT5e   D. CAT1

18. You are troubleshooting an issue where a computer is not connecting to 18.____
the Internet employing a wireless access point. The computer is transferring
files locally to the other machines but is unable to reach the Internet. The IP
address and default gateways are both on the 182.158.1.0/24. The problem is
that the computer
    A. gateway is not routing to a public IP address
    B. is using an invalid IP address
    C. is not using a private IP address
    D. none of the above

19. You have to set up a connection that enables visitors to connect to the 19.____
Internet but not the server, while employees will be able to connect to both.
The same switch manages all of the connections. What should be used to
meet these requirements?
    A. OSPF   B. RIP   C. Post trunking   D. VLAN

20. An employee kitchen area is added to your office. No changes have been 20.____
made in the work area and equipment, but the employees are having a
wireless connectivity problem. What is the cause of the problem?
    A. Interference   B. Distance
    C. Encryption   D. None of the above

21. If the staff is trained about Implementing a set of procedures and policies 21.____
that makes clear that corporation information is confidential, _____ can be
prevented.
    A. social engineering   B. patch management
    C. smurf attacks   D. none of the above

22. A user support analyst must be able to manage 22.____
    A. his time
    B. his client's time
    C. both A and B
    D. managing time is not necessary in this matter

23. A user support analyst must be able to 23.____
    A. consider the relative costs
    B. consider the benefits of potential actions to select the most appropriate one
    C. both A and B
    D. none of the above

24. A user support analyst should   24.____
    A. always solve the problems himself
    B. teach users to solve the minor problems themselves
    C. never let users solve the problem
    D. none of the above

25. The user support analyst should have the ability to   25.____
    A. communicate information and ideas
    B. read and understand information
    C. identify and understand the speech of another person
    D. all of the above

KEY (CORRECT ANSWERS)

1.	B		11.	A
2.	C		12.	A
3.	C		13.	A
4.	A		14.	A
5.	D		15.	C
6.	A		16.	D
7.	A		17.	C
8.	A		18.	A
9.	B		19.	D
10.	D		20.	A

21.	A
22.	C
23.	C
24.	B
25.	D

TEST 4

DIRECTIONS: Each question or incomplete statement is followed by several suggested answers or completions. Select the one that BEST answers the question or completes the statement. *PRINT THE LETTER OF THE CORRECT ANSWER IN THE SPACE AT THE RIGHT.*

1. You are troubleshooting the phone service at a site and discover that there is no dial tone present in the connection on block 65. Which tool would you use to check the connection at the demarcation point?
    A. Toner probe   B. Multimeter   C. Cable tester   D. Butt set

    1._____

2. A client calls you to troubleshoot his machine and you need to open connections and see the current NetBIOS configuration. Which command would you use to display this information?
    A. nbstat   B. msconfig   C. netstat   D. ipconfig

    2._____

3. A client asks you to implement a new wireless network and run the highest level of wireless encryption. You should run
    A. WEP   B. WPA2 TKIP   C. WPAS AES   D. TTL

    3._____

4. Which of the following tools is used for capturing username and passwords on a network?
    A. Proxy server   B. Sniffer   C. Firewall   D. Honey pot

    4._____

5. A company consists of one headquarters and eight remote sites. The remote sites just need to communicate with the headquarters. Which topology is BEST for the company?
    A. Mesh   B. Star   C. Hybrid   D. Ring

    5._____

6. Which of the following command line tools would you use to verify DNS functionality?
    A. netstat   B. arp   C. dig   D. traceroute

    6._____

7. Which of the following would you use to provide the highest level of security to a newly installed wireless router?
    A. SSL   B. WEP   C. WPA   D. IPSec

    7._____

8. An application layer firewall can filter _____, while a network layer firewall cannot.
    A. HTTP URLs   B. ICMP
    C. Telnet traffic   D. HTTP traffic

    8._____

9. What should be used for the purpose of connecting multiple network hosts when the physical signal is being repeated to all ports?
    A. Bridge   B. Hub   C. Router   D. Switch

    9._____

10. While troubleshooting you need to catch a specific NICs MAC address. While you know the IP address of the NIC, _____ would enable you to discover the MAC address without going to that specific computer physically.
    A. netstat   B. ping   C. nbstat   D. arp

            10.____

11. A VoIP telephone with a built-in hub is plugged into a single network, using both of the ports (hub port and telephone port). Suddenly, the network starts to experience lag because of the increase in traffic. What would help to avoid this situation in the future?
    A. VLANs   B. Trunking
    C. Port mirroring   D. Spanning tree

            11.____

12. _____ is the MOST secure access method.
    A. RSH   B. SNMPv1   C. SFTP   D. RCP

            12.____

13. If you need to access files on a remote server, _____ would be used.
    A. ARP   B. FTP   C. SIP   D. NTP

            13.____

14. _____ is 568B standard.
    A. Logical network diagram   B. Network baseline
    C. Wiring schematic   D. None of the above

            14.____

15. A user complains that on a wireless network he can connect to local resources but cannot connect to the Internet. Which of the following might be the reason?
    A. The gateway is not configured on the router
    B. The wireless network card is not in range
    C. The wireless network card is not working
    D. None of the above

            15.____

16. _____ is a client-server based authentication software system that keeps user profiles in a central database.
    A. RADIUS   B. MSCHAp   C. EAP   D. CHAP

            16.____

17. _____ is an authentication protocol the employs plain text for transmitting passwords over the internet.
    A. Kerberos   B. CHAP   C. PAP   D. RADIUS

            17.____

18. A user wants to bond his new printer with his PDA. What is the BEST technology to describe the type of wireless printer?
    A. Wi-Fi   B. Bluetooth   C. IEEE 1394   D. 802.11a

            18.____

19. Many workstations have lost network connectivity in network. Which of the following steps should you take to troubleshoot the issue?
    A. Document all possible causes
    B. Reboot the computer
    C. Escalate the issue to a senior network associate
    D. None of the above

            19.____

20. You need to provide a solution that will allow 500 users of a remote site to access the Internet using only one public routable IP address, allowing direct user access to the Internet. What is the BEST technology to implement?   20.____
    A. DNS   B. PAT   C. VPN   D. DHCP

21. You discover that unencrypted passwords are being sent over the network. Which network monitoring utility was used to find this out?   21.____
    A. Network scanner   B. Packet sniffer
    C. Throughput tester   D. None of the above

22. _____ would need to be installed to connect a fiber NIC with an Ethernet backbone.   22.____
    A. Bridge   B. Hub
    C. Repeater   D. None of the above

23. _____ is the MOST essential component for providing user support.   23.____
    A. Communication   B. Knowledge
    C. Experience   D. None of the above

24. To get to the heart of the problem, the support analyst must   24.____
    A. listen to the user   B. not ask questions to the user
    C. ask the right question   D. both A and C

25. The user should be kept _____ by the support analyst.   25.____
    A. informed of progress   B. informed of expected next steps
    C. both A and B   D. informed of all technical details

KEY (CORRECT ANSWERS)

1.	D		11.	D
2.	A		12.	C
3.	C		13.	B
4.	B		14.	C
5.	D		15.	A
6.	C		16.	A
7.	C		17.	C
8.	A		18.	B
9.	B		19.	C
10.	D		20.	C

21.	B
22.	B
23.	A
24.	D
25.	C

EXAMINATION SECTION

TEST 1

DIRECTIONS: Each question or incomplete statement is followed by several suggested answers or completions. Select the one that BEST answers the question or completes the statement. *PRINT THE LETTER OF THE CORRECT ANSWER IN THE SPACE AT THE RIGHT.*

1. _____ is the data that has been organized or presented in a meaningful fashion.   1._____
   A. A process   B. Software   C. Storage   D. Information

2. Of the following data processing functions, which one is NOT a data   2._____
   processing function of a computer?
   A. Data gathering   B. Processing data into information
   C. Analyzing the data or information   D. Storing the data or information

3. In electronic data processing systems, which standard data code is used   3._____
   commonly to represent alphabetical, numerical and punctuation characters?
   A. ASCII   B. EBCDIC   C. BCD   D. All of the above

4. Data processing performed by several separate computers/networks, at   4._____
   several different locations, linked by a communications facility is known as
   _____ processing.
   A. distributed   B. centralized   C. on-line   D. batch

5. Which process is utilized by large retailers to study market trends?   5._____
   A. Data conversion   B. Data mining
   C. Data selection   D. Pos

6. In normalization, second normal form (2NF) eliminates in Tables   6._____
   A. all hidden dependencies
   B. the possibility of insertion anomalies
   C. all non-key fields depend on the whole primary key
   D. none of the above

7. Which of the following is a bottom-up approach for database design which is   7._____
   designed by examining the relationship between attributes?
   A. Functional dependency   B. Normalization
   C. Decomposition   D. None of the above

8. Which is the process that is used to restore data that has been stored in a   8._____
   computer?
   A. Retrieve   B. Backup   C. Recovery   D. Deadlock

9. Which term BEST explains the homogenous data type? 9.____
   A. Data items of same length
   B. Data items of same type
   C. Data items of different length
   D. Numerical and character date items

10. For any category of data being processed and any type of device used for this 10.____
    purpose, all data processing systems perform the same steps. Which is the
    CORRECT sequence?
    A. Analyzing, coding and execution
    B. Input, processing and output
    C. Input, organizing and processing
    D. Processing, storage and distribution

11. Which of the following e-data processing methods works on data that 11.____
    is accumulated from more than location and records that are updated instantly?
    A. Minicomputer system   B. Batch processing system
    C. On-line, real-time system   D. Micro computer system

12. Suppose you are employed by the Air Transport Company to design a 12.____
    database for an airline transaction system. The database has to capture the
    detailed level of data related to the tickets booked by the user and the updating
    made by them with timestamp. Which database model would be your
    preference?
    A. Dimensional model
    B. It can be either dimensional model or on-line transaction processing
       model
    C. On-line transaction processing model
    D. None of the above

13. In the database management system, what are the after triggers functions? 13.____
    A. Triggers generated after a particular operation
    B. Triggers run after an insert, update or delete on a table
    C. Triggers run after an insert, views, update or delete on a table
    D. None of the above

14. For trigger creation, a CREATE TRIGGER statement is used. So, clause 14.____
    _____ specifies the table name on which the trigger is to be attached. Also,
    _____ specifies that it is an AFTER INSERT trigger.
    A. for insert; on   B. on; for insert
    C. for; insert   D. none of the above

15. Which part of a data flow diagram (DFD) represents the people and 15.____
    organizations that send data that the system being modeled uses or produces?
    A. Processes   B. Data source   C. Data store   D. Data flow

16. The purpose of cryptography is 16.____
    A. deadlock removal   B. job scheduling
    C. protection   D. file management

17. _____ memory allocation method suffers from external fragmentation.   17.____
   A. Segmentation   B. Demand paging
   C. Swapping   D. Paging

18. When working with a time-sharing operating system, when the time slot   18.____
    given to a process is completed, the process goes from the running state to the
    _____ state.
   A. blocked   B. ready   C. complete   D. terminated

19. The purpose of real-time systems   19.____
   A. is primarily used on mainframe computers
   B. monitors events instantly as they occur
   C. is employed in program development
   D. none of the above

20. What are the causes of process termination?   20.____
   A. Process is removed from all queues and process's PCB is de-allocated
   B. Process is completed
   C. Process control block is never de-allocated
   D. None of the above

21. Fragmentation of the file system   21.____
   A. occurs only if the file system is used improperly
   B. can always be prevented
   C. can be temporarily removed by compaction
   D. is a characteristic of all file systems

22. _____ scheduling is most suitable for a time-shared interactive system. It   22.____
    assigns the CPU to the first process in the ready queue for q time units. After q
    time units, if the process is not handed over to the CPU, it is blocked, and the
    process is put at the tail of the ready queue (done).
   A. Shortest-job-first (SJF)   B. CPU
   C. Round-robin (RR)   D. None of the above

23. Backup can BEST be explained as   23.____
   A. a tool that must be offered by Windows operating system like Windows
      XP and 7 that checks when your system hardware and software need a
      new OS
   B. copy files from a computer to another medium, such as tape, DVD,
      another hard drive, or a removable drive
   C. a term that is used to move from one operating system to another, which
      may or may not involve implementing a new computer
   D. none of the above

24. As a Technical Support Officer for a large organization, at times you have   24.____
to deal with login authentication problems of user computers. Which of the
following is NOT a best practice for password policy?
   A. Restriction on password reuse
   B. Password encryption
   C. Having changed passwords every two years
   D. Deciding maximum age of password
   E. None of the above

25. When working in a team environment, the BEST adopted problem-solving   25.____
technique in which all members of a team fully accept and support a decision is
   A. compromise   B. goal
   C. consensus   D. none of the above

_____

KEY (CORRECT ANSWERS)

1.	D		11.	C
2.	C		12.	C
3.	A		13.	B
4.	A		14.	B
5.	B		15.	B
6.	A		16.	C
7.	B		17.	A
8.	A		18.	B
9.	B		19.	B
10.	B		20.	A

21.	A
22.	C
23.	B
24.	C
25.	C

_____

TEST 2

DIRECTIONS: Each question or incomplete statement is followed by several suggested answers or completions. Select the one that BEST answers the question or completes the statement. *PRINT THE LETTER OF THE CORRECT ANSWER IN THE SPACE AT THE RIGHT.*

1. A collection of facts like drawings, pictures and stock figures is called   1.____
   A. quantity   B. product
   C. data   D. collector's item
   E. information

2. The electronic data processing technique that collects data into groups to permit   2.____
   convenient and efficient processing is known as
   A. document-count processing   B. batch-processing
   C. generalized-audit processing   D. multiprogramming

3. Lee runs a grocery store; he wants to keep a record of daily sold items. Lee   3.____
   uses a bar chart for this purpose to show many breads he sold per day. Each
   day has its own bar. How could he find the total number of breads sold?
   A. Finding the height of the tallest bar
   B. Adding together the heights of all the bars in the chart
   C. Counting the number of bars
   D. Finding the average of the values of each bar

4. A summary level view of a system and the highest-level DFD is provided to   4.____
   the reader with the help of
   A. data store   B. data source
   C. context diagram   D. documentation

5. Which option BEST explains the *triggers*?   5.____
   A. A statement that enables the start of any DBMS
   B. A statement that is executed by the user when debugging an application
      program
   C. A statement that is executed automatically by the system as a side effect
      of modification to the database
   D. None of the above

6. Virtual memory technique is implemented with the help of   6.____
   A. segmentation   B. fragmentation
   C. paging   D. none of the above

7. Which diagram is used to represent the relationship between the input,   7.____
   processing and output of an AIS?
   A. Flowchart   B. Data flow diagram
   C. Document flowchart   D. System flowcharts

8. _____ scheduling is the simplest scheduling technique that forces the short processes to wait for very long processes.
   A. Round-robin (RR)
   B. Last-in, first out (LIFO)
   C. Shortest-job-first (SJF)
   D. First-come, first-served (FCFS)

   8.____

9. Mapping of file is managed by
   A. paging table
   B. virtual memory
   C. file system
   D. file metadata

   9.____

10. On-line analytical processing is also called _____ processing.
    A. decision support
    B. on-line transactional
    C. transaction control
    D. none of the above

    10.____

11. When working in large organizations, you have to deal with different access authentication situations. To ensure security, you have multiple options in such conditions. Which of the following is the LEAST secure method of authentication for your organization?
    A. Key card
    B. Fingerprint
    C. Retina pattern
    D. Password

    11.____

12. DML stands for
    A. data management language
    B. data markup language
    C. data manipulation language
    D. none of the above

    12.____

13. Which term BEST explains the characteristics of a computer to run several operations simultaneously?
    A. Concurrency   B. Deadlock   C. Backup   D. Recovery

    13.____

14. In DBMS, what is the BEST way to represent the attributes in a large database?
    A. Relational-and
    B. Concatenation
    C. Dot representation
    D. All of the above

    14.____

15. Database locking mechanism is used to rectify the problem of
    A. lost update
    B. uncommitted dependency
    C. inconsistent data
    D. none of the above

    15.____

16. In the scheme (dept name, size), we have relations (total inst 2010, total inst 2013). Which dependency has led to this relation?
    A. Company name, year->size
    B. Year->size
    C. Company name->size
    D. Size->year

    16.____

17. Which is the BEST possible option to evaluate any scheduling algorithm?
    A. CPU utilization
    B. Throughput
    C. Waiting time
    D. All of the above

    17.____

18. When the round robin CPU scheduling technique is adopted in a time-shared system,
    A. very large time slice degenerates into first-come, first-served algorithm
    B. extremely small time slices improve performance
    C. extremely small time slices degenerates into LIFO algorithm
    D. medium sized time slices leads to shortest request time first algorithm

18.____

19. A priority scheduling BIGGEST issue is
    A. definite blocking
    B. starvation
    C. priority queues
    D. none of the above

19.____

20.

The above figure is called a(n) _____ in use case diagram.
    A. person
    B. substitute
    C. actor (symbol)
    D. flow directive

20.____

21. Use case models can be summed up into
    A. use case diagram
    B. use case description
    C. all of the above
    D. none of the above

21.____

22. Prototype
    A. is a working model of different parts at different levels or all of a final product
    B. does not represent any sort of models
    C. can never consist of full size
    D. all of the above

22.____

23. Kim has been given some official documents to type. While typing, he notices that some of the words are automatically changing. He is very interested to understand the purpose of this feature in MS Word. AutoCorrect is designed to replace _____ words as you type.
    A. short, repetitive
    B. grammatically incorrect
    C. misspelled
    D. none of the above

23.____

24. As a computer associate, you have to write different reports like weekly departmental updates and specially designed tasks to analyze the different areas of an organization. Of the following, which is considered good reporting practices?
    A. Report factual observations, not opinions
    B. Identify proper personnel
    C. Formalize your inspection criteria
    D. None of the above

24.____

25. To improve the competency of teams, members of a(n) _____ team have been cross-trained so that each person is capable of performing the duties of all the other team members.
    A. functional   B. cross-functional
    C. multifunctional   D. self-directed

25.____

KEY (CORRECT ANSWERS)

1.	C		11.	D
2.	B		12.	C
3.	B		13.	A
4.	C		14.	B
5.	C		15.	C
6.	C		16.	A
7.	D		17.	D
8.	C		18.	A
9.	D		19.	B
10.	A		20.	C

21.	C
22.	A
23.	C
24.	A
25.	D

TEST 3

DIRECTIONS: Each question or incomplete statement is followed by several suggested answers or completions. Select the one that BEST answers the question or completes the statement. *PRINT THE LETTER OF THE CORRECT ANSWER IN THE SPACE AT THE RIGHT.*

1. Information is _____ unfinished data. 1.____
   A. always   B. not   C. occasionally   D. none of these

2. Which option BEST explains Beta software? 2.____
   A. An early development version of software in which there are likely to be bugs.
   B. Software will expire in 30 days after its download.
   C. Software that has successfully passed the alpha test stage.
   D. Up-gradation of software is not possible.

3. Jane drew a bar chart to show the number of different cars he saw daily on his way back home. There was no bar above the Mercedes. What does this mean? 3.____
   A. He did not see any Mercedes during his trip
   B. No Mercedes exist in his city
   C. He selected a wrong type of chart
   D. He has never seen a Mercedes before

4. A flowchart is a picture representation of a program. Flows should initiate from top to bottom and from right to left. This flowcharting principle is commonly known as the _____ rule. 4.____
   A. narrative   B. sandwich   C. direction   D. consistency

5. The database designing approach which is based on a bottom-up approach that is designed by examining the relationship between attributes is 5.____
   A. functional dependency   B. database modeling
   C. normalization   D. decomposition

6. In an operating system, a situation occurs in which one process is in a waiting queue on another process that is also waiting on another process and the last one is waiting on the first process so no process is progressing in this waiting circular. This is called 6.____
   A. deadlock   B. starvation
   C. dormant   D. none of the above

7. Which access control method is considered the BEST approach for restricting system access to authorized users? 7.____
   A. Role-based access control   B. Process-based access control
   C. Job-based access control   D. None of the above

8. Which of the following is a disadvantage of a distributed system? 8.____
   A. Incremental growth   B. Reliability
   C. Resource sharing   D. All of the above

9. Which of the following is the BEST example of batch processing?
    A. Video game control   B. Online reservation system
    C. Preparing pay bills of employees   D. None of the above

    9.____

10. Which of the following techniques was initiated to keep both CPU and the I/O devices busy because it was not possible with the single job?
    A. Time-sharing   B. Spooling
    C. Preemptive scheduling   D. Multiprogramming

    10.____

11. Distributed operating system is based on the principle of
    A. single system image   B. multi-system image
    C. wireless networks   D. none of the above

    11.____

12. The following components are helpful in a successful database environment EXCEPT
    A. users   B. database
    C. separate files   D. database administrator

    12.____

13. In DBMS, which of the following is NOT schema?
    A. Database schema   B. Logical schema
    C. None of the above

    13.____

14. Of the following, which SQL Query is used to remove the table and all its data from the database?
    A. Drop table   B. Delete table
    C. Alter table   D. None of the above

    14.____

15. *Ellipses* in DBMS means
    A. weak entity set   B. attributes
    C. primary key   D. none of the above

    15.____

16. The method which performs a set of union of two "similarly structured" tables is called
    A. union   B. join
    C. addition   D. none of the above

    16.____

17. All details about the files, its ownership, permissions, and location of file contents are stored in
    A. file control block (FCB)   B. computer history
    C. file system   D. none of the above

    17.____

18. The drawback of a file management system to store data is
    A. data redundancy and inconstancy
    B. difficulty in accessing data
    C. data isolation
    D. all of the above

    18.____

19. Which of the following is a feature of the machine independent operating system?   19.____
   A. Management of real time memory   B. File processing
   C. I/O supervision   D. Job scheduling
   E. B and D   F. A and C

20. As a computer support officer, you are given details for your company's customers,   20.____
   consisting of two lists of names and addresses. You need to produce it in an
   individual document that consists of both names and address list. For this
   purpose, which mail merge would you prefer?
   A. Main document   B. Data source
   C. Mail merge   D. Merge field

21. After once creating a customer list with mail merge, which button will help   21.____
   you to add, delete or update your customer list?
   A. *Data Source* button   B. *Edit* button
   C. *Edit Data Source* button   D. *Data Editing* button

22. Which of the following steps is NOT a part of the three basic *Mail Merge*   22.____
   Helper steps?
   A. Merge the two files   B. Create the main document
   C. Set the mailing list parameters   D. Create the data source

23. As a computer support officer, while completing your assigned document   23.____
   typed in MS Word 2013, you need to insert the page number in the footer, but
   when you click on the insert tab > footer, it appears as *1*, but you wish to show *i*
   (roman numbers). What procedure will be followed?
   A. From Home, select bullets and numbering and configure the necessary
      setting
   B. From Insert Tab, choose Page Number and specify necessary setting
   C. Click on Page Number Icon and select Format Page Number and specify
      required setting
   D. All of the above

24. The problem statement contains the _____, which consists of these lists: 24.____
   I.   Lists specific input programs
   II.   Precise output values
   III. Perfect program would return for those input values

   A. Testing plan   B. Error handler
   C. Requirement list   D. Input-output specification

25. As a computer support officer who knows the stages of team development   25.____
   that will lead this team to a winning combination, what are the stages in proper
   sequence?
   A. Forming, storming, norming and performing
   B. Forming, norming, performing and finalizing
   C. Forming, storming, norming and playing
   D. None of the above

KEY (CORRECT ANSWERS)

1.	B		11.	B
2.	C		12.	C
3.	A		13.	B
4.	C		14.	C
5.	C		15.	B
6.	A		16.	A
7.	A		17.	A
8.	B		18.	D
9.	C		19.	E
10.	D		20.	C

21.	C
22.	C
23.	C
24.	A
25.	A

TEST 4

DIRECTIONS: Each question or incomplete statement is followed by several suggested answers or completions. Select the one that BEST answers the question or completes the statement. *PRINT THE LETTER OF THE CORRECT ANSWER IN THE SPACE AT THE RIGHT.*

1.   Data users are those who   1.____
     A. use data for their own advantage, breaking the law
     B. store files and data for their specific purposes
     C. use the data in databases
     D. none of the above

2.   Which type of chart would be the BEST choice for showing how the   2.____
     temperature of a pizza changes over time when it is put in the oven?
     A. Pie chart   B. Line graph
     C. Bar chart   D. None of the above

3.   As a computer support officer, you have to continuously update and   3.____
     organize your directories, folders and files on your computer. Which of the
     following BEST suits your requirement?
     A. Microsoft Word   B. Any spreadsheet application
     C. Windows Explorer   D. Microsoft Internet Explorer

4.   Upgrade installation means   4.____
     A. preparation for installation, installation itself, any required or optional
         steps following the installation
     B. completely formatting the operating system on hardware and install new
         software
     C. type of system installation on a computer that already has an earlier
         version of the operating system
     D. none of the above

5.   The main job of an operating system is   5.____
     A. command resources   B. manage resources
     C. provide utilities   D. none of the above

6.   The MOST common source of change data in refreshing a data warehouse   6.____
     is _____ change data.
     A. queryable   B. cooperative   C. logged   D. snapshot

7.   Which of the following is NOT an advantage of multiprogramming?   7.____
     A. Increased throughput
     B. Shorter response time
     C. Decreased operating system overhead
     D. Ability to assign priorities to jobs

8. In ERD, the rectangles are divided into two parts that show   8.____
       A. entity set   B. relationship set
       C. set of attributes   D. primary key

9. The MAXIMUM numbers of entities that can be participating in a relationship   9.____
    are designed with
       A. minimum cardinality   B. maximum cardinality
       C. entity relation diagram   D. none of the above

10. Which of the following is a multi-valued attribute?   10.____
       A. Phone number   B. Name
       C. Date of birth   D. Place of birth
       E. None of the above

11. Which term is used to refer to a specific record in your medicine database;   11.____
    for instance, information stored about a specific illness?
       A. Relation   B. Instance
       C. Table   D. None of the above

12. The relation stud (ID, name, house no., credit, house no., city, department)   12.____
    is decomposed into stud1 (ID, name)   stud2 (name, house no., city,
    department). This type of decomposition is called
       A. lossless decomposition   B. lossless-join decomposition
       C. both A and B   D. none of the above

13. As a technical support officer for a large organization, you have to ensure   13.____
    the uninterrupted availability of data by creating backup to deal with every
    possible data loss. Backup is taken by
       A. erasing all previous records and creating new records
       B. sending all log records from primary site to the remote backup site
       C. sending only selected records from main site to the alternate site
       D. none of the above

14. Verbal exchange of information between parents and a school staff when a   14.____
    student is moved from one department to another is a report which includes
    necessary information to maintain a consistent support for students of one
    department to another. This report is known as a
       A. transfer report   B. hand-off report
       C. graphic record   D. report

15. Which portable storage device would you prefer for backups or showing   15.____
    your photographs to your friend?
       A. USB stick   B. Hard drive
       C. Joystick   D. None of the above

16. Which is the exact step for problem solving?   16.____
    A. Observe, evaluate and adjust
    B. Collect and analyze data
    C. Identify and analyze the problem
    D. Consider possible solutions

17. The software that maintains the time of a microprocessor to assure that   17.____
all time critical events are processed as efficiently as possible and also system
activities are divided into independent tasks is known as
    A. shell processor   B. kernel
    C. device driver   D. none of the above

18. Which of the following is the MOST appropriate scheduling technique in   18.____
real time operating systems?
    A. Round robin   B. FCFS
    C. Pre-emptive scheduling   D. Random scheduling

19. Use case diagrams consist of   19.____
    A. actor   B. prototype
    C. none of the above   D. all of the above

20. Data warehouse means   20.____
    A. the actual directory of a knowledge
    B. the stage of selecting the right data for a KDD process
    C. a subject-oriented integrated time variant non-volatile collection of data in
         support of management
    D. all of the above

21. Jane wants to advertise her home-based bakery. For this purpose she needs   21.____
to develop a two-column promotion for the daily local newspaper. She selected
MS Word for this purpose, but does not know exactly which option to use. Of
the following, what would you suggest she use for newspaper style columns?
    A. Insert Tab > Smart Art   B. Table > Insert Table
    C. Insert Tab > Textbox   D. Page Layout Tab > Columns

22. Of the following, what would you suggest Jane in Question 21 use to add   22.____
Shimmer and Sparkle text in her advertisement to make it more attractive and
eye capturing?
    A. Word Art   B. Font styles
    C. Text effects   D. Font effects

23. In MS Word, which indent marker is specific to control all the lines excluding   23.____
the first line?
    A. First Line Indent Marker   B. Left Indent Marker
    C. Hanging Indent Marker   D. Right Indent Marker

24. When working as a computer support officer, you receive a help call from   24.____
one of the users. The problem is that the user has just deleted an entire folder
of important office notes. He needs to retrieve the data. Which method would
you adopt to retrieve the contents?
    A. Empty the recycle bin
    B. Restore the folder from the recycle bin
    C. Once deleted, its contents cannot be retrieved
    D. No need to worry. Only the folder has been deleted, not its contents.

25. Documentation can be explained as   25.____
    A. a procedure used to provide technical information to specific audiences
       who have specific needs for that information
    B. an explanation about all procedures and their mechanisms
    C. a method that specifies the author, source and related detail about
       information
    D. none of the above

_____

KEY (CORRECT ANSWERS)

1.	B		11.	A
2.	B		12.	D
3.	C		13.	B
4.	C		14.	A
5.	B		15.	A
6.	E		16.	C
7.	C		17.	B
8.	A		18.	C
9.	B		19.	D
10.	A		20.	C

21.	D
22.	D
23.	B
24.	B
25.	C

_____

EXAMINATION SECTION
TEST 1

DIRECTIONS: Each question or incomplete statement is followed by several suggested answers or completions. Select the one that BEST answers the question or completes the statement. *PRINT THE LETTER OF THE CORRECT ANSWER IN THE SPACE AT THE RIGHT.*

1. In the computer lab, students are getting ready to print a report for your class.   1._____
   However, when they try to print, they find that the printer is not receiving any
   print commands, so what should you do?
   - A. Call your principal so he can buy a new printer
   - B. Purchase new ink cartridges and replace the old ones
   - C. Reset the printer's properties
   - D. Look at the computer's default printer settings

2. File compression software has led to which types of files being downloaded   2._____
   more often, resulting in greater risk to intellectual property rights?
   - A. Smaller files such as e-mails and company memos
   - B. Larger files such as movies, songs and software
   - C. Smaller files like PowerPoint presentations with audio
   - D. None of these are at risk from file-compressing software

3. Copyright laws dictate that a program can be legally copied on a personal   3._____
   computer if and only if it is
   - A. for educational purposes
   - B. purchased with a site license exception
   - C. used to archive the software in case of maintenance/repair
   - D. not sold to someone else by the original user

4. Which of the following would strengthen a technology director's role within a   4._____
   school district?
   - A. Cooperating with teachers to help recognize and integrate appropriate
     technology resolutions
   - B. Finding out the cost and benefits of integrating proposed technology
   - C. Keeping current with technology improvements
   - D. Instruct subordinates so they understand technology improvements

5. When looking at the total cost of owning programs that track student   5._____
   information, finance, curriculum and more, a technology director can
   - A. identify all systems and their relative costs
   - B. determine the pragmatism of purchasing and implementing a new
     technology
   - C. find out the staff requirements and skill levels needed
   - D. get an approximation of replacement cycles and costs

6. Your students are searching for a research topic in the library and they want two of their terms to appear on the same page. Which BOOLEAN entry would the librarian tell them to use in order to achieve this purpose?   6._____
    A. And
    B. Or
    C. In Addition
    D. Not

7. A touch screen is closely related to which of the following devices?   7._____
    A. Scanner
    B. Light pen
    C. Joystick
    D. Keyboard

8. Within a disk, blocks of data are written into _____ sector(s).   8._____
    A. one
    B. two
    C. three
    D. two or more

9. Student A and Student B are arguing online and Student A makes a racist comment about Student B. Since it was online, there is a record of what Student A said, so his school has proof to suspend him for his comments. What is the lesson about online etiquette that Student A could benefit from?   9._____
    A. Don't share your opinion because people will twist it to make you sound awful
    B. Always put a smiley face at the end of every text line so people will know you are joking
    C. Be careful what you say because it may be saved and could come back to haunt you
    D. Don't post racist comments online because that is illegal and could result in jail time

10. Which of the following situations does NOT need an online citation?   10._____
    A. Using information from an online article that you put in your own words
    B. Using an image from a website for your assignment
    C. Writing that Yahoo is a commonly used search engine
    D. You need to cite in every one of these situations

11. Which of the following is a common injury from too much computer usage?   11._____
    A. Posture-related injuries
    B. Depression
    C. Eyestrain
    D. Both A and C

12. Microsoft Windows is a(n)   12._____
     A. character user interface
     B. operating system
     C. operating environment
     D. none of these

13. A condition where a ping program sends tons and tons of packets to a server   13._____
    in an effort to overwhelm its ability to handle high amounts of traffic is called a
     A. ping storm
     B. pagejacking
     C. jam sync
     D. jumbogram

14. Which of the following is a method of verification used when you need to   14._____
    check for errors in data that has been transmitted on a communications link?
     A. BeOS
     B. Remailer
     C. Cyclic redundancy checking
     D. Traceroute

15. Which software development phase allows users to sample the product so   15._____
    developers can troubleshoot?
     A. Out of the box
     B. Lexical scoping
     C. Regression testing
     D. Beta test

16. The audio signal given out by a computer to announce the result of a short   16._____
    diagnostic testing sequence the computer performs when first powering up is
    called a
     A. birdie
     B. beep code
     C. click
     D. hiccup

17. Ethics on the Internet is known as   17._____
     A. nethics
     B. net-manners
     C. netiquette
     D. net ethical and moral behaviors

18. Jon finds himself in an ethical dilemma related to an e-mail correspondence   18._____
    he is having with another person. He comes to you to ask what he should do.
    You tell him to
     A. e-mail a college professor who teaches about ethical behaviors
     B. think about how he would act in a real face-to-face scenario and
        follow that lead
     C. talk to someone with more experience in these matters
     D. do whatever he feels like because he likely won't get caught

19. You are reviewing your colleague's e-mail to an educational journal and notice that he has signed it with a smiley face at the end. You tell him
    A. to erase the smiley face as it is too informal and inappropriate
    B. replace the smiley with something more clever or comical
    C. nothing; it's his responsibility to understand Internet etiquette
    D. nothing; a smiley face never hurt anyone

19._____

20. Which of the following things should you NEVER do in an online chat setting?
    A. Post your home address
    B. Post your picture
    C. Post your comments on an assignment
    D. Post a reply to someone else's comments that you disagree with

20._____

21. You are trying to convince your board of education to purchase "ergonomic" keyboards but one board member raises his hand and asks you to define ergonomics. What should you tell him?
    A. It ensures that your hardware will be reliable and won't break down
    B. It helps make sure there are no work accidents
    C. It is the latest in environmentally friendly green technology
    D. It is a scientific look into designing safe and comfortable equipment

21._____

22. Which of the following situations would NOT be considered a health and safety issue concerned with computers?
    A. Exposed wires running underneath desks and chairs
    B. A coffee pot plugged into nearby outlets and placed beside a group of computers
    C. Wires tied, labeled and fed directly to wall and ceiling outlets
    D. Overloaded electrical sockets

22._____

23. One of the administrative assistants at the district office complains of injuries due to repetitive strain. Which of the following computer-related activities likely caused the injury?
    A. Recording and uploading notes from meetings every day
    B. Clicking on advertisements that pop up from a personal e-mail account
    C. Typing for hours each day
    D. Both A and B

23._____

24. When the first Unix OS was in its development stage, it was written in _____ language.
    A. C
    B. assembly
    C. B
    D. none of these

24._____

25. You go to your local library to log onto your Facebook page and on the wall   25._____
next to the computer the following message is posted: "Lurk before you leap."
What do the librarians mean by this message to their patrons?
  - A. Make sure to always be anonymous when on the Internet
  - B. Lurking is always an acceptable method of approach on the Internet
  - C. It is important to know everyone in your social media area before you jump into conversations, that way you can do so with names and important information
  - D. None of the above

_____

KEY (CORRECT ANSWERS)

1. D	11. D
2. B	12. B
3. C	13. A
4. A	14. C
5. A	15. D
6. A	16. B
7. B	17. C
8. D	18. B
9. C	19. A
10. C	20. A

21. D
22. C
23. C
24. B
25. C

_____

TEST 2

DIRECTIONS: Each question or incomplete statement is followed by several suggested answers or completions. Select the one that BEST answers the question or completes the statement. *PRINT THE LETTER OF THE CORRECT ANSWER IN THE SPACE AT THE RIGHT.*

1. Of the following devices, which would not be classified as input?   1._____
    A. Printer
    B. Keyboard
    C. Optical character reader
    D. Joystick

2. Which input device should you use if you want to play a computer game?   2._____
    A. Mouse
    B. Touch screen
    C. Joystick
    D. Keyboard

3. A teacher notices that one of her students has failed to properly give credit for   3._____
    a persuasive phrase that the student took from another source. This failure
    to properly credit a source is best known as
    A. paraphrasing
    B. fair-use policy
    C. laziness
    D. plagiarism

4. Which of the following would NOT be a violation of computer copyright laws?   4._____
    A. A student accidently breaks your CD you were going to use for next
       class. You decide to make a copy of other important discs so this
       won't happen again.
    B. A geology teacher has more students and computers than software.
       He decides to burn several extra copies so that each student can work
       on their own computer.
    C. A student downloads a new film from the Internet and uses a clip from
       it for his project
    D. All are in violation of copyright laws

5. A signal that is used to synchronize transmission between two or more   5._____
    systems is referred to as
    A. preamble
    B. ringtone
    C. Synclink
    D. semaphore

6. In TCP/IP, the algorithm that makes it possible to recover data packets is   6._____
    A. fast retransmit and recovery
    B. concatenation
    C. talkback
    D. cache coherence

7. When you talk with students about the plagiarism, which of the following should you make clear is a potential consequence?
    A. Receiving a zero for the assignment
    B. Having their high school diploma suspended or revoked
    C. Legal issues with the original author of the plagiarized work
    D. Both A and C

7._____

8. A student is viewing her professor's lecture online and she wants to use the professor's notes in her essay. However, the professor did not share the source used for the lecture notes. What should the student do?
    A. Cite the professor's lecture as the source
    B. Search for that information on the Internet hoping to find the original source
    C. Use the information and don't worry about citing it
    D. Don't use the information; she should only use information when it has the source attached to it

8._____

9. Which of the following programs tailored to a business that costs more than a software suite?
    A. Graphics/Multimedia
    B. Custom
    C. Home
    D. Business

9._____

10. This type of application software is legally protected, but can be freely downloaded for a short trial period.
    A. Freeware
    B. Shareware
    C. Restricted Trial
    D. Open Source

10._____

11. The technology director of your district is worried that recently purchased software might be installed on more computers than the school district has licenses for. What should she do in order to avoid legal issues?
    A. Use a pass code
    B. Have someone from the company assist the installation
    C. Use product activation
    D. Use an encryption code

11._____

12. What is used as the interface between a computer user, his or her application software, and the computer hardware?
    A. System software
    B. Allusion software
    C. Application crossing
    D. Utilities program

12._____

13. Which of the following would NOT be categorized as system software?   13._____
    A. Windows Vista
    B. Mac Snow Leopard
    C. OS
    D. None of the above

14. A specific mixture of letters, numbers and special characters used to identify   14._____
    files is more simply known as file _____.
    A. record
    B. extension
    C. name
    D. query

15. If a student wants to type a letter, a memo or even create a Web page,   15._____
    which of the following should s/he use?
    A. Spreadsheet database
    B. Word processing software
    C. Presentation software
    D. Publishing software

16. A computer's operating system is tasked with performing which of the   16._____
    following functions?
    A. Detecting viruses
    B. Compressing data
    C. Defragging disks
    D. Managing memory

17. Your students are about to post in your English class blog online. Which of   17._____
    the following are reminders you should give them before they start posting?
    A. Be clear
    B. Be knowledgeable
    C. Be succinct
    D. All of the above

18. In a computer class, students are tasked with organizing files and folders on   18._____
    their own computers. Which of the following would best help them
    understand how to do this?
    A. Explain the importance of different file extensions
    B. Have students create folders and move different files into each one
    C. Show how files are physically stored versus when in the cloud
    D. Make students create files and store them to the cloud

19. A high school English teacher wants his students to learn about the
relationship between writing and literacy. He has his students in small
groups and they will eventually demonstrate their findings in front of the
class. The teacher is not sure which of the following activities should be
used. What would be the best option for him?
    A. Have students use Microsoft Excel to present their findings
    B. Have students find articles on the Internet and show them to the class
    C. Have students print off articles from an encyclopedia from CD-ROM
    D. Have students create a database from which they can draw analysis
       of statistics

19._____

20. A technology director is in the process of gathering technology-integrated
lessons for the district. Which of the following would be the MOST essential
contemplations when creating curriculum to meet instructional goals?
    A. How interested the teachers are in technology
    B. How original the lessons are
    C. How adaptable the technology lessons are
    D. How talented teachers are with the technology

20._____

21. Your class just finished a unit and you want to do a self-reflection piece to
figure out just how well the unit taught students to research on the Internet.
What activity would help you determine how effective this lesson was?
    A. Make your students engage in a formal debate about the best ways to
       find significant information on the Internet
    B. Have students look back through their Internet search history and
       compile a list of the websites they used
    C. Give a lengthy short-answer quiz on the practices of Internet research
    D. Individually conference with each student and have them explain the
       process through which they created their projects

21._____

22. As technology director, you talk with teachers who constantly ask you for the
latest versions of software for their classroom computers. How should you
decide to upgrade to the newest available software?
    A. The simple desire to own the latest version Is enough
    B. A cost-benefit analysis with benefits outweighing costs
    C. Analyzing how many users can be added to the newer version
    D. Analyzing how long the current software has been used

22._____

23. Mr. Jones is attending a conference in which the presenter will speak about
technology integration into lesson plans. Which of the following would help
Mr. Jones the MOST in trying to integrate technology into his curriculum?
    A. The presenter asks the group ahead of time about their future units so
       everyone can work on specific ways to incorporate technology
    B. The presenter provides the group with a database of lesson plans
       that successfully use technology
    C. The presenter demonstrates the different kinds of programs and
       computers that are available for schools to purchase
    D. The conference organizers dispense a list of technology tools that the
       group might find handy

23._____

24. Teachers coaching other teachers can be a great way to develop professionally in educational technology because it   24._____
    A. offers a way for principals to informally assess teachers' skill in using technology
    B. gives educators the ability to have experts train them one-to-one assistance that can be customized
    C. provides teachers with a technology support system based on whatever needs they might have
    D. creates a network of teachers who can provide each other with feedback and support in educational technology

25. If a school district operates on a low technology budget, how should a technology director go about solving technology problems between the high school, middle school and elementary school?   25._____
    A. Request that a technology trained staff member be in each school's computer labs at all times
    B. Give all teachers the network access password so they can deal with the problems themselves
    C. Train a few tech savvy people how to solve simpler technology issues before calling in the tech director
    D. Make sure all teachers know the tech director's personal phone number so they can contact the tech director at all times

_____

KEY (CORRECT ANSWERS)

1. A		11. C	
2. C		12. A	
3. D		13. D	
4. D		14. C	
5. A		15. B	
6. A		16. D	
7. D		17. D	
8. A		18. B	
9. B		19. D	
10. B		20. C	

21. D
22. B
23. A
24. D
25. C

_____

TEST 3

DIRECTIONS: Each question or incomplete statement is followed by several suggested answers or completions. Select the one that BEST answers the question or completes the statement. *PRINT THE LETTER OF THE CORRECT ANSWER IN THE SPACE AT THE RIGHT.*

1. A person who software is designed for is known as a(n)   1._____
   A. end user
   B. programmer
   C. customer
   D. professional

2. How can multimedia help school-age children?   2._____
   A. It can replace direct reading from a textbook
   B. It can aid students in learning different and inspiring ways that will allow them to creatively express what they know
   C. It gives complete control of learning over to the students
   D. It will replace teachers in the future

3. In order to keep track of your dietary habits over the course of a month, which of the following would be the BEST method of conducting this task?   3._____
   A. Spreadsheet
   B. Word processor
   C. Database
   D. Bar graph

4. A teacher complains one day that he had his personal information stolen through a fake e-mail he responded to. Which of the following scams did the teacher fall victim to?   4._____
   A. Trolling
   B. Tracking
   C. Phishing
   D. Hacking

5. An example of a peripheral device associated with technology would be all of the following EXCEPT   5._____
   A. keyboard
   B. external hard drive
   C. printer
   D. motherboard

6. Which of the following would be the best method for educating students in how to use Microsoft Word?   6._____
   A. Coaching
   B. Lecture to them
   C. Scaffold lessons
   D. Have students recite information back to you

7. Students are placed into groups for a project and they are required to assign themselves to roles they have never been in before. What is the major advantage of this strategy?
   A. The teacher can identify student weaknesses in addition to strengths
   B. This provides a way for groups to cover for weaker group members
   C. Students will be forced to reinforce what they've learned by teaching their peers about roles they've held previously
   D. It allows the students to observe their own progress by juxtaposing with their peers

7._____

8. A teacher hands his Computers class a reflection assignment so he can improve his curriculum in the future. Students report that they loved the animation unit, but were bored with the unit on type. Using this information, what should the teacher do for future classes?
   A. Nothing; these students don't get to determine what he teaches
   B. A project that has students design their own typefaces
   C. An extra animation project in which students create a character and put it in a scene
   D. An assignment that involves students animating the text of a sound recording

8._____

9. A Junior English class is about to begin a unit in which students will be required to participate in blogs. Before the unit begins, which of the following should the teacher make sure the students understand?
   A. Online etiquette rules and regulations
   B. How to code in HTML
   C. The objectives and rules of the blog website
   D. None of the above

9._____

10. A small black-and-white photograph is put into a slideshow and appears to have lost image quality. When did this likely happen to the photo?
   A. When it was enlarged to fit the slide
   B. When it was scanned into the computer
   C. When it was desaturated
   D. When it was inserted into the presentation

10._____

11. Which of the following best defines the "golden section"?
   A. The text body that stays the same at the head of a document
   B. The middle 85% of a video image where all text should appear
   C. The cross section of fake lines that forces the viewer's eyes on a specific focal point
   D. A ratio that is used in art and design that shows a balanced, pleasing image

11._____

12. The process color model
   A. creates a final tone through subtracting the brightness from white
   B. adds color to the process
   C. measures the color values in pixels
   D. is usually used in computer programs

12._____

13. Which of the following BEST defines computer-based training?　　　　　13._____
    - A. Video games
    - B. Training a computer to reject viruses
    - C. A program that allows people to learn at their own pace with interactive software
    - D. A virtual program that trains computers to perform routine tasks

14. Which of the following BEST illustrates the benefits of groupware?　　　　14._____
    - A. Group members can share programs, files and other resources
    - B. Members can read e-mails from other group members
    - C. Group members can feel like they belong somewhere
    - D. It allows people to rely on others to do their work

15. Which historical event is thought to be primarily responsible for creating a new way of communicating, better known now as the Internet?　　　15._____
    - A. The Cold War
    - B. Vietnam War
    - C. World War II
    - D. Korean War

16. What is the best definition of the commonly known term "multimedia"?　　16._____
    - A. Images and text that moves throughout a website
    - B. Integrating both still and moving images, text and sounds through computer technology
    - C. Images and audio
    - D. None of the above

17. A student in your online class keeps posting messages in all caps. When you e-mail her, you explain that she should　　　　　17._____
    - A. keep using the all caps because it helps get her point across
    - B. change to all lowercase letters because it doesn't feel as formal
    - C. avoid using all caps because it conveys an aggressive tone and is not correct form
    - D. none of the above

18. Why would someone use acronyms in an online setting?　　　　　18._____
    - A. They are hilarious to look at
    - B. They save time and keystrokes
    - C. They make a user appear more literate
    - D. Acronyms serve no real purpose

19. You want to hire a group of programmers whose job it is to expose security errors in new software so that your computer network will not fail. Which group should you hire?　　　　　19._____
    - A. ERM Group
    - B. Computer Emergency Response Team
    - C. Microsoft Certified Systems Engineers
    - D. Tiger team

20. What is the diagnostic test sequence called that a computer input/output system will run to find out if the keyboard, RAM, disc drives and other hardware are working properly?
    A. NetBIOS
    B. Safe mode
    C. Initial program load
    D. POST

20._____

21. One of your colleagues is chatting with you through Google Hangouts and sends the message "BRB." What did that colleague just communicate with you?
    A. "Be right back"
    B. "Been really bad"
    C. "Be really brief"
    D. It's an inside joke

21._____

22. The golden rule of online etiquette most closely resembles which of the following?
    A. Remember that you are speaking to another human being online
    B. Don't spam others unless you want to be spammed
    C. Never send viruses to your friends
    D. Be friendly and kind in online forums and through e-mails

22._____

23. When a help desk personnel member describes a problem that is user-related and not software/hardware-related, they may refer to the problem as which of the following?
    A. Cuckoo egg
    B. Mouse potato
    C. PEBCAK
    D. Silicon cockroach

23._____

24. The Clark County school board and superintendent decide it is time to start using social media for its school communications. What is the first step the technology committee should take in order to implement this project?
    A. Come up with a list of commonly used jargon and grammar style for people unfamiliar with social media
    B. Find out which employees already use social media
    C. Create personal accounts for employees on Twitter, Facebook and YouTube
    D. Look back at the district policies already in place with regards to teacher use of social media

24._____

25. Teachers in your district constantly ask for professional development regarding technology. Which of the following would best help them become more adept with using technology in their classrooms?

    A. Giving teachers access to district technology resources and programs at all times

    B. Planning and developing staff skilled in online instruction and digital resources

    C. Creating specific learning modules for teachers and new staff

    D. Budgeting for staff members to be trained on district-owned resources

25._____

KEY (CORRECT ANSWERS)

1. A	11. D
2. B	12. B
3. A	13. C
4. C	14. A
5. D	15. A
6. A	16. B
7. C	17. C
8. D	18. B
9. C	19. D
10. A	20. D

21. A
22. A
23. C
24. D
25. B

TEST 4

DIRECTIONS: Each question or incomplete statement is followed by several suggested answers or completions. Select the one that BEST answers the question or completes the statement. *PRINT THE LETTER OF THE CORRECT ANSWER IN THE SPACE AT THE RIGHT.*

1. For a technology to be successfully implemented into a district, which of the following MUST happen?
   A. You must attain the support of the local community leaders
   B. You must acquire the support from knowledge-workers in advance
   C. You should perform a survey among students to find their readiness levels
   D. You must assuage parental concerns through proper channels

   1._____

2. What statistic would best show that students are getting equal access to technology resources within a district?
   A. Frequency of use as reported by students
   B. Number of devices per school
   C. Cost per student for technology
   D. Ratio of students to technology devices

   2._____

3. What is an important step a technology director should take to encourage teachers to use interactive technology in the classroom?
   A. Have teachers share examples of lessons that used interactive technology
   B. Create a curriculum plan that uses interactive technology and make teachers use it
   C. Look at the district technology plan and structure to make sure interactive technology can be enabled
   D. None of the above are important steps to take

   3._____

4. A 9th grade English teacher asks you to assist him in implementing the school's multimedia resources into a unit on *To Kill A Mockingbird*. How should you determine what technology the English teacher should use?
   A. How comfortable the teacher is with technology in the classroom
   B. The objectives outlined by the unit being presented
   C. The ability of the resources and presentation to entertain students
   D. How much time will be given in class to the unit

   4._____

5. A program that allows students to enter a combination of keys one key at a time instead of pressing multiple keys at the same time would most benefit which type of student?
   A. One who lacks self-assurance in using the keyboard
   B. A pupil who has the use of only one hand when entering data on a keyboard
   C. Someone who prefers to use the mouse rather than the keyboard for all tasks
   D. A student who uses an oversized keyboard because of visual impairment

   5._____

6. Mrs. Stephenson borrows a software program from Mr. Jones and installs it on her own computer to use for her classroom. Which of the following describes this situation?

    6._____

    A. This was not a copyright violation because both teachers are from the same school
    B. This was not a copyright violation because the teachers made sure to never use the software at the same time
    C. This was a violation of copyright law because it is contrary to the licensing agreement
    D. This was only a copyright violation if Mr. Jones already made a backup copy of the software

7. In their upcoming unit, students will need to write and edit at a computer and meet with their teacher to conference on their work. Which question about learning is an important one for the teacher to consider before the unit starts?

    7._____

    A. Will the type of word-processing software affect the quality of work for each student?
    B. Should students be allowed to publish their drafts unedited or should they have to wait until teacher review?
    C. Will students be allowed to use software tools to help them gain technological literacy?
    D. How will the amount of time spent on the computer influence social interaction between students in the classroom?

8. A firewall is put into place to protect the school from viruses and malware. Which of the following could compromise the firewall?

    8._____

    A. A teacher allowing students to download and save files from the Web
    B. A teacher using a phone outlet to connect an external modem to their computer
    C. Leaving a computer connected to the Internet all day even though it is not used
    D. A teacher downloading a newer version of a free Web browser and installing it on classroom computers

9. Which of the following file extensions is MOST likely to contain a virus?

    9._____

    A. .pdf
    B. .wav
    C. .jpg
    D. .exe

10. In a Windows OS, the Device Manager should be used for which of the following functions?

    10._____

    A. Uninstalling Microsoft Word
    B. Changing the interrupt used by a modem
    C. Configuring a printer to use draft settings
    D. None of the above

11. A middle school technology committee has recently convened to find and implement the best software for improving students' keyboarding skills. What is the first step the committee should take?
    A. Create and agree upon the objectives that the keyboarding software should meet
    B. Create a needs assessment to determine the importance of keyboarding skills in each classroom
    C. Figure out which interface would be most appropriate for the users
    D. Download a trial version of the most popular software to evaluate

11._____

12. During a Distance Learning course, students complain that the video keeps halting and audio does not match with the video being displayed. What is the most likely factor for this technology glitch?
    A. Quality of the camera
    B. The display resolution
    C. Available bandwidth
    D. Computer compatibility between two locations

12._____

13. The school decides it wants to update its website so that it's available and accessible to visually impaired students. What is the best way to do this?
    A. Href tags for hyperlinks
    B. Image maps for navigating the site
    C. Alt tags to describe images
    D. Automatic refresh for all pages

13._____

14. In a jazz band class, the teacher records a rehearsal and finds that the audio playback is very poor. Which of the following indicates the BEST way to solve the problem?
    A. Rerecord the rehearsal through MIDI devices
    B. A surge in digital sampling rate
    C. Play the audio file through the computer's internal speaker
    D. Save the file in MP3 format and then play that file back

14._____

15. You create a teacher web page using web authoring software only to find out your page appears on the intranet, but not on the Internet. What concept are you missing from creating your web page?
    A. FTP protocol
    B. Bandwidth
    C. Firewall
    D. Web server

15._____

16. In order to create a successful technology systems plan, what is the MOST important thing to do?
    A. Generate a plan that figures in the total cost of ownership
    B. Create procedures for technology access by teachers and students
    C. Form a replacement schedule for old and faulty equipment
    D. None of the above

16._____

17. How many bits does a byte represent?   17._____
    A. 10
    B. 40
    C. 8
    D. 22

18. _____ is a standard code used to share information between a data   18._____
    processor and a communication system.
    A. ACM
    B. APL
    C. ANSI
    D. ASCII

19. Which of these would a mouse be connected to?   19._____
    A. LPT1 port
    B. LPT2 port
    C. the serial port
    D. none

20. According to the E-Rate, a discount schools receive for telecom services, 20._____
    schools can also get discounts on which of the following?
    A. Internal network wiring and connections
    B. Computers for school classrooms
    C. Professional development for staff members
    D. Educational software packages

21. Which of the following is NOT a type of computer network?   21._____
    A. LAN (Local)
    B. RAN (Remote)
    C. MAN (Metropolitan)
    D. PAN (Personal)

22. Which color coding of cable is used to connect two similar devices?   22._____
    A. Straight cable
    B. Cross over cable
    C. Serial cable
    D. All of the above

23. The protocol for specifying and controlling network traffic so that certain 23._____
    traffic types get precedence is known as
    A. differentiated services
    B. specification of a sequence of flow objects (sosofo)
    C. order of magnitude
    D. flow control

24. Mr. Jones is creating a unit on online communication and he is currently working on a lesson that features the differences between online and face-to-face communication. What is one absolutely critical difference that Mr. Jones should mention?

    A. A user's face cannot be seen, making it more difficult to show thoughts and intentions. This could lead to misunderstandings.

    B. You can use swear words in your real life, but it is not allowed online

    C. When speaking it is okay to be informal and use slang, but writing online should be polished and formal

    D. Online, it is way easier to get away with stuff. Go ahead and do whatever you want.

24._____

25. After opening an e-mail in your class, a student receives a message that states "Warning: your computer may be infected with a virus." What should he do?

    A. Make sure he forwards the e-mail to everyone else in the class

    B. Ignore the warning and continue checking his e-mail

    C. Call you over so you can go to a security website to check if there is a real virus attached to the computer

    D. Flag you down so you can tell the principal who will shut down the whole lab so the virus cannot spread

25._____

KEY (CORRECT ANSWERS)

1. B	11. A
2. A	12. C
3. C	13. C
4. B	14. A
5. B	15. D
6. C	16. A
7. D	17. C
8. A	18. D
9. D	19. D
10. B	20. A

21. B
22. B
23. A
24. A
25. C

OFFICE RECORD KEEPING

EXAMINATION SECTION

TEST 1

DIRECTIONS: Each question or incomplete statement is followed by several suggested answers or completions. Select the one that BEST answers the question or completes the statement. *PRINT THE LETTER OF THE CORRECT ANSWER IN THE SPACE AT THE RIGHT.*

Questions 1-5.

DIRECTIONS: Questions 1 through 5 are to be answered on the basis of the following chart to check for address and zip code errors.

    A. No errors
    B. Address only
    C. Zip code only
    D. Both

	Correct List Address	Zip Code	List to be Checked Address	Zip Code	
1.	44-A Western Avenue Bethesda, MD	65564	44-A Western Avenue Bethesda, MD	65654	1.____
2.	567 Opera Lane Jackson, MO	28218	567 Opera Lane Jacksen, MO	28218	2.____
3.	200 W. Jannine Dr. Missoula, MT	30707	200 W. Jannine Dr. Missoula, MT	30307	3.____
4.	28 Champaline Dr. Reno, NV	34101	28 Champaine Way Reno, NV	43101	4.____
5.	65156 Rodojo Parsimony, KY	44590-7326	65156 Rodojo Parsimony, KY	44590-7326	5.____

6. When alphabetized correctly, which of the following would be second?   6.____
    A. flame   B. herring   C. decadence   D. emoticon

7. Which one of the following letters is as far after E as K is before R in the alphabet?   7.____
    A. J   B. K   C. H   D. M

8. How many pairs of the following sets of numbers are exactly alike?   8.____
        134232   123456   432512   561343
        564643   432123   132439   438318

    A. 0   B. 2   C. 3   D. 4

9.   When alphabetized correctly, which of the following would be FOURTH?   9.____
        A. microcosm   B. natural   C. lithe   D. nature

10.   When alphabetized correctly, which of the following would be THIRD?   10.____
        A. exoskeleton   B. euthanize   C. Europe   D. eurythmic

11.   Which one of the following letters is as far before T as S is after I in the   11.____
        alphabet?
        A. j   B. K   C. M   D. N

12.   How many pairs of the following sets of letters are exactly ALIKE?   12.____
        GIHEKE   GIHEKE
        KIWNEB   KWINEB
        PQMZJI   PMQZJI
        OPZIBS   OBZIBS
        PONEHE   POENHE

        A. 0   B. 1   C. 2   D. 4

13.   When alphabetized correctly, which of the following would be FIRST?   13.____
        A. Catalina   B. catcher   C. caustic   D. curious

14.   Which of the following letters is as far after D as U is after B in the alphabet?   14.____
        A. R   B. V   C. W   D. Z

Questions 15-19.

DIRECTIONS: Use the following information and chart to complete Questions 15 through 19.

Every theft reported to an adjuster needs to be assigned a six-letter code containing the following:

    First Letter: Type of theft
    Second Letter: Witnesses
    Third Letter: Value of stolen item
    Fourth Letter: Location
    Fifth Letter: Time of theft
    Sixth Letter: Elapsed between theft and report

Type of Theft:	Witnesses
A. Breaking and Entering	A. None
B. Retail Theft	B. 1 witness
C. Armed robbery	C. Multiple witnesses
D. Grand Theft Auto	D. Security camera

Location
A. Single Family Home
B. Apartment Building
C. Store
D. Office
E. Vehicle
F. Public Space (Parking Garage, Park, etc.)

Time Elapsed Between Theft and Report
A. 0-1 hour
B. 1-4 hours
C. 4-12 hours
D. 12-24 hours
E. 24 Hours

Time of Theft
A. 7 AM – 1 PM
B. 1 PM – 6 PM
C. 6 PM – 11 PM
D. 11 PM – 3 AM
E. 3 AM – 7 AM

Value of Stolen Items
A. $0-$100
B. $101-$250
C. $251-$500
D. $500-$1000
E. $1001-$5000
F. $5000 or more

15. At 9:30 PM, $175 worth of clothing was stolen from a store. The crime was reported right away by a single store associate. Which of the following would be the CORRECT code?
    A. BCCABB   B. BBBCCA   C. ACCBAB   D. CBCABB

15.____

16. A Crossover vehicle worth $4,500 was stolen from a park at approximately 6:45 AM this morning. It was reported stolen at 11:00 AM later that morning by the owner. There were no witnesses. What is the CORRECT code?
    A. DEECAF   B. CFECAE   C. DEFECA   D. DAEFEC

16.____

17. Although it was just reported, a breaking and entering occurred 5 days ago at 1:30 AM, according to security cameras that recorded the theft at the accounting firm. Although locks and doors were damaged, nothing was stolen. Which of the following would be the CORRECT code?
    A. ADDEEA   B. ADDDAE   C. ADADDE   D. ADEADE

17.____

18. Jill Wagner was held at knifepoint this morning at 11:30 AM when she was walking out of her apartment complex. The thief demanded money, and she gave him $54. She was the only witness and reported the crime immediately. Which of the following would be the CORRECT code?
    A. CBABAA   B. BBABAA   C. CBBABB   D. ABBBCA

18.____

19. An artifact worth $5,500 was stolen from the home of Chad Judea this early evening while he was out to dinner from 5:30 PM to 6 PM. When he arrived home at 6 PM, he immediately called the police. There were no witnesses. Which of the following would be the CORRECT code?
    A. AABBAF   B. AABFAF   C. AABABF   D. AAFABA

19.____

20. Diatribe means MOST NEARLY
    A. argument   B. cooperation   C. delicate   D. arrogance

20.____

21. Vitriolic means MOST NEARLY 21.____
    A. flammable   B. fearful   C. spiteful   D. asinine

22. Aplomb means MOST NEARLY 22.____
    A. self-righteous   B. respectable   C. dispirited   D. self-confidence

23. Pervicacious means MOST NEARLY 23.____
    A. rotten   B. immoral   C. stubborn   D. immortal

24. Detrimental means MOST NEARLY 24.____
    A. valuable   B. selfish   C. hopeless   D. harmful

25. Heinous means MOST NEARLY 25.____
    A. sweating   B. glorious   C. atrocious   D. moderate

KEY (CORRECT ANSWERS)

1.	C		11.	A
2.	B		12.	B
3.	C		13.	A
4.	D		14.	C
5.	A		15.	B
6.	D		16.	D
7.	B		17.	C
8.	A		18.	A
9.	D		19.	D
10.	B		20.	A

21.	C
22.	D
23.	C
24.	D
25.	C

TEST 2

DIRECTIONS: Each question or incomplete statement is followed by several suggested answers or completions. Select the one that BEST answers the question or completes the statement. *PRINT THE LETTER OF THE CORRECT ANSWER IN THE SPACE AT THE RIGHT.*

Questions 1-7.

DIRECTIONS: In answering Questions 1 through 7, you will be presented with analogies (known as word relationships). Select the answer choice that BEST completes the analogy.

1. Coordinated is related to movement as speech is related to   1.____
    A. predictive   B. rapid   C. prophetic   D. articulate

2. Pottery is related to shard as wood is related to   2.____
    A. acorn   B. chair   C. smoke   D. kiln

3. Poverty is related to money as famine is related to   3.____
    A. nourishment   B. infirmity   C. illness   D. care

4. Farmland is related to arable as waterway is related to   4.____
    A. impenetrable   B. maneuverable
    C. fertile   D. deep

5. 19 is related to 17 as 37 is related to   5.____
    A. 39   B. 36   C. 34   D. 31

6. Cup is related to lip as bird is related to   6.____
    A. beak   B. grass   C. forest   D. bush

7. ZRYQ is related to KCJB as PWOV is related to   7.____
    A. GBHA   B. ISJT   C. ELDK   D. EOFP

Questions 8-12.

DIRECTIONS: In answering Questions 8 through 12, each of the questions has a group. Find out which one of the given alternatives will be another member of that group.

8. Springfield, Sacramento, Tallahassee   8.____
    A. Buffalo   B. Bangor   C. Pittsburgh   D. Providence

9. Lock, Shut, Fasten   9.____
    A. Window   B. Iron   C. Door   D. Block

10. Pathology, Radiology, Ophthalmology   10.____
    A. Zoology   B. Hematology   C. Geology   D. Biology

11. Karate, Jujitsu, Boxing   11.____
    A. Polo   B. Pole-vault   C. Judo   D. Swimming

12. Newspaper, Hoarding, Television   12.____
    A. Press   B. Rumor   C. Media   D. Broadcast

Questions 13-18.

DIRECTIONS: Questions 13 through 18 are to be answered on the basis of the following pie chart.

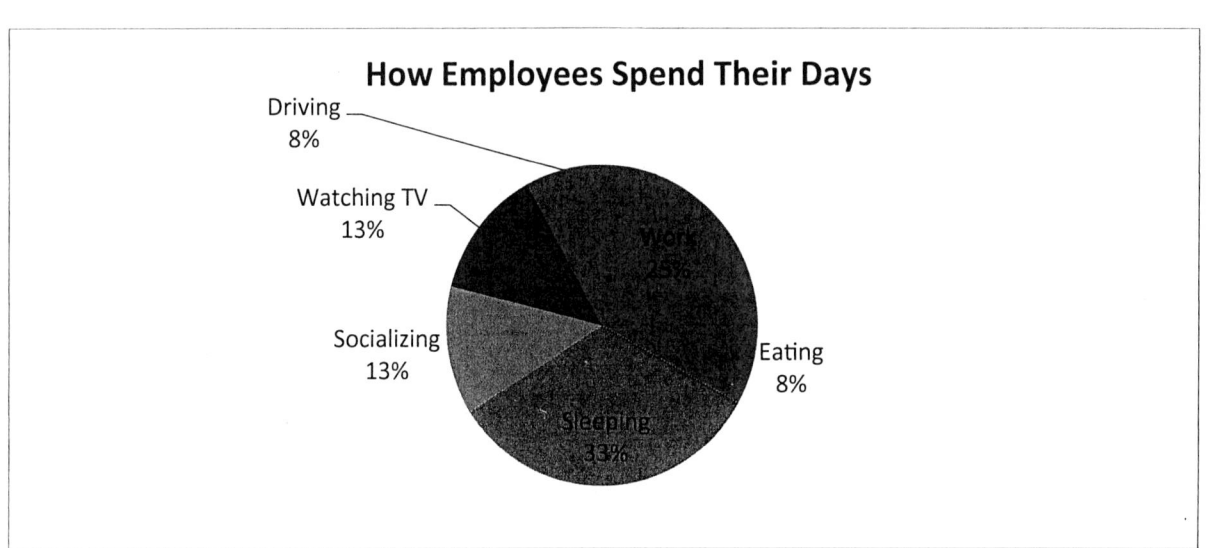

How Employees Spend Their Days

13. Approximately how many hours a day are spent eating?   13.____
    A. 2 hours   B. 5 hours   C. 1 hour   D. 30 minutes

14. According to the graph, for each 48 hour period, about how many hours are   14.____
    spent socializing and watching TV?
    A. 9 hours   B. 6 hours   C. 12 hours   D. 3 hours

15. If an employee ate two-thirds of their meals at a restaurant, what percentage 15.____
    of the total day is spent eating at home?
    A. 2.5%   B. 5.3%   C. 8%   D. 1.4%

16. About how many hours a day are spent working and sleeping?   16.____
    A. 7   B. 10   C. 12   D. 14

17. Which of the following equations could be used to figure out how much time 17.____
    an employee spends watching TV during a week? T equals the total amount of
    time watching TV during the week.
    A. T = 13% x 24 x 7   B. T = 24 x 13 x 7
    C. T = 24/13% x 7   D. T = 1.3 x 7 x 24

18. How many hours a week does the average employee spend socializing?   18.____
    A. 20   B. 22   C. 23   D. 24

Questions 19-25.

DIRECTIONS: Questions 19 through 25 are to be answered on the basis of the following charts.

DIAL DIRECT	WEEKDAY FULL RATE		EVENING 40% DISCOUNT		WEEKEND 60% DISCOUNT	
SAMPLE RATES FROM SEATTLE TO	FIRST MINUTE	EACH ADDITIONAL MINUTE	FIRST MINUTE	EACH ADDITIONAL MINUTE	FIRST MINUTE	EACH ADDITIONAL MINUTE
Savannah, GA	.52	.23	.31	.14	.21	.08
Providence, RI	.52	.223	.31	.14	.21	.08
Golden, CO	.52	.23	.31	.14	.21	.08
Indianapolis, IN	.48	.19	.29	.11	.19	.07
San Diego, CA	.54	.24	.32	.14	.22	.09
Tallahassee, FL	.54	.24	.32	.14	.22	.09
Milwaukee, WI	.57	.27	.34	.16	.23	.09
Minneapolis, MN	.49	.22	.29	.13	.20	.08
Baton Rouge, LA	.52	.23	.31	.14	.21	.08
Buffalo, NY	.52	.23	.31	.14	.21	.08
Annapolis, MD	.54	.24	.32	.14	.22	.09
Washington, DC	.52	.23	.31	.14	.21	.08

OPERATOR ASSISTED		
STATION-TO-STATION		PERSON-TO-PERSON
1 – 10 MILES	$.75	$3.00 FEE FOR ALL MILEAGES
11 - 22 MILES	$1.10	*NOTE: Add to this base charge – the minute rates from the above chart
23-3000 MILES	$1.55	

19. What is the price of a 6-minute dial direct call to Annapolis, MD when you call on a weekend?
    A. $0.59   B. $0.54   C. $0.67   D. $0.49

19._____

20. What is the difference in cost between a 10 minute dial direct to Buffalo, NY and a 10 minute person-to-person call to Buffalo, NY?
    A. $1.55   B. $3.00   C. $0.55   D. $4.55

20._____

21. What is the price of a 15-minute operator-assisted Station-to-Station call to Indianapolis, IN on a Monday at noon?
    A. $3.74   B. $7.80   C. $3.45   D. $4.69

21._____

22. What is the difference in price between an 11-minute dial direct call to Milwaukee, WI at 11:00 AM on a Wednesday and the same call made at 9 PM that night?
    A. $2.27   B. $3.00   C. $1.55   D. $1.336

22._____

23. Which of the following is NOT a type of charge for a dial direct call?   23.____
    A. Holiday   B. Evening   C. Weekend   D. Weekday

24. If a 3.5% tax applied to the total cost of any call, what would be the TOTAL   24.____
    cost of a 13-minute weekday, dial direct call to Golden, CO?
    A. $3.28   B. $3.39   C. $4.94   D. $6.39

25. What is the amount of discount from a dial direct, weekday call to   25.____
    Tallahassee, FL cost as compared to a dial direct, weekend call to
    Tallahassee?
    A. 45%   B. 30%   C. 60%   D. 20%

KEY (CORRECT ANSWERS)

1.	D		11.	C
2.	B		12.	D
3.	A		13.	A
4.	C		14.	C
5.	D		15.	A
6.	A		16.	D
7.	C		17.	A
8.	D		18.	B
9.	D		19.	C
10.	B		20.	B

21. D
22. D
23. A
24. B
25. C

TEST 3

DIRECTIONS: Each question or incomplete statement is followed by several suggested answers or completions. Select the one that BEST answers the question or completes the statement. *PRINT THE LETTER OF THE CORRECT ANSWER IN THE SPACE AT THE RIGHT.*

Questions 1-7.

DIRECTIONS: Questions 1 through 7 are to be answered on the basis of the following graph.

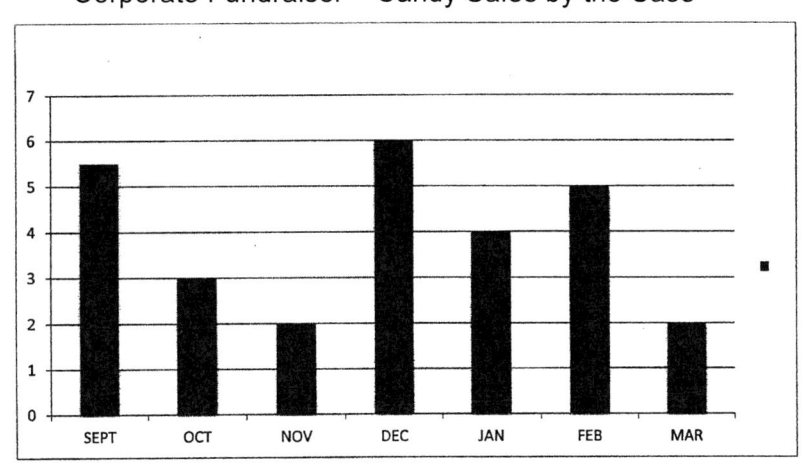

Corporate Fundraiser – Candy Sales by the Case

1. The vertical scale ranging from 0 to 7 represents the number of   1.____
    A. students selling candy
    B. candy sold in each case
    C. days each month that candy was sold
    D. cases of candy sold

2. Which two months had approximately the same amount of candy sold?   2.____
    A. November and March   B. September and February
    C. November and October   D. October and March

3. Which month showed a 100% increase in sales over the month of November?   3.____
    A. March   B. January   C. April   D. December

4. From month-to-month, which month saw an approximate 33% drop in sales   4.____
    from the previous month?
    A. March   B. September   C. January   D. October

5. The amount of candy sold in December is twice the amount of candy sold   5.____
    in which other month?
    A. October   B. March   C. January   D. September

6. What was the total amount of candy sold during the months shown on the graph?

    A. 44 cases   B. 35.5 cases   C. 23.5 cases   D. 27.5 cases

6.____

7. If the fundraiser extended the additional five months of the year and added an additional 65% in sales, approximately how many cases would be sold in total for an entire year?

    A. 40.5 cases   B. 37 cases   C. 45 cases   D. 27.5 cases

7.____

Questions 8-11.

DIRECTIONS: Questions 8 through 11 are to be answered on the basis of the following chart.

S = 10 students
s = 5 students

Mr. Hucklebee	S S S S s
Ms. Shopenhauer	S S S
Mr. White	S S S s
Mrs. Mulrooney	S S S

8. The size of Mr. White's class is _____ students.

    A. 30   B. 35   C. 40   D. 4

8.____

9. The total of all students in all four classes is _____ students.

    A. 150   B. 140   C. 125   D. 14

9.____

10. The average class size based on the above chart is _____ students.

    A. 140   B. 45   C. 35   D. 30

10.____

11. In order to ensure each teacher has the same amount of students in each class, how many students would need to transfer out of Mr. Hucklebee's class?

    A. 10
    B. 5
    C. 0
    d. 15 would need to transfer into his class

11.____

12. When alphabetized correctly, which of the following would be THIRD?

    A. box   B. departed   C. electrical   D. elemental

12.____

13. When alphabetized correctly, which of the following would be SECOND?

    A. polarize   B. omnipotent   C. polygraph   D. omniscient

13.____

14. When alphabetized correctly, which of the following would be THIRD?

    A. Macklemore, Jonathan   B. Mackelmore, J.
    C. DiCastro, Darian   D. Castro, Darren Henry

14.____

15. The group fought through the fog, *shambling* through the night, doing their best to stay upright.
The word *shambling* means
    A. frozen in place
    B. running
    C. walking awkwardly
    D. shivering uncontrollably

15.____

16. Many doctors agree that Gen-aspirin is the best for fighting headaches. It comes in different flavors and is easy to swallow.
Is this a valid or invalid argument?
    A. Invalid
    B. Valid

16.____

Questions 17-21.

DIRECTIONS: Questions 17 through 21 are to be answered on the basis of the following paragraph.

Hospital workers and volunteers often ask Mr. Ansley to educate children who are hospitalized with primary ciliary dyskinesia (PCD). As he goes through the precautionary cleaning process (scrubbing, donning sterilized clothes, etc.) in order to see his students, Mr. Ansley wonders why their parents add the stress and pressure of schooling and trying to play catch-up because of the amount of time spent in the hospital and not in the classroom, which is an unfortunate side effect of patients with PCD. These children go through so many painful treatments on a given day that it seems punishing to subject them to schooling as normal children do, especially with life expectancy being as short as it is.

17. What is meant by *precautionary* in the second sentence?
    A. Careful   B. Protective   C. Sterilizing   D. Medical

17.____

18. What is the MAIN idea of this passage?
    A. The preparation to visit a patient with primary ciliary dyskinesia is extensive.
    B. Children with PCD are unable to live normal lives.
    C. Children with PCD die young.
    D. Certain allowances should be made for children with PCD.

18.____

19. What is the author's purpose?
    A. To advise
    B. To educate
    C. To establish credibility
    D. To amuse

19.____

20. What is the author's tone?
    A. Cruel
    B. Sympathetic
    C. Disbelieving
    D. Cheerful

20.____

21. How is Mr. Ansley so familiar with the procedures used when visiting a child with PCD?
    A. He has read about it
    B. He works in the hospital.
    C. His child has PCD.
    D. He tutors them on a regular basis.

21.____

Questions 22-25.

DIRECTIONS: One of the underlined words in Questions 22 through 25 should be changed. Select the one that should be changed and print the letter of the word that would change the underlined word.

22. After we <u>washed</u> the fruit that had <u>growing</u> in the garden, we knew there <u>was</u> a store that would buy them.
   A. washing   B. grown   C. is   D. No change
      22.____

23. When the temperature <u>drops</u> under 32 degrees (F), the water on the lake <u>freezes</u>, which <u>allowed</u> children to skate across it.
   A. dropped   B. froze   C. allows   D. No change
      23.____

24. My friend's bulldog, while <u>chasing</u> cars in the street, always <u>manages</u> to <u>knock</u> over our garbage bins.
   A. chased   B. manage   C. knocks   D. No change
      24.____

25. Some of the ice on the driveway <u>has melted</u>.
   A. having melted   B. have melted
   C. has melt   D. No change
      25.____

KEY (CORRECT ANSWERS)

1.	D		11.	A
2.	A		12.	C
3.	B		13.	D
4.	C		14.	B
5.	A		15.	C
6.	D		16.	A
7.	C		17.	C
8.	B		18.	D
9.	B		19.	A
10.	C		20.	B

21.	D
22.	B
23.	C
24.	D
25.	D

TEST 4

DIRECTIONS: Each question or incomplete statement is followed by several suggested answers or completions. Select the one that BEST answers the question or completes the statement. *PRINT THE LETTER OF THE CORRECT ANSWER IN THE SPACE AT THE RIGHT.*

Questions 1-2.

DIRECTIONS: One of the underlined words in Questions 1 and 2 should be changed. Select the one that should be changed and print the letter of the word that would change the underlined word.

1. You can get to Martha's Vineyard by driving from Boston to Woods Hole. Once there, you can travel over on a boat, but you may find traveling by airplane to be more exciting.
   A. they   B. visitors   C. it   D. No change

1._____

2. When John wants to go to the store looking for milk and eggs, you must remember to bring his wallet.
   A. them   B. he   C. its   D. No change

2._____

3. An item that sells for $400 is put on sale at $145. What is the percentage of decrease?
   A. 25%   B. 28%   C. 64%   D. 36%

3._____

4. Two Junior College Mathematics courses have a total of 510 students. The 9:00 AM class has 60 more than the 12:30 PM class. How many students are in the 12:30 class?
   A. 225   B. 285   C. 255   D. 205

4._____

5. If a car gets 26 miles per gallon and it has driven 75,210 miles, approximately what is the number of gallons of gas that it has used?
   A. 3,000   B. 2,585   C. 165   D. 1,800

5._____

6. Which one of the following sentences about proper telephone usage is NOT always correct? When answering a telephone, you should
   A. know who you are speaking to
   B. give the caller your undivided attention
   C. identify yourself to the caller
   D. obtain the information your caller wishes before you do other work

6._____

7. You are part of the "Safety at Work" committee, which is dedicated to ensuring safety of employees. During your regular shift, you notice an employee in violation of one of your committee's rules. Which of the following actions should you take FIRST?
    A. Speak with the employee about the safety rules and mandate them to stop breaking the rules.
    B. Speak to the employee about safety rules and point out the rule they violated.
    C. Bring up the issue during the next committee meeting.
    D. Report the violation to the employee's superiors.

7.____

8. Part of your duties is overseeing employee confidential information. A friend and coworker of ours asks to obtain information concerning another employee. Which is the BEST action to take?
    A. Ask the coworker if you can share the information.
    B. Ask your supervisor if you can give the information to your friend.
    C. Refuse to give the information to your friend.
    D. Give the information to your friend.

8.____

9. Which of the following words means the OPPOSITE of protract?
    A. Extend   B. Hesitant   C. Curtail   D. Plethora

9.____

10. Which of the following words means the OPPOSITE of conserve?
    A. Relinquish   B. Waste   C. Proficient   D. Rigid

10.____

11. Which of the following words means the SAME as dissipate?
    A. Scatter   B. Emancipate
    C. Engage   D. Accumulate

11.____

12. Your office just purchased 14 fax machines. Each fax machine costs $79.99. How much did the 14 fax machines cost?
    A. $1,119.86   B. $1,108.77   C. $1,201.44   D. $1,788.22

12.____

Questions 13-19.

DIRECTIONS: Questions 13 through 19 are to be answered on the basis of the following chart.

Office City	Sales Rank	Production Materials Produced	Rank for Production	Damaged Materials	Employees	Percent of Profit	Sales Points	Weeks Without Injuries
Springfield	13.6	271	12	1	34	35	36	7
Philadelphia	17	274	4	3	25	41	20	4
Gary	16	260	10	5	34	34	21	3
Boulder	5	10	6	9	38	15	20	8
Miami	81	3	81	77	133	4	2	0
Houston	2	370	2	0	95	66	100	16
Battle Creek	82	290	82	81	91	13	9	2

13. Between Philadelphia and Battle Creek, how many damaged materials were there?

    A. 84   B. 78   C. 45   D. 86

13.____

14. How many offices have had 5 or more weeks without injuries?

    A. 3   B. 4   C. 2   D. 0

14.____

15. What was the TOTAL number of damaged materials for the offices in Boulder, Miami, Houston, and Springfield offices?

    A. 91   B. 87   C. 80   D. 77

15.____

16. What were the TOTAL sales points of Houston, Battle Creek, and Gary?

    A. 115   B. 145   C. 160   D. 130

16.____

17. Which of the offices had the LOWEST number of weeks without an injury?

    A. Battle Creek   B. Miami   C. Gary   D. Philadelphia

17.____

18. If worker efficiency is a percentage based on the number of workers at an office and the amount of materials produced, which office has the GREATEST worker efficiency?

    A. Philadelphia   B. Springfield   C. Boulder   D. Gary

18.____

19. If the company was looking to close a facility, which of the following factors would NOT be a reason to close the Miami office?

    A. Weeks without injury   B. Sales rank
    C. Production materials produced   D. Employees

19.____

Questions 20-25.

DIRECTIONS: In answering Questions 20 through 25, select the sentence in which the underlined word is used correctly.

20. A. Jon needs to increase his <u>capitol</u> by 30% to invest in my business.
    B. The organization is reevaluating <u>it's</u> decision to purchase the building.
    C. The office supply store sells computer paper and <u>stationery</u>.
    D. The quarterback and running back left <u>there</u> helmets on the bus.

20.____

21. A. The police sergeant <u>sited</u> me for disorderly conduct and driving without a license.
    B. The votes have <u>already</u> been counted.
    C. The professor's theory contradicts the <u>principals</u> of Einstein and Newton.
    D. <u>Who's</u> glass of water is on the table?

21.____

22. A. The board of trustees decided to <u>accept</u> the CEO's resignation.
    B. <u>Lose</u> hats will help keep your head from hurting.
    C. She <u>complemented</u> me on my exquisite dinner tastes.
    D. Jamaal offered him some sound <u>advise</u>.

22.____

23. A. In class today, Maya <u>lead</u> us in the reciting of the pledge.
    B. Doctors worry about the <u>affects</u> of drinking red wine right before bed.
    C. The workers used sledge hammers to <u>break</u> up the pavement.
    D. The teacher gave her students wise <u>council</u>.

23.____

24. A. This building was <u>formerly</u> the site of one of the city's oldest department stores.
    B. In his position, Albert must be very <u>discrete</u> in handling confidential information.
    C. He was <u>to</u> tired to continue the race.
    D. Each of his mortgage payments as about evenly divided between <u>principle</u> and interest.

24.____

25. A. The police spent several hours at the <u>cite</u> of the accident.
    B. A majority of the public support <u>capitol</u> punishment.
    C. The magician used mirrors to create a convincing <u>illusion</u>.
    D. The heiress <u>flouted</u> her wealth by wearing expensive jewelry.

25.____

KEY (CORRECT ANSWERS)

1.	D	11.	A
2.	B	12.	A
3.	C	13.	A
4.	A	14.	A
5.	A	15.	B
6.	D	16.	D
7.	B	17.	B
8.	C	18.	A
9.	C	19.	D
10.	B	20.	C

21.	B
22.	A
23.	C
24.	A
25.	C

READING COMPREHENSION
UNDERSTANDING AND INTERPRETING WRITTEN MATERIAL

EXAMINATION SECTION
TEST 1

DIRECTIONS: Each question or incomplete statement is followed by several suggested answers or completions. Select the one that BEST answers the question or completes the statement. *PRINT THE LETTER OF THE CORRECT ANSWER IN THE SPACE AT THE RIGHT.*

Questions 1-7.

DIRECTIONS: Questions 1 through 7 are to be answered SOLELY on the basis of the following passage.

The first step in establishing a programming development schedule is to rate the programs to be developed or to be maintained on the basis of complexity, size, and input-output complexity. The most experienced programmer should rate the program complexity based on the system flow chart. The same person should do all of the rating so that all programs are rated in the same manner. If possible, the same person who rates the complexity should estimate the program size based on the number of pages of coding. This rating can easily be checked, after coding has been completed, against the number of pages of coding actually produced. If there is consistent error in the estimates for program size, all future estimates should be corrected for this error or the estimating method reviewed.

The input-output rating is a mechanical count of the number of input and output units or tapes which the program uses. The objective is to measure the number of distinct files which the program must control.

After the ratings have been completed, the man-days required for each of the tasks can be calculated. Good judgment or, if available, a table of past experience is used to translate the ratings into man-days, the units in which the schedule is expressed. The calculations should keep the values for each task completely separate so that a later evaluation can be made by program, programmer, and function.

After the values have been calculated, it is a simple matter to establish a development schedule. This can be a simple bar chart which assigns work to specific programmers, a complex computer program using the *PERT* technique of critical path scheduling, or other useful type of document.

1. The rating and estimating of the programs should be performed by   1.____

    A. the person who will do the programming
    B. a programmer trainee
    C. the most experienced programmer
    D. the operations supervisor

2. The measurement used to express the programming schedule is the number of

    A. distinct files controlled by the programmer
    B. man-days
    C. pages of coding
    D. programmers

3. A mechanical count of the number of input and output units or tapes should be considered as a(n)

    A. input-output rating
    B. measure of the number of man-days required
    C. rating of complexity
    D. estimate of the number of pages of coding

4. Programming development scheduling methods are for

    A. new programs only
    B. programs to be developed and maintained
    C. large and complicated programs only
    D. maintenance programs only

5. If there is a consistent error in the estimates for program size, all estimates should be

    A. adjusted for future programs
    B. eliminated for all programs
    C. replaced by rating of complexity
    D. replaced by input-output rating

6. It is intimated that

    A. the calculations should keep the valuations for each task completely separated
    B. it is a simple matter to establish a development schedule
    C. the man-days required for each of the tasks can be calculated
    D. a later evaluation will be made

7. Complexity of programs can be checked

    A. before coding has been completed
    B. after future estimates have been corrected for error
    C. as a first step in establishing a complex computer program
    D. with reference to the number of pages of coding produced

Questions 8-13.

DIRECTIONS: Questions 8 through 13 are to be answered SOLELY on the basis of the following passage.

The purposes of program testing are to determine that the program has been coded correctly, that the coding matches the logical design, and that the logical design matches the basic requirements of the job as set down in the specifications. Program errors fall into the following categories: errors in logic, clerical errors, misidentification of the computer components' functions, misinterpretation of the requirements of the job, and system analysis errors.

The number of errors in a program will average one for each 125 instructions, assuming that the programmer has been reasonably careful in his coding system. The number of permutations and combinations of conditions in a program may reach into the billions before each possibility has been thoroughly checked out. It is, therefore, a practical impossibility to check out each and every possible combination of conditions—the effort would take years, even in the simplest program. As a result, it is quite possible for errors to remain latent for a number of years, suddenly appearing when a particular combination is reached which had not previously occurred.

Latent program errors will remain in operating programs, and their occurrence should be minimized by complete and thorough testing. The fact that the program is operative and reaches end-of-job satisfactorily does not mean that all of the exception conditions and their permutations and combinations have been tested. Quite the contrary, many programs reach end-of-job after very few tests, since the *straight-line* part of the program is often simplest. However, the exceptions programmed to deal with a minimal percentage of the input account for a large percentage of the instructions. It is, therefore, quite possible to reach the end-of-job halt with only 10% of the program checked out.

8. One of the MAIN points of this passage is that 8.____

    A. it is impossible to do a good job of programming
    B. reaching end-of-job means only 10% of the program is checked out
    C. standard testing procedures should require testing of every possible combination of conditions
    D. elimination of all errors can never be assured, but the occurrence of errors can be minimized by thorough testing

9. Latent program errors GENERALLY 9.____

    A. evade detection for some time
    B. are detected in the last test run
    C. test the number of permutations and combinations in a program
    D. allow the program to go to end-of-job

10. Which one of the following statements pertaining to errors in a program is CORRECT? 10.____

    A. If the program has run to a normal completion, then all program errors have been eliminated.
    B. Program errors, if not caught in testing, will surely be detected in the first hundred runs of the program.
    C. It is practically impossible to verify that the typical program is free of errors.
    D. A program that is coded correctly is free of errors.

11. Among other things, program testing is designed to 11.____

    A. assure that the documentation is correct
    B. assure that the coding is correct
    C. determine the program running time
    D. measure programmer's performance

12. The difficulty in detecting errors in programs is due to　　12._

    A. the extremely large number of conditions that exist in a program
    B. poor analysis of work errors
    C. very sophisticated and clever programming
    D. reaching the end-of-job halt with only 10% of the program checked out

13. If the program being tested finally reaches the end-of-job halt, it means that　　13._

    A. one path through the program has been successfully tested
    B. less than 10% of the program has been tested
    C. the program has been coded correctly
    D. the logical design is correct

Questions 14-20.

DIRECTIONS: Questions 14 through 20 are to be answered SOLELY on the basis of the following passage.

     Systems analysis represents a major link in the chain of translations from the problem to its machine solution. After the problem and its requirements for solution have been stated in clear terms, the systems analyst defines the broad outlines of the machine solution. He must know the overall capabilities of the equipment, and he must be familiar with the application. The ultimate output of the analysis is a detailed job specification containing all the tools necessary to produce a series of computer programs. The purpose of the specifications is to document and describe the system by defining the problem and the proposed solution, explain system outputs and functions, state system requirements for programmers, and to avoid misunderstandings among involved departments. The specification serves as a link between the analysis of the problem and the next function, programming. Systems analysis relies on creativity rather than rote analysis to develop effective computer systems. But this creativity must be channeled and documented effectively if lasting value is to be obtained.

14. According to the above paragraph, the systems analyst MUST be familiar with　　14._

    A. programming and the machine solution
    B. the machine solution and the next function
    C. the application and programming
    D. the application and the equipment capabilities

15. According to the above paragraph, the time that systems analysis MUST be performed is　　15._

    A. *after* the problem analysis
    B. *after* programming
    C. *before* problem definition
    D. *before* problem analysis

16. According to the above paragraph, the MAIN task performed by the systems analyst is to　　16._

    A. write the program
    B. analyze the problem
    C. define the overall capacities of the equipment
    D. define the machine solution of the problem

17. According to the above paragraph, the document produced by the systems analyst as his main output does NOT normally include

17.____

    A. an explanation of system outputs
    B. system requirements for programmers
    C. a statement of the problem
    D. performance standards

18. According to the above paragraph, the systems analysis function is

18.____

    A. relatively straightforward, requiring little creative effort
    B. extremely complex, making standard procedures impossible
    C. primarily a rote memory procedure
    D. a creative effort

19. According to the above paragraph, the specification

19.____

    A. is a major link in the sequence from problem to machine solution
    B. states the problem and its requirements for solution
    C. is chiefly concerned with the overall capabilities of the equipment
    D. represents the ultimate product of systems analysis

20. According to the above paragraph, the sequential function after the analysis of the program is

20.____

    A. documentation   B. application
    C. definition   D. programming

Questions 21-25.

DIRECTIONS: Questions 21 through 25 are to be answered SOLELY on the basis of the following passage.

Currently, memory represents one of the main limitations on computer performance and, as a result, is one of the areas where technological improvements will prove most fruitful.

Historically, the main problem of computer memories has been a very unfavorable cost-to-speed ratio. Memory devices which have great speed cost disproportionately more than those with less speed. This problem has forced computer designers to use minimum amounts of rapid access memory and to rely mainly on slower, large capacity storage. This practice has resulted in a *memory tree,* where a hierarchy of memory devices provides various increments of storage at different costs and speeds for various purposes.

To achieve better speed/cost ratios, designers are increasingly turning to memory media other than the traditional ferrite cores. These cores now account for over 90% of the memory market. Plated wire and semiconductors are the media most likely to supplant ferrite cores. Semiconductors are expected to rapidly displace cores, starting with higher speed memories. Their costs are dropping sharply and are expected to drop as much as five-fold by the middle of this decade, while their speeds are at least doubling.

Despite the increasing use of competing technologies, ferrite cores will probably still dominate the extended random access storage area. Since the largest increment of storage is associated with ferrite core memory devices, their share of the internal memory market was well over 50% by 1980. The only factor militating against this is the possibility that the largest manufacturers of computers may abandon the extended internal storage concept.

Memory developments likely to happen later in this decade include the progressive replacement of magnetic drums by magnetic disks. The latter were themselves displaced near the end of the seventies by electro optical units, followed by magnetic bubble storage. It also may prove possible to show the feasibility of associative processors. Under this concept, which is still experimental, data access would be considerably speeded through use of Contents-Addressable-Memories (CAM).

21. According to the above passage, a hierarchy of memory devices which provides various increments of storage at different costs and speeds has been used by designers because

    A. one of the larger manufacturers of computers might abandon the extended internal storage concept
    B. of the very unfavorable cost-to-speed ratio of computer memories
    C. magnetic disks have progressively replaced magnetic drums in the mid-seventies
    D. data access is expected to be appreciably speeded up through the use of Content-Addressable-Memories

21._

22. According to the above passage, which of the following memory developments is MOST likely to have occurred by 1980?

    A. Designers will turn to memories other than core for 90% of their needs.
    B. Cores and semiconductors will largely replace plated wire memories.
    C. Cores and semiconductors will largely be replaced by electro optical and magnetic bubble storage.
    D. Ferrite core will continue to dominate the internal memory market.

22._

23. According to the above passage, the speed/cost ratio for semiconductors is

    A. becoming more favorable
    B. the same as the speed/cost ratio for plated wire
    C. remaining constant
    D. less favorable than the speed/cost ratio for ferrite core

23._

24. According to the information in the passage, development of improved memory technology is IMPORTANT because

    A. it demonstrates the feasibility of associative processors
    B. memory represents one of the chief limitations on computer performance today
    C. semiconductors are expected to largely replace core which now represents about half of the memory market
    D. data can now be speeded through the use of CAM

24._

25. Three types of memory media which are discussed in the above passage are

    A. core, plated wire, semiconductors
    B. high speed buffer, magnetic disks, rotating magnetic storage
    C. ferrite cores, magnetic drums, remote data terminals
    D. high speed buffers, magnetic disks, magnetic drums

25._

KEY (CORRECT ANSWERS)

1.	C	11.	B
2.	B	12.	A
3.	A	13.	A
4.	B	14.	D
5.	A	15.	A
6.	D	16.	D
7.	D	17.	D
8.	D	18.	D
9.	A	19.	D
10.	C	20.	D

21.	B
22.	D
23.	A
24.	B
25.	A

TEST 2

Each question or incomplete statement is followed by several suggested answers or completions. Select the one that BEST answers the question or completes the statement. *PRINT THE LETTER OF THE CORRECT ANSWER IN THE SPACE AT THE RIGHT.*

Questions 1-5.

DIRECTIONS: Questions 1 through 5 are to be answered SOLELY on the basis of the following paragraph.

Work standards presuppose an ability to measure work. Measurement in office management is needed for several reasons. First, it is necessary to evaluate the overall efficiency of the office itself. It is then essential to measure the efficiency of each particular section or unit and that of the individual worker. To plan and control the work of sections and units, one must have measurement. A program of measurement goes hand in hand with a program of standards. One can have measurement without standards, but one cannot have work standards without measurement. Providing data on amount of work done and time expended, measurement does not deal with the amount of energy expended by an individual although, in many cases, such energy may be in direct proportion to work output. Usually from two-thirds to three-fourths of all work can be measured. However, less than two-thirds of all work is actually measured because measurement difficulties are encountered when office work is non-repetitive and irregular, or when it is primarily mental rather than manual. These obstacles are often used as excuses for non-measurement far more frequently than is justified.

1. According to the above paragraph, an office manager cannot set work standards unless he can

   A. plan the amount of work to be done
   B. control the amount of work that is done
   C. estimate accurately the quantity of work done
   D. delegate the amount of work to be done to efficient workers

   1.__

2. According to the above paragraph, the type of office work that would be MOST difficult to measure would be

   A. checking warrants for accuracy of information
   B. recording payroll changes
   C. processing applications
   D. making up a new system of giving out supplies

   2.__

3. According to the above paragraph, the ACTUAL amount of work that is measured is _____ of all work.

   A. less than two-thirds
   B. two-thirds to three-fourths
   C. less than three-sixths
   D. more than three-fourths

   3.__

4. Which of the following would be MOST difficult to determine by using measurement techniques?

   A. The amount of work that is accomplished during a certain period of time
   B. The amount of work that should be planned for a period of time
   C. How much time is needed to do a certain task
   D. The amount of incentive a person must have to do his job

   4.__

5. The one of the following which is the MOST suitable title for the above paragraph is
    5.____
    A. HOW MEASUREMENT OF OFFICE EFFICIENCY DEPENDS ON WORK STAN-
       DARDS
    B. USING MEASUREMENT FOR OFFICE MANAGEMENT AND EFFICIENCY
    C. WORK STANDARDS AND THE EFFICIENCY OF THE OFFICE WORKER
    D. MANAGING THE OFFICE USING MEASURED WORK STANDARDS

Questions 6-9.

DIRECTIONS: Questions 6 through 9 are to be answered SOLELY on the basis of the follow-
              ing passage.

Work measurement concerns accomplishment or productivity. It has to do with results; it
does not deal with the amount of energy used up, although in many cases this may be in
direct proportion to the work output. Work measurement not only helps a manager to distribute work loads fairly, but it also enables him to define work success in actual units, evaluate
employee performance, and determine where corrective help is needed. Work measurement
is accomplished by measuring the amount produced, measuring the time spent to produce it,
and relating the two. To illustrate, it is common to speak of so many orders processed within a
given time. The number of orders processed becomes meaningful when related to the
amount of time taken.

Much of the work in an office can be measured fairly accurately and inexpensively. The
extent of work measurement possible in any given case will depend upon the particular type
of office tasks performed, but usually from two-thirds to three-fourths of all work in an office
can be measured. It is true that difficulty in work measurement is encountered, for example,
when the office work is irregular and not repeated often, or when the work is primarily mental
rather than manual. These are problems, but they are used as excuses for doing no work
measurement far more frequently than is justified.

6. According to the above passage, which of the following BEST illustrates the type of information obtained as a result of work measurement?
    6.____

    A. Clerk takes one hour to file 150 folders
    B. Typist types five letters
    C. Stenographer works harder typing from shorthand notes than she does typing from
       a typed draft
    D. Clerk keeps track of employees' time by computing sick leave, annual leave, and
       overtime leave

7. The above passage does NOT indicate that work measurement can be used to help a
   supervisor to determine
    7.____

    A. *why* an employee is performing poorly on the job
    B. *who* are the fast and slow workers in the unit
    C. *how* the work in the unit should be divided up
    D. *how* long it should take to perform a certain task

8. According to the above passage, the kind of work that would be MOST difficult to measure would be such work as
    8.____

A. sorting mail
B. designing a form for a new procedure
C. photocopying various materials
D. answering inquiries with form letters

9. The excuses mentioned in the above passage for failure to perform work measurement   9._
can be BEST summarized as the

A. repetitive nature of office work
B. costs involved in carrying out accurate work measurement
C. inability to properly use the results obtained from work measurement
D. difficulty involved in measuring certain types of work

Questions 10-13.

DIRECTIONS: Questions 10 through 13 are to be answered SOLELY on the basis of the following passage.

Job analysis combined with performance appraisal is an excellent method of determining
training needs of individuals. The steps in this method are to determine the specific duties of
the job, to evaluate the adequacy with which the employee performs each of these duties,
and finally to determine what significant improvements can be made by training.

The list of duties can be obtained in a number of ways: asking the employee, asking the
supervisor, observing the employee, etc. Adequacy of performance can be estimated by the
employee, but the supervisor's evaluation must also be obtained. This evaluation will usually
be based on observation.

What does the supervisor observe? The employee, while he is working; the employee's
work relationships; the ease, speed, and sureness of the employee's actions; the way he
applies himself to the job; the accuracy and amount of completed work, its conformity with
established procedures and standards; the appearance of the work; the soundness of judgment it shows; and, finally, signs of good or poor communication, understanding, and cooperation among employees.

Such observation is a normal and inseparable part of the everyday job of supervision.
Systematically recorded, evaluated, and summarized, it highlights both general and individual
training needs.

10. According to the above passage, job analysis may be used by the supervisor in   10._

A. increasing his own understanding of tasks performed in his unit
B. increasing efficiency of communication within the organization
C. assisting personnel experts in the classification of positions
D. determining in which areas an employee needs more instruction

11. According to the above passage, the FIRST step in determining the training needs of   11._
employees is to

A. locate the significant improvements that can be made by training
B. determine the specific duties required in a job
C. evaluate the employee's performance
D. motivate the employee to want to improve himself

12. On the basis of the above passage, which of the following is the BEST way for a supervisor to determine the adequacy of employee performance?   12.____

    A. Check the accuracy and amount of completed work
    B. Ask the training officer
    C. Observe all aspects of the employee's work
    D. Obtain the employee's own estimate

13. Which of the following is NOT mentioned by the above passage as a factor to be taken into consideration in judging the adequacy of employee performance?   13.____

    A. Accuracy of completed work
    B. Appearance of completed work
    C. Cooperation among employees
    D. Attitude of the employee toward his supervisor

Questions 14-15.

DIRECTIONS: Questions 14 and 15 are to be answered SOLELY on the basis of the following paragraph.

The fundamental characteristic of the type of remote control which management needs to bridge the gap between itself and actual operations is the more effective use of records and reports — more specifically, the gathering and interpretation of the facts contained in records and reports. Facts, for management purposes, are those data (narrative and quantitative) which express in simple terms the current standing of the agency's program, work, and resources in relation to the plans and policies formulated by management. They are those facts or measures (1) which permit management to compare current status with past performance and with its forecasts for the immediate future, and (2) which provide management with a reliable basis for long-range forecasting.

14. For management purposes, facts are, according to the above paragraph,   14.____

    A. forecasts which can be compared to current status
    B. data which can be used for certain control purposes
    C. a fundamental characteristic of a type of remote control
    D. the data contained in records and reports

15. An inference which can be drawn from this statement is that   15.____

    A. management which has a reliable basis for long-range forecasting has at its disposal a type of remote control which is needed to bridge the gap between itself and actual operations
    B. data which do not express in simple terms the current standing of the agency's program, work, and resources in relationship to the plans and policies formulated by management may still be facts for management purposes
    C. data which express relationships among the agency's program, work, and resources are management facts
    D. the gap between management and actual operations can only be bridged by characteristics which are fundamentally a type of remote control

Questions 16-17.

DIRECTIONS: Questions 16 and 17 are to be answered SOLELY on the basis of the following passage.

Two approaches are available in developing criteria for the evaluation of plans. One approach, designated <u>Approach A</u>, is a review and analysis of characteristics that differentiate successful plans from unsuccessful plans. These criteria are descriptive in nature and serve as a checklist against which the plan under consideration may be judged. These characteristics have been observed by many different students of planning, and there is considerable agreement concerning the characteristics necessary for a plan to be successful.

A second approach to the development of criteria for judging plans, designated <u>Approach B</u>, is the determination of the degree to which the plan under consideration is economic. The word *economic* is used here in its broadest sense; i.e., effective in its utilization of resources. In order to determine the economic worth of a plan, it is necessary to use a technique that permits the description of any plan in economic terms and to utilize this technique to the extent that it becomes a *way of thinking* about plans.

16.   According to <u>Approach B</u>, the MOST successful plan is *generally* one which   16._

    A.   costs least to implement
    B.   gives most value for resources expended
    C.   uses the least expensive resources
    D.   utilizes the greatest number of resources

17.   According to <u>Approach A</u>, a successful plan is one which is   17._

    A.   descriptive in nature
    B.   lowest in cost
    C.   similar to other successful plans
    D.   agreed upon by many students of planning

Questions 18-20.

DIRECTIONS: Questions 18 through 20 are to be answered SOLELY on the basis of the following passage.

The primary purpose of control reports is to supply information intended to serve as the basis for corrective action if needed. At the same time, the significance of control reports must be kept in proper perspective. Control reports are only a part of the planning-management information system. Control information includes nonfinancial as well as financial data that measure performance and isolate variances from standard. Control information also provides feedback so that planning information may be updated and corrected. Whenever possible, control reports should be designed so that they provide feedback for the planning process as well as provide information of immediate value to the control process.

Since the culmination of the control process is the taking of necessary corrective action to bring performance in line with standards, it follows that control information must be directed to the person who is organizationally responsible for taking the required action. Usually the same information, though in a somewhat abbreviated form, is given to the responsible manager's superior. A district sales manager needs a complete daily record of the performance of each of his salesmen; yet, the report forwarded to the regional sales manager summarizes only the performance of each sales district in his region. In preparing reports for higher echelons of management, summary statements and recommendations for action should appear on the first page; substantiating data, usually the information presented to the person directly responsible for the operation, may be included if needed.

18. A control report serves its primary purpose as part of the process which leads DIRECTLY to

    18.____

    A. better planning for future action
    B. increasing the performance of district salesmen
    C. the establishment of proper performance standards
    D. taking corrective action when performance is poor

19. The one of the following which would be the BEST description of a control report is that a control report is a form of

    19.____

    A. planning
    B. communication
    C. direction
    D. organization

20. If control reports are to be effective, the one of the following which is LEAST essential to the effectiveness of control reporting is a system of

    20.____

    A. communication
    B. standards
    C. authority
    D. work simplification

Questions 21-23.

DIRECTIONS: Questions 21 through 23 are to be answered SOLELY on the basis of the following passage.

The need for the best in management techniques has given rise to the expression *scientific management.* Within reasonable limits, management can be scientific, but it will probably be many decades before it becomes truly scientific either in the factory or in the office. As long as it is impossible to measure accurately individual performance and to equate human behavior, so long will it be impossible to develop completely scientific techniques of office management. There is a likelihood, of course, that management might be reduced to a science when it is applied to inanimate objects which facilitate operations such as machinery, office equipment and furnishings, and forms. The limiting factor, therefore, is the human element.

21. The above passage is concerned PRIMARILY with the

    21.____

    A. value of scientific office management
    B. methods for the development of scientific office management
    C. need for the best office management techniques
    D. possibility of reducing office management to a science

22. According to the above passage, the realization of truly scientific office management is dependent upon the

    22.____

    A. expression of management techniques
    B. development of accurate personnel measurement techniques

    C.   passage of many decades, most probably
    D.   elimination of individual differences in human behavior

23.   According to the above passage, the scientific management of inanimate objects   23._

    A.   occurs automatically because there is no human factor
    B.   cannot occur in a factory, but can occur in an office
    C.   could be achieved without the concurrent achievement of truly scientific office management
    D.   is not a necessary component of truly scientific office management

Questions 24-25.

DIRECTIONS: Questions 24 and 25 are to be answered SOLELY on the basis of the following paragraph.

    Your role as human resources utilization experts is to submit your techniques to operating administrators, for the program must, in reality, be theirs, not yours. We, in personnel, have been guilty of encouraging operating executives to believe that these important matters affecting their employees are personnel department matters, not management matters. We should hardly be surprised, as a consequence, to find these executives playing down the role of personnel and finding personnel routines a nuisance, for these are not in the mainstream of managing the enterprise – or so we have encouraged them to believe.

24.   The BEST of the following interpretations of the above paragraph is that   24._

    A.   personnel people have been guilty of *passing the buck* on personnel functions
    B.   operating officials have difficulty understanding personnel techniques
    C.   personnel employees have tended to usurp some functions rightfully belonging to management
    D.   matters affecting employees should be handled by the personnel department

25.   The BEST of the following interpretations of the above paragraph is that   25._

    A.   personnel departments have aided and abetted the formulation of negative attitudes on the part of management
    B.   personnel people are labor relations experts and should carry out these duties
    C.   personnel activities are not really the responsibility of management
    D.   management is now being encouraged by personnel experts to assume some responsibility for personnel functions

KEY (CORRECT ANSWERS)

1.	C	11.	B
2.	D	12.	C
3.	A	13.	D
4.	D	14.	B
5.	B	15.	C
6.	A	16.	B
7.	A	17.	C
8.	B	18.	D
9.	D	19.	B
10.	D	20.	D

21.	D
22.	B
23.	C
24.	C
25.	A

—————

TEST 3

DIRECTIONS: Each question or incomplete statement is followed by several suggested answers or completions. Select the one that BEST answers the question or completes the statement. *PRINT THE LETTER OF THE CORRECT ANSWER IN THE SPACE AT THE RIGHT.*

Questions 1-3

DIRECTIONS: Questions 1 through 3 are to be answered SOLELY on the basis of the following paragraph.

Prior to revising its child care program, a department feels that it is necessary to get some information from the mothers served by the existing program in order to determine where changes are required. A questionnaire is to be constructed to obtain this information.

1. Of the following points which can be taken into consideration in the construction of the questionnaire, the one which is of LEAST importance is

    A. that the data are to be put into punch cards
    B. the aspects of the program which seem to be in need of change
    C. the type of person who will fill out the questionnaire
    D. testing the questionnaire for ambiguity in advance of general distribution
    E. setting up a control group so that answers received can be compared to a standard

1.___

2. To discuss this questionnaire with all mothers who have been asked to answer it, before they actually fill it out, is

    A. *desirable;* the mothers may be able to offer valuable suggestions for changes in the form of the questionnaire
    B. *undesirable;* it is of some value but consumes too much valuable time
    C. *desirable;* cooperation and uniform interpretation will tend to be achieved
    D. *undesirable;* it may cause the answers to be biased
    E. *desirable;* the group will tend to support the program

2.___

3. Of the following items included in the questionnaire, the one which will be of LEAST assistance for comparing attitudes toward the program among different kinds of persons is

    A. name   B. address   C. age
    D. place of birth   E. education

3.___

Questions 4-6.

DIRECTIONS: Questions 4 through 6 are to be answered SOLELY on the basis of the following paragraph.

The supervisor of a large clerical and statistical division has assigned to one of the units under his supervision the preparation of a special statistical report required by the department head. The unit head accepted the assignment without comment but soon ran into considerable difficulty because no one in his unit had had any statistical training.

4. If a result of this lack of training is that the report is not completed on time, although everyone has done all that could be expected, the responsibility for the failure rests with

    A. the department head   B. the supervisor
    C. the unit head   D. the employees in the unit
    E. no one

4.___

5. This incident indicates that the supervisory staff has insufficient knowledge of employee   5.____

    A. capabilities
    B. reaction to increased demands
    C. on-the-job training needs
    D. work habits
    E. ability to perform ordinary assignments

6. After working on the report for two days, the unit head notifies the supervisor that he will   6.____
not be able to get the report out in the required time. He states that his staff will be completely trained in another day or two and that after that preparing the report will be a simple matter. At this stage, the supervisor decides to have the statistical unit prepare the report. This action on the part of the supervisor is

    A. *undesirable;* the unit head should be given an incentive to continue with his training program which may produce good results
    B. *desirable;* it is the most effective way in which the supervisor can show his displeasure with the unit head's failure
    C. *undesirable;* it may adversely affect the morale of the unit
    D. *desirable;* it will generally result in a better report completed in a shorter time
    E. *undesirable;* the time spent on training the unit will be completely wasted

Questions 7-9.

DIRECTIONS: Questions 7 through 9 are to be answered SOLELY on the basis of the following paragraph.

The regressive uses of discipline are ubiquitous. Administrative architects who seek the optimum balance between structure and morale must accordingly look toward the identification and isolation of disciplinary elements. The whole range of disciplinary sanctions, from the reprimand to the dismissal, presents opportunities for reciprocity and accommodation of institutional interests. When rightly seized upon, these opportunities may provide the moment and the means for fruitful exercise of leadership and collaboration.

7. The one of the following ways of reworking the ideas presented in the above paragraph in   7.____
order to be BEST suited for presentation In an in-service training course in supervision is:

    A. When one of your men does something wrong, talk it over with him. Tell him what he should have done. This is a chance for you to show the man that you are on his side and that you would welcome him on your side.
    B. It is not necessary to reprimand or to dismiss an employee because he needs disciplining. The alert foreman will lead and collaborate with his subordinates, making discipline unnecessary.
    C. A good way to lead the men you supervise is to take those opportunities which present themselves to use the whole range of disciplinary sanctions from reprimand to dismissal as a means for enforcing collaboration.
    D. Chances to punish a man in your squad should be welcomed as opportunities to show that you are a *good guy* who does not bear a grudge.
    E. Before you talk to a man or have him report to the office for something he has done wrong, attempt to lead him and get him to work with you. Tell him that his actions were wrong, that you expect him not to repeat the same wrong act, and that you will take a firmer stand if the act is repeated.

8. Of the following, the PRINCIPAL point made in the paragraph above is that   8._

    A. discipline is frequently used improperly
    B. it is possible to isolate the factors entering into a disciplinary situation
    C. identification of the disciplinary elements is desirable
    D. disciplinary situations may be used to the advantage of the organization
    E. obtaining the best relationship between organizational form and spirit depends
        upon the ability to label disciplinary elements

9. The MOST novel idea presented in the above paragraph is that   9._

    A. discipline is rarely necessary
    B. discipline may be a joint action of man and supervisor
    C. there are disciplinary elements which may be identified
    D. a range of disciplinary sanctions exists
    E. it is desirable to seek for balance between structure and morale.

Questions 10-11.

DIRECTIONS: Questions 10 and 11 are to be answered SOLELY on the basis of the following
               paragraph.

   People must be selected to do the tasks involved and must be placed on a payroll in jobs
fairly priced. Each of these people must be assigned those tasks which he can perform best;
the work of each must be appraised, and good and poor work singled out appropriately. Skill
in performing assigned tasks must be developed, and the total work situation must be condu-
cive to sustained high performance. Finally, employees must be separated from the work
force either voluntarily or involuntarily because of inefficient or unsatisfactory performance or
because of curtailment of organizational activities.

10. A personnel function which is NOT included in the above description is   10._

    A. classification   B. training   C. placement
    D. severance   E. service rating

11. The underlying implied purpose of the policy enunciated in the above paragraph is   11._

    A. to plan for the curtailment of the organizational program when it becomes neces-
        sary
    B. to single out appropriate skill in performing assigned tasks
    C. to develop and maintain a high level of performance by employees
    D. that training employees in relation to the total work situation is essential if good and
        poor work are to be singled out
    E. that equal money for equal work results in a total work situation which insures
        proper appraisal

Questions 12-16.

DIRECTIONS: Questions 12 through 16 are to be answered SOLELY on the basis of the fol-
               lowing sections which appeared in a report on the work production of two
               bureaus of a department. Throughout the report, assume that each month has
               4 weeks.

Each of the two bureaus maintains a chronological file. In Bureau A, every 9 months on the average, this material fills a standard legal size file cabinet sufficient for 12,000 work units. In Bureau B, the same type of cabinet is filled in 18 months. Each bureau maintains three complete years of information plus a current file. When the current file cabinet is filled, the cabinet containing the oldest material is emptied, the contents disposed of, and the cabinet used for current material. The similarity of these operations makes it possible to consolidate these files with little effort.

Study of the practice of using typists as filing clerks for periods when there is no typing work showed (1) Bureau A has for the past 6 months completed a total of 1500 filing work units a week using on the average 200 man-hours of trained file clerk time and 20 man-hours of typist time, (2) Bureau B has in the same period completed a total of 2000 filing work units a week using on the average 125 man-hours of trained file clerk time and 60 hours of typist time. This includes all work in chronological files. Assuming that all clerks work at the same speed and that all typists work at the same speed, this indicates that work other than filing should be found for typists or that they should be given some training in the filing procedures used.... It should be noted that Bureau A has not been producing the 1,600 units of technical (not filing) work per 30 day period required by Schedule K, but is at present 200 units behind. The Bureau should be allowed 3 working days to get on schedule.

12. What percentage (approximate) of the total number of filing work units completed in both units consists of the work involved in the maintenance of the chronological files?   12.____

    A. 5%   B. 10%   C. 15%   D. 20%   E. 25%

13. If the two chronological files are consolidated, the number of months which should be allowed for filling a cabinet is   13.____

    A. 2   B. 4   C. 6   D. 8   E. 14

14. The MAXIMUM number of file cabinets which can be released for other uses as a result of the consolidation recommended is   14.____

    A. 0
    B. 1
    C. 2
    D. 3
    E. not determinable on the basis of the data given

15. If all the filing work for both units is consolidated without any diminution in the amount to be done and all filing work is done by trained file clerks, the number of clerks required (35-hour work week) is   15.____

    A. 4   B. 5   C. 6   D. 7   E. 8

16. In order to comply with the recommendation with respect to Schedule K, the present work production of Bureau A must be increased by   16.____

    A. 50%   B. 100%
    C. 150%   D. 200%
    E. an amount which is not determinable on the basis of the data given

Questions 17-18.

DIRECTIONS: Questions 17 and 18 are to be answered SOLELY on the basis of the following paragraph.

Production planning is mainly a process of synthesis. As a basis for the positive act of bringing complex production elements properly together, however, analysis is necessary, especially if improvement is to be made in an existing organization. The necessary analysis requires customary means of orientation and preliminary fact gathering with emphasis, however, on the recognition of administrative goals and of the relationship among work steps.

17.   The entire process described is PRIMARILY one of   17._

    A.   taking apart, examining, and recombining
    B.   deciding what changes are necessary, making the changes and checking on their value
    C.   fact finding so as to provide the necessary orientation
    D.   discovering just where the emphasis in production should be placed and then modifying the existing procedure so that it is placed properly
    E.   recognizing administrative goals and the relationship among work steps

18.   In production planning, according to the above paragraph, analysis is used PRIMARILY   18._
as

    A.   a means of making important changes in an organization
    B.   the customary means of orientation and preliminary fact finding
    C.   a development of the relationship among work steps
    D.   a means for holding the entire process intact by providing a logical basis
    E.   a method to obtain the facts upon which a theory can be built

Questions 19-21.

DIRECTIONS: Questions 19 through 21 are to be answered SOLELY on the basis of the following paragraph.

Public administration is policy-making. But it is not autonomous, exclusive, or isolated policy-making. It is policy-making on a field where mighty forces contend, forces engendered in and by society. It is policy-making subject to still other and various policy makers. Public administration is one of a number of basic political processes by which these people achieve and control government.

19.   From the point of view expressed in the above paragraph, public administration is   19._

    A.   becoming a technical field with completely objective processes
    B.   the primary force in modern society
    C.   a technical field which should be divorced from the actual decision-making function
    D.   basically anti-democratic
    E.   intimately related to politics

20. According to the above paragraph, public administration is NOT entirely   20._____

    A.   a force generated in and by society
    B.   subject at times to controlling influences
    C.   a social process
    D.   policy-making relating to administrative practices
    E.   related to policy-making at lower levels

21. The above paragraph asserts that public administration   21._____

    A.   develops the basic and controlling policies
    B.   is the result of policies made by many different forces
    C.   should attempt to break through its isolated policymaking and engage on a broader field
    D.   is a means of directing government
    E.   is subject to the political processes by which acts are controlled

Questions 22-24.

DIRECTIONS: Questions 22 through 24 are to be answered SOLELY on the basis of the following paragraph.

    In order to understand completely the source of an employee's insecurity on his job, it is necessary to understand how he came to be, who he is, and what kind of a person he is away from his job. This would necessitate an understanding of those personal assets and liabilities which the employee brings to the job situation. These arise from his individual characteristics and his past experiences and established patterns of interpersonal relations. This whole area is of tremendous scope, encompassing everything included within the study of psychiatry and interpersonal relations. Therefore, it has been impracticable to consider it in detail. Attention has been focused on the relatively circumscribed area of the actual occupational situation. The factors considered – those which the employee brings to the job situation and which arise from his individual characteristics and his past experience and established patterns of interpersonal relations – are: intellectual level or capacity, specific aptitudes, education, work experience, health, social and economic background, patterns of interpersonal relations and resultant personality characteristics.

22. According to the above paragraph, the one of the following fields of study which would be   22._____
of LEAST importance in the study of the problem is the

    A.   relationships existing among employees
    B.   causes of employee insecurity in the job situation
    C.   conflict, if it exists, between intellectual level and work experience
    D.   distribution of intellectual achievement
    E.   relationship between employee characteristics and the established pattern of interpersonal relations in the work situation

23. According to the above paragraph, in order to make a thoroughgoing and comprehensive   23._____
study of the sources of employee insecurity, the field of study should include

    A.   only such circumscribed areas as are involved in extra-occupational situations
    B.   a study of the dominant mores of the period
    C.   all branches of the science of psychology

D. a determination of the characteristics, such as intellectual capacity, which an employee should bring to the job situation

E. employee personality characteristics arising from previous relationships with other people

24. It is implied by the above paragraph that it would be of GREATEST advantage to bring to this problem a comprehensive knowledge of   24.__

A. all established patterns of interpersonal relations
B. the milieu in which the employee group is located
C. what assets and liabilities are presented in the job situation
D. methods of focusing attention on relatively circumscribed regions
E. the sources of an employee's insecurity on his job

Questions 25-26.

DIRECTIONS: Questions 25 and 26 are to be answered SOLELY on the basis of the following paragraph.

If, during a study, some hundreds of values of a variable (such as annual number of latenesses for each employee in a department) have been noted merely in the arbitrary order in which they happen to occur, the mind cannot properly grasp the significance of the record; the observations must be ranked or classified in some way before the characteristics of the series can be comprehended, and those comparisons, on which arguments as to causation depend, can be made with other series. A dichotomous classification is too crude; if the values are merely classified according to whether they exceed or fall short of some fixed value, a large part of the information given by the original record is lost. Numerical measurements lend themselves with peculiar readiness to a manifold classification.

25. According to the above paragraph, if the values of a variable which are gathered during a study are classified in a few subdivisions, the MOST likely result will be   25.__

A. an inability to grasp the significance of the record
B. an inability to relate the series with other series
C. a loss of much of the information in the original data
D. a loss of the readiness with which numerical measurements lend themselves to a manifold classification
E. that the order in which they happen to occur will be arbitrary

26. The above paragraph advocates, with respect to numerical data, the use of   26.__

A. arbitrary order
B. comparisons with other series
C. a two value classification
D. a many value classification
E. all values of a variable

Question 27.

DIRECTIONS: Question 27 is to be answered SOLELY on the basis of the following paragraph.

A more significant manifestation of the concern of the community with the general welfare is the collection and dissemination of statistics. This statement may cause the reader to smile, for statistics seem to be drab and prosaic things. The great growth of statistics, however, is one of the most remarkable characteristics of the age. Never before has a community kept track from month to month, and in some cases from week to week, of how many people are born, how many die and from what causes, how many are sick, how much is being produced, how much is being sold, how many people are at work, how many people are unemployed, how long they have been out of work, what prices people pay, how much income they receive and from what sources, how much they owe, what they intend to buy. These elaborate attempts of the country to keep informed about what is happening mean that the community is concerned with how its members are faring and with the conditions under which they live. For this reason, the present age may take pride in its numerous and regular statistical reports and in the rapid increase in the number of these reports. No other age has evidenced such a keen interest in the conditions of the people.

27. The writer implies that statistics are   27.____

    A. too scientific for general use
    B. too elaborate and too drab
    C. related to the improvement of living conditions
    D. frequently misinterpreted
    E. a product of the machine age

KEY (CORRECT ANSWERS)

1.	E	11.	C
2.	C	12.	C
3.	A	13.	C
4.	B	14.	B
5.	A	15.	D
6.	D	16.	E
7.	A	17.	A
8.	D	18.	E
9.	B	19.	E
10.	A	20.	D

21.	D
22.	D
23.	E
24.	B
25.	C
26.	D
27.	C

GLOSSARY OF COMPUTER TERMS

Contents

GLOSSARY OF COMPUTER TERMS

Basic

application & **app**
An application (often called "app" for short) is simply a program with a GUI. Note that it is different from an applet.

boot
Starting up an OS is booting it. If the computer is already running, it is more often called rebooting.

browser
A browser is a program used to browse the web. Some common browsers include Netscape, MSIE (Microsoft Internet Explorer), Safari, Lynx, Mosaic, Amaya, Arena, Chimera, Opera, Cyberdog, HotJava, etc.

bug
A bug is a mistake in the design of something, especially software. A really severe bug can cause something to crash.

chat
Chatting is like e-mail, only it is done instantaneously and can directly involve multiple people at once. While e-mail now relies on one more or less standard protocol, chatting still has a couple competing ones. Of particular note are IRC and Instant Messenger. One step beyond chatting is called MUDding.

click
To press a mouse button. When done twice in rapid succession, it is referred to as a double-click.

cursor
A point of attention on the computer screen, often marked with a flashing line or block. Text typed into the computer will usually appear at the cursor.

database
A database is a collection of data, typically organized to make common retrievals easy and efficient. Some common database programs include Oracle, Sybase, Postgres, Informix, Filemaker, Adabas, etc.

desktop
A desktop system is a computer designed to sit in one position on a desk somewhere and not move around. Most general purpose computers are desktop systems. Calling a system a desktop implies nothing about its platform. The fastest desktop system at any given time is typically either an Alpha or PowerPC based system, but the SPARC and PA-RISC based systems are also often in the running. Industrial strength desktops are typically called workstations.

directory
Also called "folder", a directory is a collection of files typically created for organizational purposes. Note that a directory is itself a file, so a directory can generally contain other directories. It differs in this way from a partition.

disk
A disk is a physical object used for storing data. It will not forget its data when it loses power. It is always used in conjunction with a disk drive. Some disks can be removed from their drives, some cannot. Generally it is possible to write new information to a disk in addition to reading data from it, but this is not always the case.

1

drive

A device for storing and/or retrieving data. Some drives (such as disk drives, zip drives, and tape drives) are typically capable of having new data written to them, but some others (like CD-ROMs or DVD-ROMs) are not. Some drives have random access (like disk drives, zip drives, CD-ROMs, and DVD-ROMs), while others only have sequential access (like tape drives).

e-book

The concept behind an e-book is that it should provide all the functionality of an ordinary book but in a manner that is (overall) less expensive and more environmentally friendly. The actual term e-book is somewhat confusingly used to refer to a variety of things: custom software to play e-book titles, dedicated hardware to play e-book titles, and the e-book titles themselves. Individual e-book titles can be free or commercial (but will always be less expensive than their printed counterparts) and have to be loaded into a player to be read. Players vary wildly in capability level. Basic ones allow simple reading and bookmarking; better ones include various features like hypertext, illustrations, audio, and even limited video. Other optional features allow the user to mark-up sections of text, leave notes, circle or diagram things, highlight passages, program or customize settings, and even use interactive fiction. There are many types of e-book; a couple popular ones include the Newton book and Palm DOC.

e-mail

E-mail is short for electronic mail. It allows for the transfer of information from one computer to another, provided that they are hooked up via some sort of network (often the Internet. E-mail works similarly to FAXing, but its contents typically get printed out on the other end only on demand, not immediately and automatically as with FAX. A machine receiving e-mail will also not reject other incoming mail messages as a busy FAX machine will; rather they will instead be queued up to be received after the current batch has been completed. E-mail is only seven-bit clean, meaning that you should not expect anything other than ASCII data to go through uncorrupted without prior conversion via something like uucode or bcode. Some mailers will do some conversion automatically, but unless you know your mailer is one of them, you may want to do the encoding manually.

file

A file is a unit of (usually named) information stored on a computer.

firmware

Sort of in-between hardware and software, firmware consists of modifiable programs embedded in hardware. Firmware updates should be treated with care since they can literally destroy the underlying hardare if done improperly. There are also cases where neglecting to apply a firmware update can destroy the underlying hardware, so user beware.

floppy

An extremely common type of removable disk. Floppies do not hold too much data, but most computers are capable of reading them. Note though that there are different competing format used for floppies, so that a floppy written by one type of computer might not directly work on another. Also sometimes called "diskette".

format

The manner in which data is stored; its organization. For example, VHS, SVHS, and Beta are three different formats of video tape. They are not 100% compatible with each other, but information can be transferred from one to the other with the proper equipment (but not always without loss; SVHS contains more information than either of the other two). Computer information can be stored in literally hundreds of different formats, and can represent text, sounds, graphics, animations, etc. Computer information can be exchanged via different computer types provided both computers can interpret the format used.

function keys

On a computer keyboard, the keys that start with an "F" that are usually (but not always) found on the top row. They are meant to perform user-defined tasks.

graphics

Anything visually displayed on a computer that is not text.

hardware

The physical portion of the computer.

hypertext

A hypertext document is like a text document with the ability to contain pointers to other regions of (possibly other) hypertext documents.

Internet

The Internet is the world-wide network of computers. There is only one Internet, and thus it is typically capitalized (although it is sometimes referred to as "the 'net"). It is different from an intranet.

keyboard

A keyboard on a computer is almost identical to a keyboard on a typewriter. Computer keyboards will typically have extra keys, however. Some of these keys (common examples include Control, Alt, and Meta) are meant to be used in conjunction with other keys just like shift on a regular typewriter. Other keys (common examples include Insert, Delete, Home, End, Help, function keys,etc.) are meant to be used independently and often perform editing tasks. Keyboards on different platforms will often look slightly different and have somewhat different collections of keys. Some keyboards even have independent shift lock and caps lock keys. Smaller keyboards with only math-related keys are typically called "keypads".

language

Computer programs can be written in a variety of different languages. Different languages are optimized for different tasks. Common languages include Java, C, C++, ForTran, Pascal, Lisp, and BASIC. Some people classify languages into two categories, higher-level and lower-level. These people would consider assembly language and machine language lower-level languages and all other languages higher-level. In general, higher-level languages can be either interpreted or compiled; many languages allow both, but some are restricted to one or the other. Many people do not consider machine language and assembly language at all when talking about programming languages.

laptop

A laptop is any computer designed to do pretty much anything a desktop system can do but run for a short time (usually two to five hours) on batteries. They are designed to be carried around but are not particularly convenient to carry around. They are significantly more expensive than desktop systems and have far worse battery life than PDAs. Calling a system a laptop implies nothing about its platform. By far the fastest laptops are the PowerPC based Macintoshes.

memory

Computer memory is used to temporarily store data. In reality, computer memory is only capable of remembering sequences of zeros and ones, but by utilizing the binary number system it is possible to produce arbitrary rational numbers and through clever formatting all manner of representations of pictures, sounds, and animations. The most common types of memory are RAM, ROM, and flash.

MHz & **megahertz**

One megahertz is equivalent to 1000 kilohertz, or 1,000,000 hertz. The clock speed of the main processor of many computers is measured in MHz, and is sometimes (quite misleadingly) used to represent the overall speed of a computer. In fact, a computer's speed is based upon many factors, and since MHz only reveals how many clock cycles the main processor has per second (saying nothing about how much is actually accomplished per cycle), it can really only accurately be used to gauge two computers with the same generation and family of processor plus similar configurations of memory, co-processors, and other peripheral hardware.

modem

A modem allows two computers to communicate over ordinary phone lines. It derives its name

3

from **mod**ulate / **dem**odulate, the process by which it converts digital computer data back and forth for use with an analog phone line.

monitor

The screen for viewing computer information is called a monitor.

mouse

In computer parlance a mouse can be both the physical object moved around to control a pointer on the screen, and the pointer itself. Unlike the animal, the proper plural of computer mouse is "mouses".

multimedia

This originally indicated a capability to work with and integrate various types of things including audio, still graphics, and especially video. Now it is more of a marketing term and has little real meaning. Historically the Amiga was the first multimedia machine. Today in addition to AmigaOS, IRIX and Solaris are popular choices for high-end multimedia work.

NC

The term **n**etwork **c**omputer refers to any (usually desktop) computer system that is designed to work as part of a network rather than as a stand-alone machine. This saves money on hardware, software, and maintenance by taking advantage of facilities already available on the network. The term "Internet appliance" is often used interchangeably with NC.

network

A network (as applied to computers) typically means a group of computers working together. It can also refer to the physical wire etc. connecting the computers.

notebook

A notebook is a small laptop with similar price, performance, and battery life.

organizer

An organizer is a tiny computer used primarily to store names, addresses, phone numbers, and date book information. They usually have some ability to exchange information with desktop systems. They boast even better battery life than PDAs but are far less capable. They are extremely inexpensive but are typically incapable of running any special purpose applications and are thus of limited use.

OS

The **o**perating **s**ystem is the program that manages a computer's resources. Common OSes include Windows '95, MacOS, Linux, Solaris, AmigaOS, AIX, Windows NT, etc.

PC

The term **p**ersonal **c**omputer properly refers to any desktop, laptop, or notebook computer system. Its use is inconsistent, though, and some use it to specifically refer to x86 based systems running MS-DOS, MS-Windows, GEOS, or OS/2. This latter use is similar to what is meant by a WinTel system.

PDA

A **p**ersonal **d**igital **a**ssistant is a small battery-powered computer intended to be carried around by the user rather than left on a desk. This means that the processor used ought to be power-efficient as well as fast, and the OS ought to be optimized for hand-held use. PDAs typically have an instant-on feature (they would be useless without it) and most are grayscale rather than color because of battery life issues. Most have a pen interface and come with a detachable stylus. None use mouses. All have some ability to exchange data with desktop systems. In terms of raw capabilities, a PDA is more capable than an organizer and less capable than a laptop (although some high-end PDAs beat out some low-end laptops). By far the most popular PDA is the Pilot, but other common types include Newtons, Psions, Zauri, Zoomers, and Windows CE hand-helds. By far the fastest current PDA is the Newton (based around a StrongARM RISC processor). Other PDAs are optimized for other tasks; few computers are as personal as PDAs and care must be taken in their purchase. Feneric's PDA / Handheld Comparison Page is perhaps the most detailed comparison of PDAs and handheld computers to be found anywhere on the web.

platform

Roughly speaking, a platform represents a computer's family. It is defined by both the processor type on the hardware side and the OS type on the software side. Computers belonging to different platforms cannot typically run each other's programs (unless the programs are written in a language like Java).

portable

If something is portable it can be easily moved from one type of computer to another. The verb "to port" indicates the moving itself.

printer

A printer is a piece of hardware that will print computer information onto paper.

processor

The processor (also called central processing unit, or CPU) is the part of the computer that actually works with the data and runs the programs. There are two main processor types in common usage today: CISC and RISC. Some computers have more than one processor and are thus called "multiprocessor". This is distinct from multitasking. Advertisers often use megahertz numbers as a means of showing a processor's speed. This is often extremely misleading; megahertz numbers are more or less meaningless when compared across different types of processors.

program

A program is a series of instructions for a computer, telling it what to do or how to behave. The terms "application" and "app" mean almost the same thing (albeit applications generally have GUIs). It is however different from an applet. Program is also the verb that means to create a program, and a programmer is one who programs.

run

Running a program is how it is made to do something. The term "execute" means the same thing.

software

The non-physical portion of the computer; the part that exists only as data; the programs. Another term meaning much the same is "code".

spreadsheet

An program used to perform various calculations. It is especially popular for financial applications. Some common spreadsheets include Lotus 123, Excel, OpenOffice Spreadsheet, Octave, Gnumeric, AppleWorks Spreadsheet, Oleo, and GeoCalc.

user

The operator of a computer.

word processor

A program designed to help with the production of textual documents, like letters and memos. Heavier duty work can be done with a desktop publisher. Some common word processors include MS-Word, OpenOffice Write, WordPerfect, AbiWord, AppleWorks Write, and GeoWrite.

www

The **W**orld-**W**ide-**W**eb refers more or less to all the publically accessible documents on the Internet. It is used quite loosely, and sometimes indicates only HTML files and sometimes FTP and Gopher files, too. It is also sometimes just referred to as "the web".

Reference

65xx

The 65xx series of processors includes the 6502, 65C02, 6510, 8502, 65C816, 65C816S, etc. It is a CISC design and is not being used in too many new stand-alone computer systems, but is still being used in embedded systems, game systems (such as the Super NES), and processor enhancement add-ons for older systems. It was originally designed by MOS Technologies, but is now produced by The Western Design Center, Inc. It was the primary processor for many extremely popular systems no longer being produced, including the Commodore 64, the Commodore 128, and all the Apple][series machines.

68xx

The 68xx series of processors includes the 6800, 6805, 6809, 68000, 68020, 68030, 68040, 68060, etc. It is a CISC design and is not being used in too many new stand-alone computer systems, but is still being used heavily in embedded systems. It was originally designed by Motorola and was the primary processor for older generations of many current machines, including Macintoshes, Amigas, Sun workstations, HP workstations, etc. and the primary processor for many systems no longer being produced, such as the TRS-80. The PowerPC was designed in part to be its replacement.

a11y

Commonly used to abbreviate the word "accessibility". There are eleven letters between the "a" and the "y".

ADA

An object-oriented language at one point popular for military and some academic software. Lately C++ and Java have been getting more attention.

AI

Artificial intelligence is the concept of making computers do tasks once considered to require thinking. AI makes computers play chess, recognize handwriting and speech, helps suggest prescriptions to doctors for patients based on imput symptoms, and many other tasks, both mundane and not.

AIX

The industrial strength OS designed by IBM to run on PowerPC and x86 based machines. It is a variant of UNIX and is meant to provide more power than OS/2.

AJaX

AJaX is a little like DHTML, but it adds asynchronous communication between the browser and Web site via either XML or JSON to achieve performance that often rivals desktop applications.

Alpha

An Alpha is a RISC processor invented by Digital and currently produced by Digital/Compaq and Samsung. A few different OSes run on Alpha based machines including Digital UNIX, Windows NT, Linux, NetBSD, and AmigaOS. Historically, at any given time, the fastest processor in the world has usually been either an Alpha or a PowerPC (with sometimes SPARCs and PA-RISCs making the list), but Compaq has recently announced that there will be no further development of this superb processor instead banking on the release of the somewhat suspect Merced.

AltiVec

AltiVec (also called the "Velocity Engine") is a special extension built into some PowerPC CPUs to provide better performance for certain operations, most notably graphics and sound. It is similar to MMX on the x86 CPUs. Like MMX, it requires special software for full performance benefits to be realized.

Amiga

A platform originally created and only produced by Commodore, but now owned by Gateway 2000 and produced by it and a few smaller companies. It was historically the first multimedia machine and gave the world of computing many innovations. It is now primarily used for audio / video applications; in fact, a decent Amiga system is less expensive than a less capable video editing system. Many music videos were created on Amigas, and a few television series and movies had their special effects generated on Amigas. Also, Amigas can be readily synchronized with video cameras, so typically when a computer screen appears on television or in a movie and it is not flickering wildly, it is probably an Amiga in disguise. Furthermore, many coin-operated arcade games are really Amigas packaged in stand-up boxes. Amigas have AmigaOS for their OS. New Amigas have either a PowerPC or an Alpha for their main processor and a 68xx processor dedicated to graphics manipulation. Older (and low end) Amigas do everything with just a 68xx processor.

AmigaOS

The OS used by Amigas. AmigaOS combines the functionality of an OS and a window manager and is fully multitasking. AmigaOS boasts a pretty good selection of games (many arcade games are in fact written on Amigas) but has limited driver support. AmigaOS will run on 68xx, Alpha, and PowerPC based machines.

Apple][

The Apple][computer sold millions of units and is generally considered to have been the first home computer with a 1977 release date. It is based on the 65xx family of processors. The earlier Apple I was only available as a build-it-yourself kit.

AppleScript

A scripting language for Mac OS computers.

applet

An applet differs from an application in that is not meant to be run stand-alone but rather with the assistance of another program, usually a browser.

AppleTalk

AppleTalk is a protocol for computer networks. It is arguably inferior to TCP/IP.

Aqua

The default window manager for Mac OS X.

Archie

Archie is a system for searching through FTP archives for particular files. It tends not to be used too much anymore as more general modern search engines are significantly more capable.

ARM

An ARM is a RISC processor invented by Advanced RISC Machines, currently owned by Intel, and currently produced by both the above and Digital/Compaq. ARMs are different from most other processors in that they were not designed to maximize speed but rather to maximize speed per power consumed. Thus ARMs find most of their use on hand-held machines and PDAs. A few different OSes run on ARM based machines including Newton OS, JavaOS, and (soon) Windows CE and Linux. The StrongARM is a more recent design of the original ARM, and it is both faster and more power efficient than the original.

ASCII

The ASCII character set is the most popular one in common use. People will often refer to a bare text file without complicated embedded format instructions as an ASCII file, and such files can usually be transferred from one computer system to another with relative ease. Unfortunately there are a few minor variations of it that pop up here and there, and if you receive a text file that seems subtly messed up with punctuation marks altered or upper and lower case reversed, you are probably encountering one of the ASCII variants. It is usually fairly straightforward to translate from one ASCII variant to another, though. The ASCII character set is seven bit while pure binary is usually eight bit, so transferring a binary file through ASCII channels will result in corruption and loss of data. Note also that the ASCII character set is a subset of the Unicode character set.

ASK
A protocol for an infrared communications port on a device. It predates the IrDA compliant infrared communications protocol and is not compatible with it. Many devices with infrared communications support both, but some only support one or the other.

assembly language
Assembly language is essentially machine language that has had some of the numbers replaced by somewhat easier to remember mnemonics in an attempt to make it more human-readable. The program that converts assembly language to machine language is called an assembler. While assembly language predates FORTRAN, it is not typically what people think of when they discuss computer languages.

Atom
Atom is an intended replacement for RSS and like it is used for syndicating a web site's content. It is currently not nearly as popular or well-supported by software applications, however.

authoring system
Any GUIs method of designing new software can be called an authoring system. Any computer language name with the word "visual" in front of it is probably a version of that language built with some authoring system capabilities. It appears that the first serious effort to produce a commercial quality authoring system took place in the mid eighties for the Amiga.

AWK
AWK is an interpreted language developed in 1977 by Aho, Weinberger, & Kernighan. It gets its name from its creators' initials. It is not particularly fast, but it was designed for creating small throwaway programs rather than full-blown applications -- it is designed to make the writing of the program fast, not the program itself. It is quite portable with versions existing for numerous platforms, including a free GNU version. Plus, virtually every version of UNIX in the world comes with AWK built-in.

BASIC
The **B**eginners' **A**ll-purpose **S**ymbolic **I**nstruction **C**ode is a computer language developed by Kemeny & Kurtz in 1964. Although it is traditionally interpreted, compilers exist for many platforms. While the interpreted form is typically fairly slow, the compiled form is often quite fast, usually faster than Pascal. The biggest problem with BASIC is portability; versions for different machines are often completely unlike each other; Amiga BASIC at first glance looks more like Pascal, for example. Portability problems actually go beyond even the cross platform level; in fact, most machines have multiple versions of incompatible BASICs available for use. The most popular version of BASIC today is called Visual BASIC. Like all BASICs it has portability issues, but it has some of the advantages of an authoring system so it is relatively easy to use.

baud
A measure of communications speed, used typically for modems indicating how many bits per second can be transmitted.

BBS
A **b**ulletin **b**oard **s**ystem is a computer that can be directly connected to via modem and provides various services like e-mail, chatting, newsgroups, and file downloading. BBSs have waned in popularity as more and more people are instead connecting to the Internet, but they are still used for product support and local area access. Most current BBSs provide some sort of gateway connection to the Internet.

bcode
Identical in intent to uucode, bcode is slightly more efficient and more portable across different computer types. It is the preferred method used by MIME.

BeOS
A lightweight OS available for both PowerPC and x86 based machines. It is often referred to simply as "Be".

beta

A beta version of something is not yet ready for prime time but still possibly useful to related developers and other interested parties. Expect beta software to crash more than properly released software does. Traditionally beta versions (of commercial software) are distributed only to selected testers who are often then given a discount on the proper version after its release in exchange for their testing work. Beta versions of non-commercial software are more often freely available to anyone who has an interest.

binary

There are two meanings for binary in common computer usage. The first is the name of the number system in which there are only zeros and ones. This is important to computers because all computer data is ultimately a series of zeros and ones, and thus can be represented by binary numbers. The second is an offshoot of the first; data that is not meant to be intepreted through a common character set (like ASCII) is typically referred to as binary data. Pure binary data is typically eight bit data, and transferring a binary file through ASCII channels without prior modification will result in corruption and loss of data. Binary data can be turned into ASCII data via uucoding or bcoding.

bit

A bit can either be on or off; one or zero. All computer data can ultimately be reduced to a series of bits. The term is also used as a (very rough) measure of sound quality, color quality, and even procesor capability by considering the fact that series of bits can represent binary numbers. For example (without getting too technical), an eight bit image can contain at most 256 distinct colors while a sixteen bit image can contain at most 65,536 distinct colors.

bitmap

A bitmap is a simplistic representation of an image on a computer, simply indicating whether or not pixels are on or off, and sometimes indicating their color. Often fonts are represented as bitmaps. The term "pixmap" is sometimes used similarly; typically when a distinction is made, pixmap refers to color images and bitmap refers to monochrome images.

blog

Short for web log, a blog (or weblog, or less commonly, 'blog) is a web site containing periodic (usually frequent) posts. Blogs are usually syndicated via either some type of RSS or Atom and often supports TrackBacks. It is not uncommon for blogs to function much like newspaper columns. A blogger is someone who writes for and maintains a blog.

boolean

Boolean algebra is the mathematics of base two numbers. Since base two numbers have only two values, zero and one, there is a good analogy between base two numbers and the logical values "true" & "false". In common usage, booleans are therefore considered to be simple logical values like true & false and the operations that relate them, most typically "and", "or" and "not". Since everyone has a basic understanding of the concepts of true & false and basic conjunctions, everyone also has a basic understanding of boolean concepts -- they just may not realize it.

byte

A byte is a grouping of bits. It is typically eight bits, but there are those who use non-standard byte sizes. Bytes are usually measured in large groups, and the term "kilobyte" (often abbreviated as K) means one-thousand twenty-four (1024) bytes; the term "megabyte" (often abbreviated as M) means one-thousand twenty-four (1024) K; the term gigabyte (often abbreviated as G) means one-thousand twenty-four (1024) M; and the term "terabyte" (often abbreviated as T) means one-thousand twenty-four (1024) G. Memory is typically measured in kilobytes or megabytes, and disk space is typically measured in megabytes or gigabytes. Note that the multipliers here are 1024 instead of the more common 1000 as would be used in the metric system. This is to make it easier to work with the binary number system. Note also that some hardware manufacturers will use the smaller 1000 multiplier on M & G quantities to make

9

their disk drives seem larger than they really are; buyer beware.

bytecode

Sometimes computer languages that are said to be either interpreted or compiled are in fact neither and are more accurately said to be somewhere in between. Such languages are compiled into bytecode which is then interpreted on the target system. Bytecode tends to be binary but will work on any machine with the appropriate runtime environment (or virtual machine) for it.

C

C is one of the most popular computer languages in the world, and quite possibly *the* most popular. It is a compiled langauge widely supported on many platforms. It tends to be more portable than FORTRAN but less portable than Java; it has been standardized by ANSI as "ANSI C" -- older versions are called either "K&R C" or "Kernighan and Ritchie C" (in honor of C's creators), or sometimes just "classic C". Fast and simple, it can be applied to all manner of general purpose tasks. C compilers are made by several companies, but the free GNU version (gcc) is still considered one of the best. Newer C-like object-oriented languages include both Java and C++.

C#

C# is a compiled object-oriented language based heavily on C++ with some Java features.

C++

C++ is a compiled object-oriented language. Based heavily on C, C++ is nearly as fast and can often be thought of as being just C with added features. It is currently probably the second most popular object-oriented language, but it has the drawback of being fairly complex -- the much simpler but somewhat slower Java is probably the most popular object-oriented language. Note that C++ was developed independently of the somewhat similar Objective-C; it is however related to Objective-C++.

C64/128

The Commodore 64 computer to this day holds the record for being the most successful model of computer ever made with even the lowest estimates being in the tens of millions. Its big brother, the Commodore 128, was not quite as popular but still sold several million units. Both units sported ROM-based BASIC and used it as a default "OS". The C128 also came with CP/M (it was a not-often-exercized option on the C64). In their later days they were also packaged with GEOS. Both are based on 65xx family processors. They are still in use today and boast a friendly and surprisingly active user community. There is even a current effort to port Linux to the C64 and C128 machines.

CDE

The common desktop environment is a popular commercial window manager (and much more -- as its name touts, it is more of a desktop environment) that runs under X-Windows. Free work-alike versions are also available.

chain

Some computer devices support chaining, the ability to string multiple devices in a sequence plugged into just one computer port. Often, but not always, such a chain will require some sort of terminator to mark the end. For an example, a SCSI scanner may be plugged into a SCSI CD-ROM drive that is plugged into a SCSI hard drive that is in turn plugged into the main computer. For all these components to work properly, the scanner would also have to have a proper terminator in use. Device chaining has been around a long time, and it is interesting to note that C64/128 serial devices supported it from the very beginning. Today the most common low-cost chainable devices in use support USB while the fastest low-cost chainable devices in use support FireWire.

character set

Since in reality all a computer can store are series of zeros and ones, representing common things like text takes a little work. The solution is to view the series of zeros and ones instead as a sequence of bytes, and map each one to a particular letter, number, or symbol. The full mapping is called a character set. The most popular character set is commonly referred to as ASCII. The second most popular character set these days is Unicode (and it will probably eventually surpass ASCII). Other fairly common character sets include EBCDIC and PETSCII. They are generally quite different from one another; programs exist to convert between them on most platforms, though. Usually EBCDIC is only found on really old machines.

CISC

Complex **i**nstruction **s**et **c**omputing is one of the two main types of processor design in use today. It is slowly losing popularity to RISC designs; currently all the fastest processors in the world are RISC. The most popular current CISC processor is the x86, but there are also still some 68xx, 65xx, and Z80s in use.

CLI

A **c**ommand-**l**ine **i**nterface is a text-based means of communicating with a program, especially an OS. This is the sort of interface used by MS-DOS, or a UNIX shell window.

COBOL

The **Co**mmon **B**usiness **O**riented **L**anguage is a language developed back in 1959 and still used by some businesses. While it is relatively portable, it is still disliked by many professional programmers simply because COBOL programs tend to be physically longer than equivalent programs written in almost any other language in common use.

compiled

If a program is compiled, its original human-readable source has been converted into a form more easily used by a computer prior to it being run. Such programs will generally run more quickly than interpreted programs, because time was pre-spent in the compilation phase. A program that compiles other programs is called a compiler.

compression

It is often possible to remove redundant information or capitalize on patterns in data to make a file smaller. Usually when a file has been compressed, it cannot be used until it is uncompressed. Image files are common exceptions, though, as many popular image file formats have compression built-in.

cookie

A cookie is a small file that a web page on another machine writes to your personal machine's disk to store various bits of information. Many people strongly detest cookies and the whole idea of them, and most browsers allow the reception of cookies to be disabled or at least selectively disabled, but it should be noted that both Netscape and MSIE have silent cookie reception enabled by default. Sites that maintain shopping carts or remember a reader's last position have legitimate uses for cookies. Sites without such functionality that still spew cookies with distant (or worse, non-existent) expiration dates should perhaps be treated with a little caution.

CP/M

An early DOS for desktops, CP/M runs on both Z80 and the x86 based machines. CP/M provides only a CLI and there really is not any standard way to get a window manager to run on top of it. It is fairly complex and tricky to use. In spite of all this, CP/M was once the most popular DOS and is still in use today.

crash

If a bug in a program is severe enough, it can cause that program to crash, or to become inoperable without being restarted. On machines that are not multitasking, the entire machine will crash and have to be rebooted. On machines that are only partially multitasking the entire machine will sometimes crash and have to be rebooted. On machines that are fully multitasking, the machine should never crash and require a reboot.

Cray

A Cray is a high-end computer used for research and frequently heavy-duty graphics applications. Modern Crays typically have Solaris for their OS and sport sixty-four RISC processors; older ones had various other configurations. Current top-of-the-line Crays can have over 2000 processors.

crippleware

Crippleware is a variant of shareware that will either self-destruct after its trial period or has built-in limitations to its functionality that get removed after its purchase.

CSS

Cascading style sheets are used in conjunction with HTML and XHTML to define the layout of web pages. While CSS is how current web pages declare how they should be displayed, it tends not to be supported well (if at all) by ancient browsers. XSL performs this same function more generally.

desktop publisher

A program for creating newspapers, magazines, books, etc. Some common desktop publishing programs include FrameMaker, PageMaker, InDesign, and GeoPublish.

DHTML

Dynamic **HTML** is simply the combined use of both CSS and JavaScript together in the same document; a more extreme form is called AJaX. Note that DHTML is quite different from the similarly named DTML.

dict

A protocol used for looking up definitions across a network (in particular the Internet).

digital camera

A digital camera looks and behaves like a regular camera, except instead of using film, it stores the image it sees in memory as a file for later transfer to a computer. Many digital cameras offer additional storage besides their own internal memory; a few sport some sort of disk but the majority utilize some sort of flash card. Digital cameras currently lack the resolution and color palette of real cameras, but are usually much more convenient for computer applications. Another related device is called a scanner.

DIMM

A physical component used to add RAM to a computer. Similar to, but incompatible with, SIMMs.

DNS

Domain name service is the means by which a name (like www.saugus.net or ftp.saugus.net) gets converted into a real Internet address that points to a particular machine.

DoS

In a denial of service attack, many individual (usually compromised) computers are used to try and simultaneously access the same public resource with the intent of overburdening it so that it will not be able to adequately serve its normal users.

DOS

A disk operating system manages disks and other system resources. Sort of a subset of OSes, sort of an archaic term for the same. MS-DOS is the most popular program currently calling itself a DOS. CP/M was the most popular prior to MS-DOS.

download

To download a file is to copy it from a remote computer to your own. The opposite is upload.

DR-DOS

The DOS currently produced by Caldera (originally produced by Design Research as a successor to CP/M) designed to work like MS-DOS. While similar to CP/M in many ways, it utilizes simpler commands. It provides only a CLI, but either Windows 3.1 or GEOS may be run on top of it to provide a GUI. It only runs on x86 based machines.

driver

A driver is a piece of software that works with the OS to control a particular piece of hardware, like a printer or a scanner or a mouse or whatever.

DRM

Depending upon whom you ask, DRM can stand for either Digital Rights Management or Digital Restrictions Management. In either case, DRM is used to place restrictions upon the usage of digital media ranging from software to music to video.

DTML

The **D**ocument **T**emplate **M**ark-up **L**anguage is a subset of SGML and a superset of HTML used for creating documents that dynamically adapt to external conditions using its own custom tags and a little bit of Python. Note that it is quite different from the similarly named DHTML.

EDBIC

The EDBIC character set is similar to (but less popular than) the ASCII character set in concept, but is significantly different in layout. It tends to be found only on old machines..

emacs

Emacs is both one of the most powerful and one of the most popular text editing programs in existence. Versions can be found for most platforms, and in fact multiple companies make versions, so for a given platform there might even be a choice. There is even a free GNU version available. The drawback with emacs is that it is not in the least bit lightweight. In fact, it goes so far in the other direction that even its advocates will occasionally joke about it. It is however extremely capable. Almost anything that one would need to relating to text can be done with emacs and is probably built-in. Even if one manages to find something that emacs was not built to do, emacs has a built-in Lisp interpreter capable of not only extending its text editing capabilities, but even of being used as a scripting language in its own right.

embedded

An embedded system is a computer that lives inside another device and acts as a component of that device. For example, current cars have an embedded computer under the hood that helps regulate much of their day to day operation.

An embedded file is a file that lives inside another and acts as a portion of that file. This is frequently seen with HTML files having embedded audio files; audio files often embedded in HTML include AU files, MIDI files, SID files, WAV files, AIFF files, and MOD files. Most browsers will ignore these files unless an appropriate plug-in is present.

emulator

An emulator is a program that allows one computer platform to mimic another for the purposes of running its software. Typically (but not always) running a program through an emulator will not be quite as pleasant an experience as running it on the real system.

endian

A processor will be either "big endian" or "little endian" based upon the manner in which it encodes multiple byte values. There is no difference in performance between the two encoding methods, but it is one of the sources of difficulty when reading binary data on different platforms.

environment

An environment (sometimes also called a runtime environment) is a collection of external variable items or parameters that a program can access when run. Information about the computer's hardware and the user can often be found in the environment.

EPOC

EPOC is a lightweight OS. It is most commonly found on the Psion PDA.

extension

Filename extensions originate back in the days of CP/M and basically allow a very rough grouping of different file types by putting a tag at the end of the name. To further complicate matters, the tag is sometimes separated by the name proper by a period "." and sometimes by a tab. While extensions are semi-enforced on CP/M, MS-DOS, and MS-Windows, they have no real meaning aside from convention on other platforms and are only optional.

FAQ

A **f**requently **a**sked **q**uestions file attempts to provide answers for all commonly asked questions related to a given topic.

FireWire

An incredibly fast type of serial port that offers many of the best features of SCSI at a lower price. Faster than most types of parallel port, a single FireWire port is capable of chaining many devices without the need of a terminator. FireWire is similar in many respects to USB but is significantly faster and somewhat more expensive. It is heavily used for connecting audio/video devices to computers, but is also used for connecting storage devices like drives and other assorted devices like printers and scanners.

fixed width

As applied to a font, fixed width means that every character takes up the same amount of space. That is, an "i" will be just as wide as an "m" with empty space being used for padding. The opposite is variable width. The most common fixed width font is Courier.

flash

Flash memory is similar to RAM. It has one significant advantage: it does not lose its contents when power is lost; it has two main disadvantages: it is slower, and it eventually wears out. Flash memory is frequently found in PCMCIA cards.

font

In a simplistic sense, a font can be thought of as the physical description of a character set. While the character set will define what sets of bits map to what letters, numbers, and other symbols, the font will define what each letter, number, and other symbol looks like. Fonts can be either fixed width or variable width and independently, either bitmapped or vectored. The size of the large characters in a font is typically measured in points.

Forth

A language developed in 1970 by Moore. Forth is fairly portable and has versions on many different platforms. While it is no longer an very popular language, many of its ideas and concepts have been carried into other computer programs. In particular, some programs for doing heavy-duty mathematical and engineering work use Forth-like interfaces.

FORTRAN

FORTRAN stands for **for**mula **tran**slation and is the oldest computer language in the world. It is typically compiled and is quite fast. Its primary drawbacks are portability and ease-of-use -- often different FORTRAN compilers on different platforms behave quite differently in spite of standardization efforts in 1966 (FORTRAN 66 or FORTRAN IV), 1978 (FORTRAN 77), and 1991 (FORTRAN 90). Today languages like C and Java are more popular, but FORTRAN is still heavily used in military software. It is somewhat amusing to note that when FORTRAN was first released back in 1958 its advocates thought that it would mean the end of software bugs. In truth of course by making the creation of more complex software practical, computer languages have merely created new types of software bugs.

FreeBSD

A free variant of Berkeley UNIX available for Alpha and x86 based machines. It is not as popular as Linux.

freeware

Freeware is software that is available for free with no strings attached. The quality is often superb as the authors are also generally users.

FTP

The **f**ile **t**ransfer **p**rotocol is one of the most commonly used methods of copying files across the Internet. It has its origins on UNIX machines, but has been adapted to almost every type of computer in existence and is built into many browsers. Most FTP programs have two modes of operation, ASCII, and binary. Transmitting an ASCII file via the ASCII mode of operation is more efficient and cleaner. Transmitting a binary file via the ASCII mode of operation will result in a broken binary file. Thus the FTP programs that do not support both modes of operation will typically only do the binary mode, as binary transfers are capable of transferring both kinds of

14

data without corruption.

gateway

A gateway connects otherwise separate computer networks.

GEOS

The **g**raphic **e**nvironment **o**perating **s**ystem is a lightweight OS with a GUI. It runs on several different processors, including the 65xx (different versions for different machines -- there are versions for the C64, the C128, and the Apple][, each utilizing the relevant custom chip sets), the x86 (although the x86 version is made to run on top of MS-DOS (or PC-DOS or DR-DOS) and is not strictly a full OS or a window manager, rather it is somewhat in between, like Windows 3.1) and numerous different PDAs, embedded devices, and hand-held machines. It was originally designed by Berkeley Softworks (no real relation to the Berkeley of UNIX fame) but is currently in a more interesting state: the company GeoWorks develops and promotes development of GEOS for hand-held devices, PDAs, & and embedded devices and owns (but has ceased further development on) the x86 version. The other versions are owned (and possibly still being developed) by the company CMD.

GHz & **gigahertz**

One gigahertz is equivalent to 1000 megahertz, or 1,000,000,000 hertz.

Glulx

A virtual machine optimized for running interactive fiction, interactive tutorials, and other interactive things of a primarily textual nature. Glulx has been ported to several platforms, and in in many ways an upgrade to the Z-machine.

GNOME

The **G**NU **n**etwork **o**bject **m**odel **e**nvironment is a popular free window manager (and much more -- as its name touts, it is more of a desktop environment) that runs under X-Windows. It is a part of the GNU project.

GNU

GNU stands for **G**NU's **n**ot **U**NIX and is thus a recursive acronym (and unlike the animal name, the "G" here is pronounced). At any rate, the GNU project is an effort by the Free Software Foundation (FSF) to make all of the traditional UNIX utilities free for whoever wants them. The Free Software Foundation programmers know their stuff, and the quality of the GNU software is on par with the best produced commercially, and often better. All of the GNU software can be downloaded for free or obtained on CD-ROM for a small service fee. Documentation for all GNU software can be downloaded for free or obtained in book form for a small service fee. The Free Software Foundation pays its bills from the collection of service fees and the sale of T-shirts, and exists mostly through volunteer effort. It is based in Cambridge, MA.

gopher

Though not as popular as FTP or http, the gopher protocol is implemented by many browsers and numerous other programs and allows the transfer of files across networks. In some respects it can be thought of as a hybrid between FTP and http, although it tends not to be as good at raw file transfer as FTP and is not as flexible as http. The collection of documents available through gopher is often called "gopherspace", and it should be noted that gopherspace is older than the web. It should also be noted that gopher is not getting as much attention as it once did, and surfing through gopherspace is a little like exploring a ghost town, but there is an interesting VR interface available for it, and some things in gopherspace still have not been copied onto the web.

GUI

A **g**raphical **u**ser **i**nterface is a graphics-based means of communicating with a program, especially an OS or window manager. In fact, a window manager can be thought of as a GUI for a CLI OS.

HP-UX

HP-UX is the version of UNIX designed by Hewlett-Packard to work with their PA-RISC and

68xx based machines.

HTML

The **H**yper**t**ext **M**ark-up **L**anguage is the language currently most frequently used to express web pages (although it is rapidly being replaced by XHTML). Every browser has the built-in ability to understand HTML. Some browsers can additionally understand Java and browse FTP areas. HTML is a proper subset of SGML.

http

The **h**yper**t**ext **t**ransfer **p**rotocol is the native protocol of browsers and is most typically used to transfer HTML formatted files. The secure version is called "https".

Hurd

The Hurd is the official GNU OS. It is still in development and is not yet supported on too many different processors, but promises to be the most powerful OS available. It (like all the GNU software) is free.

Hz & **hertz**

Hertz means cycles per second, and makes no assumptions about what is cycling. So, for example, if a fluorescent light flickers once per jiffy, it has a 60 Hz flicker. More typical for computers would be a program that runs once per jiffy and thus has a 60 Hz frequency, or larger units of hertz like kHz, MHz, GHz, or THz.

i18n

Commonly used to abbreviate the word "internationalization". There are eighteen letters between the "i" and the "n". Similar to (and often used along with) i18n.

iCalendar

The iCalendar standard refers to the format used to store calendar type information (including events, to-do items, and journal entries) on the Internet. iCalendar data can be found on some World-Wide-Web pages or attached to e-mail messages.

icon

A small graphical display representing an object, action, or modifier of some sort.

IDE

Loosely speaking, a disk format sometimes used by MS-Windows, Mac OS, AmigaOS, and (rarely) UNIX. EIDE is enhanced IDE; it is much faster. Generally IDE is inferior (but less expensive) to SCSI, but it varies somewhat with system load and the individual IDE and SCSI components themselves. The quick rundown is that: SCSI-I and SCSI-II will almost always outperform IDE; EIDE will almost always outperform SCSI-I and SCSI-II; SCSI-III and UltraSCSI will almost always outperform EIDE; and heavy system loads give an advantage to SCSI. Note that although loosely speaking it is just a format difference, it is deep down a hardware difference.

Inform

A compiled, object-oriented language optimized for creating interactive fiction.

infrared communications

A device with an infrared port can communicate with other devices at a distance by beaming infrared light signals. Two incompatible protocols are used for infrared communications: IrDA and ASK. Many devices support both.

Instant Messenger

AOL's Instant Messenger is is a means of chatting over the Internet in real-time. It allows both open group discussions and private conversations. Instant Messenger uses a different, proprietary protocol from the more standard IRC, and is not supported on as many platforms.

interactive fiction

Interactive fiction (often abbreviated "IF" or "I-F") is a form of literature unique to the computer. While the reader cannot influence the direction of a typical story, the reader plays a more active role in an interactive fiction story and completely controls its direction. Interactive fiction works come in all the sizes and genres available to standard fiction, and in fact are not always even

16

fiction per se (interactive tutorials exist and are slowly becoming more common).

interpreted

If a program is interpreted, its actual human-readable source is read as it is run by the computer. This is generally a slower process than if the program being run has already been compiled.

intranet

An intranet is a private network. There are many intranets scattered all over the world. Some are connected to the Internet via gateways.

IP

IP is the family of protocols that makes up the Internet. The two most common flavors are TCP/IP and UDP/IP.

IRC

Internet **r**elay **c**hat is a means of chatting over the Internet in real-time. It allows both open group discussions and private conversations. IRC programs are provided by many different companies and will work on many different platforms. AOL's Instant Messenger utilizes a separate incompatible protocol but is otherwise very similar.

IrDA

The **I**nfrared **D**ata **A**ssociation (IrDA) is a voluntary organization of various manufacturers working together to ensure that the infrared communications between different computers, PDAs, printers, digital cameras, remote controls, etc. are all compatible with each other regardless of brand. The term is also often used to designate an IrDA compliant infrared communications port on a device. Informally, a device able to communicate via IrDA compliant infrared is sometimes simply said to "have IrDA". There is also an earlier, incompatible, and usually slower type of infrared communications still in use called ASK.

IRI

An **I**nternationalized **R**esource **I**dentifier is just a URI with i18n.

IRIX

The variant of UNIX designed by Silicon Graphics, Inc. IRIX machines are known for their graphics capabilities and were initially optimized for multimedia applications.

ISDN

An **i**ntegrated **s**ervice **d**igital **n**etwork line can be simply looked at as a digital phone line. ISDN connections to the Internet can be four times faster than the fastest regular phone connection, and because it is a digital connection a modem is not needed. Any computer hooked up to ISDN will typically require other special equipment in lieu of the modem, however. Also, both phone companies and ISPs charge more for ISDN connections than regular modem connections.

ISP

An **I**nternet **s**ervice **p**rovider is a company that provides Internet support for other entities. AOL (America Online) is a well-known ISP.

Java

A computer language designed to be both fairly lightweight and extremely portable. It is tightly bound to the web as it is the primary language for web applets. There has also been an OS based on Java for use on small hand-held, embedded, and network computers. It is called JavaOS. Java can be either interpreted or compiled. For web applet use it is almost always interpreted. While its interpreted form tends not to be very fast, its compiled form can often rival languages like C++ for speed. It is important to note however that speed is not Java's primary purpose -- raw speed is considered secondary to portabilty and ease of use.

JavaScript

JavaScript (in spite of its name) has nothing whatsoever to do with Java (in fact, it's arguably more like Newton Script than Java). JavaScript is an interpreted language built into a browser to provide a relatively simple means of adding interactivity to web pages. It is only supported on a few different browsers, and tends not to work exactly the same on different versions. Thus its

17

use on the Internet is somewhat restricted to fairly simple programs. On intranets where there are usually fewer browser versions in use, JavaScript has been used to implement much more complex and impressive programs.

jiffy

A jiffy is 1/60 of a second. Jiffies are to seconds as seconds are to minutes.

joystick

A joystick is a physical device typically used to control objects on a computer screen. It is frequently used for games and sometimes used in place of a mouse.

JSON

The JSON is used for data interchange between programs, an area in which the ubiquitous XML is not too well-suited. JSON is lightweight and works extremely cleanly with languages languages including JavaScript, Python, Java, C++, and many others.

JSON-RPC

JSON-RPC is like XML-RPC but is significantly more lightweight since it uses JSON in lieu of XML.

KDE

The **K d**esktop **e**nvironment is a popular free window manager (and much more -- as its name touts, it is more of a desktop environment) that runs under X-Windows.

Kerberos

Kerberos is a network authentication protocol. Basically it preserves the integrity of passwords in any untrusted network (like the Internet). Kerberized applications work hand-in-hand with sites that support Kerberos to ensure that passwords cannot be stolen.

kernel

The very heart of an OS is often called its kernel. It will usually (at minimum) provide some libraries that give programmers access to its various features.

kHz & **kilohertz**

One kilohertz is equivalent to 1000 hertz. Some older computers have clock speeds measured in kHz.

l10n

Commonly used to abbreviate the word "localization". There are ten letters between the "l" and the "n". Similar to (and often used along with) i18n.

LDAP

The **L**ightweight **D**irectory **A**ccess **P**rotocol provides a means of sharing address book type of information across an intranet or even across the Internet. Note too that "address book type of information" here is pretty broad; it often includes not just human addresses, but machine addresses, printer configurations, and similar.

library

A selection of routines used by programmers to make computers do particular things.

lightweight

Something that is lightweight will not consume computer resources (such as RAM and disk space) too much and will thus run on less expensive computer systems.

Linux

Believe it or not, one of the fastest, most robust, and powerful multitasking OSes is available for free. Linux can be downloaded for free or be purchased on CD-ROM for a small service charge. A handful of companies distribute Linux including Red Hat, Debian, Caldera, and many others. Linux is also possibly available for more hardware combinations than any other OS (with the possible exception of NetBSD. Supported processors include: Alpha, PowerPC, SPARC, x86, and 68xx. Most processors currently not supported are currently works-in-progress or even available in beta. For example, work is currently underway to provide support for PA-RISC, 65xx, StrongARM, and Z80. People have even successfully gotten Linux working on PDAs. As you may have guessed, Linux can be made quite lightweight. Linux is a variant of UNIX and as such, most of the traditional UNIX software will run on Linux. This especially includes the GNU software, most of which comes with the majority of Linux distributions. Fast, reliable, stable, and inexpensive, Linux is popular with ISPs, software developers, and home hobbyists alike.

Lisp

Lisp stands for **lis**t **p**rocessing and is the second oldest computer language in the world. Being developed in 1959, it lost the title to FORTRAN by only a few months. It is typically interpreted, but compilers are available for some platforms. Attempts were made to standardize the language, and the standard version is called "Common Lisp". There have also been efforts to simplify the language, and the results of these efforts is another language called Scheme. Lisp is a fairly portable language, but is not particularly fast. Today, Lisp is most widely used with AI software.

load

There are two popular meanings for load. The first means to fetch some data or a program from a disk and store it in memory. The second indicates the amount of work a component (especially a processor) is being made to do.

Logo

Logo is an interpreted language designed by Papert in 1966 to be a tool for helping people (especially kids) learn computer programming concepts. In addition to being used for that purpose, it is often used as a language for controlling mechanical robots and other similar devices. Logo interfaces even exist for building block / toy robot sets. Logo uses a special graphics cursor called "the turtle", and Logo is itself sometimes called "Turtle Graphics". Logo is quite portable but not particularly fast. Versions can be found on almost every computer platform in the world. Additionally, some other languages (notably some Pascal versions) provide Logo-like interfaces for graphics-intensive programming.

lossy

If a process is lossy, it means that a little quality is lost when it is performed. If a format is lossy, it means that putting data into that format (or possibly even manipulating it in that format) will cause some slight loss. Lossy processes and formats are typically used for performance or resource utilization reasons. The opposite of lossy is lossless.

Lua

Lua is a simple interpreted language. It is extremely portable, and free versions exist for most platforms.

Mac OS

Mac OS is the OS used on Macintosh computers. There are two distinctively different versions of it; everything prior to version 10 (sometimes called Mac OS Classic) and everything version 10 or later (called Mac OS X).

Mac OS Classic

The OS created by Apple and originally used by Macs is frequently (albeit slightly incorrectly) referred to as Mac OS Classic (officially Mac OS Classic is this original OS running under the modern Mac OS X in emulation. Mac OS combines the functionality of both an OS and a window manager and is often considered to be the easiest OS to use. It is partially multitasking but will still sometimes crash when dealing with a buggy program. It is probably the second most popular OS, next only to Windows 'XP (although it is quickly losing ground to Mac OS X) and has excellent driver support and boasts a fair selection of games. Mac OS will run on PowerPC and 68xx based machines.

Mac OS X

Mac OS X (originally called Rhapsody) is the industrial strength OS produced by Apple to run on both PowerPC and x86 systems (replacing what is often referred to as Mac OS Classic. Mac OS X is at its heart a variant of UNIX and possesses its underlying power (and the ability to run many of the traditional UNIX tools, including the GNU tools). It also was designed to mimic other OSes on demand via what it originally refered to as "boxes" (actually high-performance emulators); it has the built-in capability to run programs written for older Mac OS (via its "BlueBox", officially called Mac OS Classic) and work was started on making it also run Windows '95 / '98 / ME software (via what was called its "YellowBox"). There are also a few rumors going around that future versions may even be able to run Newton software (via the "GreenBox"). It provides a selection of two window managers built-in: Aqua and X-Windows (with Aqua being the default).

machine language

Machine language consists of the raw numbers that can be directly understood by a particular processor. Each processor's machine language will be different from other processors' machine language. Although called "machine language", it is not usually what people think of when talking about computer languages. Machine language dressed up with mnemonics to make it a bit more human-readable is called assembly language.

Macintosh

A Macintosh (or a Mac for short) is a computer system that has Mac OS for its OS. There are a few different companies that have produced Macs, but by far the largest is Apple. The oldest Macs are based on the 68xx processor; somewhat more recent Macs on the PowerPC processor, and current Macs on the x86 processor. The Macintosh was really the first general purpose computer to employ a GUI.

MacTel

An x86 based system running some flavor of Mac OS.

mainframe

A mainframe is any computer larger than a small piece of furniture. A modern mainframe is more powerful than a modern workstation, but more expensive and more difficult to maintain.

MathML

The **Math M**ark-up **L**anguage is a subset of XML used to represent mathematical formulae and equations. Typically it is found embedded within XHTML documents, although as of this writing not all popular browsers support it.

megahertz

A million cycles per second, abbreviated MHz. This is often used misleadingly to indicate processor speed, because while one might expect that a higher number would indicate a faster processor, that logic only holds true within a given type of processors as different types of processors are capable of doing different amounts of work within a cycle. For a current example, either a 200 MHz PowerPC or a 270 MHz SPARC will outperform a 300 MHz Pentium.

Merced

The Merced is a RISC processor developed by Intel with help from Hewlett-Packard and possibly Sun. It is just starting to be released, but is intended to eventually replace both the x86 and PA-RISC processors. Curiously, HP is recommending that everyone hold off using the first release and instead wait for the second one. It is expected some day to be roughly as fast as an Alpha or PowerPC. It is expected to be supported by future versions of Solaris, Windows-NT, HP-UX, Mac OS X, and Linux. The current semi-available Merced processor is called the Itanium. Its overall schedule is way behind, and some analysts predict that it never will really be released in significant quanitities.

MFM

Loosely speaking, An old disk format sometimes used by CP/M, MS-DOS, and MS-Windows. No longer too common as it cannot deliver close to the performance of either SCSI or IDE.

middleware

Software designed to sit in between an OS and applications. Common examples are Java and Tcl/Tk.

MIME

The **m**ulti-purpose **I**nternet **m**ail **e**xtensions specification describes a means of sending non-

ASCII data (such as images, sounds, foreign symbols, etc.) through e-mail. It commonly utilizes bcode.

MMX

Multimedia extensions were built into some x86 CPUs to provide better performance for certain operations, most notably graphics and sound. It is similar to AltiVec on the PowerPC CPUs. Like AltiVec, it requires special software for full performance benefits to be realized.

MOB

A movable object is a graphical object that is manipulated separately from the background. These are seen all the time in computer games. When implemented in hardware, MOBs are sometimes called sprites.

Modula-2 & Modula-3

Modula-2 is a procedural language based on Pascal by its original author in around the 1977 - 1979 time period. Modula-3 is an intended successor that adds support for object-oriented constructs (among other things). Modula-2 can be either compiled or interpreted, while Modula-3 tends to be just a compiled language.

MOTD

A message of the day. Many computers (particularly more capable ones) are configured to display a MOTD when accessed remotely.

Motif

Motif is a popular commercial window manager that runs under X-Windows. Free work-alike versions are also available.

MS-DOS

The DOS produced by Microsoft. Early versions of it bear striking similarities to the earlier CP/M, but it utilizes simpler commands. It provides only a CLI, but either OS/2, Windows 3.1, Windows '95, Windows '98, Windows ME, or GEOS may be run on top of it to provide a GUI. It only runs on x86 based machines.

MS-Windows

MS-Windows is the name collectively given to several somewhat incompatible OSes all produced by Microsoft. They are: Windows CE, Windows NT, Windows 3.1, Windows '95, Windows '98, Windows ME, Windows 2000, and Windows XP.

MUD

A multi-user dimension (also sometimes called multi-user dungeon, but in either case abbreviated to "MUD") is sort of a combination between the online chatting abilities provided by something like IRC and a role-playing game. A MUD built with object oriented principles in mind is called a "Multi-user dimension object-oriented", or MOO. Yet another variant is called a "multi-user shell", or MUSH. Still other variants are called multi-user role-playing environments (MURPE) and multi-user environments (MUSE). There are probably more. In all cases the differences will be mostly academic to the regular user, as the same software is used to connect to all of them. Software to connect to MUDs can be found for most platforms, and there are even Java based ones that can run from within a browser.

multitasking

Some OSes have built into them the ability to do several things at once. This is called multitasking, and has been in use since the late sixties / early seventies. Since this ability is built into the software, the overall system will be slower running two things at once than it will be running just one thing. A system may have more than one processor built into it though, and such a system will be capable of running multiple things at once with less of a performance hit.

nagware

Nagware is a variant of shareware that will frequently remind its users to register.

NetBSD

A free variant of Berkeley UNIX available for Alpha, x86, 68xx, PA-RISC, SPARC, PowerPC, ARM, and many other types of machines. Its emphasis is on portability.

21

netiquette

The established conventions of online politeness are called netiquette. Some conventions vary from site to site or online medium to online medium; others are pretty standard everywhere. Newbies are often unfamiliar with the conventional rules of netiquette and sometimes embarrass themselves accordingly. Be sure not to send that incredibly important e-mail message before reading about netiquette.

newbie

A newbie is a novice to the online world or computers in general.

news

Usenet news can generally be thought of as public e-mail as that is generally the way it behaves. In reality, it is implemented by different software and is often accessed by different programs. Different newsgroups adhere to different topics, and some are "moderated", meaning that humans will try to manually remove off-topic posts, especially spam. Most established newsgroups have a FAQ, and people are strongly encouraged to read the FAQ prior to posting.

Newton

Although Newton is officially the name of the lightweight OS developed by Apple to run on its MessagePad line of PDAs, it is often used to mean the MessagePads (and compatible PDAs) themselves and thus the term "Newton OS" is often used for clarity. The Newton OS is remarkably powerful; it is fully multitasking in spite of the fact that it was designed for small machines. It is optimized for hand-held use, but will readily transfer data to all manner of desktop machines. Historically it was the first PDA. Recently Apple announced that it will discontinue further development of the Newton platform, but will instead work to base future hand-held devices on either Mac OS or Mac OS X with some effort dedicated to making the new devices capable of running current Newton programs.

Newton book

Newton books provide all the functionality of ordinary books but add searching and hypertext capabilities. The format was invented for the Newton to provide a means of making volumes of data portable, and is particularly popular in the medical community as most medical references are available as Newton books and carrying around a one pound Newton is preferable to carrying around twenty pounds of books, especially when it comes to looking up something. In addition to medical books, numerous references, most of the classics, and many contemporary works of fiction are available as Newton books. Most fiction is available for free, most references cost money. Newton books are somewhat more capable than the similar Palm DOC; both are specific types of e-books.

Newton Script

A intepreted, object-oriented language for Newton MessagePad computers.

nybble

A nybble is half a byte, or four bits. It is a case of computer whimsy; it only stands to reason that a small byte should be called a nybble. Some authors spell it with an "i" instead of the "y", but the "y" is the original form.

object-oriented

While the specifics are well beyond the scope of this document, the term "object-oriented" applies to a philosophy of software creation. Often this philosophy is referred to as object-oriented design (sometimes abbreviated as OOD), and programs written with it in mind are referred to as object-oriented programs (often abbreviated OOP). Programming languages designed to help facilitate it are called object-oriented languages (sometimes abbreviated as OOL) and databases built with it in mind are called object-oriented databases (sometimes abbreviated as OODB or less fortunately OOD). The general notion is that an object-oriented approach to creating software starts with modeling the real-world problems trying to be solved in familiar real-world ways, and carries the analogy all the way down to structure of the program. This is of course a great over-simplification. Numerous object-oriented programming languages exist including: Java, C++, Modula-2, Newton Script, and ADA.

Objective-C & ObjC

Objective-C (often called "ObjC" for short) is a compiled object-oriented language. Based heavily on C, Objective-C is nearly as fast and can often be thought of as being just C with added features. Note that it was developed independently of C++; its object-oriented extensions are more in the style of Smalltalk. It is however related to Objective-C++.

Objective-C++ & ObjC++

Objective-C++ (often called "ObjC++" for short) is a curious hybrid of Objective-C and C++, allowing the syntax of both to coexist in the same source files.

office suite

An office suite is a collection of programs including at minimum a word processor, spreadsheet, drawing program, and minimal database program. Some common office suites include MS-Office, AppleWorks, ClarisWorks, GeoWorks, Applixware, Corel Office, and StarOffice.

open source

Open source software goes one step beyond freeware. Not only does it provide the software for free, it provides the original source code used to create the software. Thus, curious users can poke around with it to see how it works, and advanced users can modify it to make it work better for them. By its nature, open souce software is pretty well immune to all types of computer virus.

OpenBSD

A free variant of Berkeley UNIX available for Alpha, x86, 68xx, PA-RISC, SPARC, and PowerPC based machines. Its emphasis is on security.

OpenDocument & ODF

OpenDocument (or ODF for short) is the suite of open, XML-based office suite application formats defined by the OASIS consortium. It defines a platform-neutral, non-proprietary way of storing documents.

OpenGL

A low-level 3D graphics library with an emphasis on speed developed by SGI.

OS/2

OS/2 is the OS designed by IBM to run on x86 based machines. It is semi-compatible with MS-Windows. IBM's more industrial strength OS is called AIX.

PA-RISC

The PA-RISC is a RISC processor developed by Hewlett-Packard. It is currently produced only by HP. At the moment only one OS runs on PA-RISC based machines: HP-UX. There is an effort underway to port Linux to them, though.

Palm DOC

Palm DOC files are quite similar to (but slightly less capable than) Newton books. They were designed for Palm Pilots but can now be read on a couple other platforms, too. They are a specific type of e-book.

Palm Pilot

The Palm Pilot (also called both just Palm and just Pilot, officially now just Palm) is the most popular PDA currently in use. It is one of the least capable PDAs, but it is also one of the smallest and least expensive. While not as full featured as many of the other PDAs (such as the Newton) it performs what features it does have quite well and still remains truly pocket-sized.

parallel

Loosely speaking, parallel implies a situation where multiple things can be done simultaneously, like having multiple check-out lines each serving people all at once. Parallel connections are by their nature more expensive than serial ones, but usually faster. Also, in a related use of the word, often multitasking computers are said to be capable of running multiple programs in parallel.

partition

Sometimes due to hardware limitations, disks have to be divided into smaller pieces. These pieces are called partitions.

Pascal

Named after the mathematician Blaise Pascal, Pascal is a language designed by Niklaus Wirth originally in 1968 (and heavily revised in 1972) mostly for purposes of education and training people how to write computer programs. It is a typically compiled language but is still usually slower than C or FORTRAN. Wirth also created a more powerful object-oriented Pascal-like language called Modula-2.

PC-DOS

The DOS produced by IBM designed to work like MS-DOS. Early versions of it bear striking similarities to the earlier CP/M, but it utilizes simpler commands. It provides only a CLI, but either Windows 3.1 or GEOS may be run on top of it to provide a GUI. It only runs on x86 based machines.

PCMCIA

The **P**ersonal **C**omputer **M**emory **C**ard **I**nternational **A**ssociation is a standards body that concern themselves with PC Card technology. Often the PC Cards themselves are referred to as "PCMCIA cards". Frequently flash memory can be found in PC card form.

Perl

Perl is an interpreted language extremely popular for web applications.

PET

The Commodore PET (**P**ersonal **E**lectronic **T**ransactor) is an early (circa 1977-1980, around the same time as the Apple][) home computer featuring a ROM-based BASIC developed by Microsoft which it uses as a default "OS". It is based on the 65xx family of processors and is the precursor to the VIC-20.

PETSCII

The PETSCII character set gets its name from "**PET ASCII**; it is a variant of the ASCII character set originally developed for the Commodore PET that swaps the upper and lower case characters and adds over a hundred graphic characters in addition to other small changes. If you encounter some text that seems to have uppercase where lowercase is expected and vice-versa, it is probably a PETSCII file.

PHP

Named with a recursive acronym (PHP: Hypertext Preprocessor), PHP provides a means of creating web pages that dynamically modify themselves on the fly.

ping

Ping is a protocol designed to check across a network to see if a particular computer is "alive" or not. Computers that recognize the ping will report back their status. Computers that are down will not report back anything at all.

pixel

The smallest distinct point on a computer display is called a pixel.

plug-in

A plug-in is a piece of software designed not to run on its own but rather work in cooperation with a separate application to increase that application's abilities.

point

There are two common meanings for this word. The first is in the geometric sense; a position in space without size. Of course as applied to computers it must take up some space in practise (even if not in theory) and it is thus sometimes synonomous with pixel. The other meaning is related most typically to fonts and regards size. The exact meaning of it in this sense will unfortunately vary somewhat from person to person, but will often mean 1/72 of an inch. Even when it does not exactly mean 1/72 of an inch, larger point sizes always indicate larger fonts.

PowerPC

The PowerPC is a RISC processor developed in a collaborative effort between IBM, Apple, and Motorola. It is currently produced by a few different companies, of course including its original developers. A few different OSes run on PowerPC based machines, including Mac OS, AIX, Solaris, Windows NT, Linux, Mac OS X, BeOS, and AmigaOS. At any given time, the fastest processor in the world is usually either a PowerPC or an Alpha, but sometimes SPARCs and PA-RISCs make the list, too.

proprietary

This simply means to be supplied by only one vendor. It is commonly misused. Currently, most processors are non-proprietary, some systems are non-proprietary, and every OS (except for arguably Linux) is proprietary.

protocol

A protocol is a means of communication used between computers. As long as both computers recognize the same protocol, they can communicate without too much difficulty over the same network or even via a simple direct modem connection regardless whether or not they are themselves of the same type. This means that WinTel boxes, Macs, Amigas, UNIX machines, etc., can all talk with one another provided they agree on a common protocol first.

Psion

The Psion is a fairly popular brand of PDA. Generally, it is in between a Palm and a Newton in capability. It runs the EPOC OS.

Python

Python is an interpreted, object-oriented language popular for Internet applications. It is extremely portable with free versions existing for virtually every platform.

queue

A queue is a waiting list of things to be processed. Many computers provide printing queues, for example. If something is being printed and the user requests that another item be printed, the second item will sit in the printer queue until the first item finishes printing at which point it will be removed from the queue and get printed itself.

QuickDraw

A high-level 3D graphics library with an emphasis on quick development time created by Apple.

RAM

Random **a**ccess **m**emory is the short-term memory of a computer. Any information stored in RAM will be lost if power goes out, but the computer can read from RAM far more quickly than from a drive.

random access

Also called "dynamic access" this indicates that data can be selected without having to skip over earlier data first. This is the way that a CD, record, laserdisc, or DVD will behave -- it is easy to selectively play a particular track without having to fast forward through earlier tracks. The other common behavior is called sequential access.

RDF

The **R**esource **D**escription **F**ramework is built upon an XML base and provides a more modern means of accessing data from Internet resources. It can provide metadata (including annotations) for web pages making (among other things) searching more capable. It is also being used to refashion some existing formats like RSS and iCalendar; in the former case it is already in place (at least for newer RSS versions), but it is still experimental in the latter case.

real-time

Something that happens in real-time will keep up with the events around it and never give any sort of "please wait" message.

Rexx

The **R**estructured **Ex**tended Executor is an interpreted language designed primarily to be embedded in other applications in order to make them consistently programmable, but also to be easy to learn and understand.

RISC

Reduced **i**nstruction **s**et **c**omputing is one of the two main types of processor design in use today, the other being CISC. The fastest processors in the world today are all RISC designs. There are several popular RISC processors, including Alphas, ARMs, PA-RISCs, PowerPCs, and SPARCs.

robot

A robot (or 'bot for short) in the computer sense is a program designed to automate some task, often just sending messages or collecting information. A spider is a type of robot designed to traverse the web performing some task (usually collecting data).

robust

The adjective robust is used to describe programs that are better designed, have fewer bugs, and are less likely to crash.

ROM

Read-only memory is similar to RAM only cannot be altered and does not lose its contents when power is removed.

RSS

RSS stands for either Rich Site Summary, Really Simple Syndication, or RDF Site Summary, depending upon whom you ask. The general idea is that it can provide brief summaries of articles that appear in full on a web site. It is well-formed XML, and newer versions are even more specifically well-formed RDF.

Ruby

Ruby is an interpreted, object-oriented language. Ruby was fairly heavily influenced by Perl, so people familiar with that language can typically transition to Ruby easily.

scanner

A scanner is a piece of hardware that will examine a picture and produce a computer file that represents what it sees. A digital camera is a related device. Each has its own limitations.

Scheme

Scheme is a typically interpreted computer language. It was created in 1975 in an attempt to make Lisp simpler and more consistent. Scheme is a fairly portable language, but is not particularly fast.

script

A script is a series of OS commands. The term "batch file" means much the same thing, but is a bit dated. Typically the same sort of situations in which one would say DOS instead of OS, it would also be appropriate to say batch file instead of script. Scripts can be run like programs, but tend to perform simpler tasks. When a script is run, it is always interpreted.

SCSI

Loosely speaking, a disk format sometimes used by MS-Windows, Mac OS, AmigaOS, and (almost always) UNIX. Generally SCSI is superior (but more expensive) to IDE, but it varies somewhat with system load and the individual SCSI and IDE components themselves. The quick rundown is that: SCSI-I and SCSI-II will almost always outperform IDE; EIDE will almost always outperform SCSI-I and SCSI-II; SCSI-III and UltraSCSI will almost always outperform EIDE; and heavy system loads give an advantage to SCSI. Note that although loosely speaking it is just a format difference, it is deep down a hardware difference.

sequential access

This indicates that data cannot be selected without having to skip over earlier data first. This is the way that a cassette or video tape will behave. The other common behavior is called random access.

serial

Loosely speaking, serial implies something that has to be done linearly, one at a time, like people being served in a single check-out line. Serial connections are by their nature less expensive than parallel connections (including things like SCSI) but are typically slower.

server

A server is a computer designed to provide various services for an entire network. It is typically either a workstation or a mainframe because it will usually be expected to handle far greater loads than ordinary desktop systems. The load placed on servers also necessitates that they utilize robust OSes, as a crash on a system that is currently being used by many people is far worse than a crash on a system that is only being used by one person.

SGML

The **S**tandard **G**eneralized **M**ark-up **L**anguage provides an extremely generalized level of mark-up. More common mark-up languages like HTML and XML are actually just popular subsets of SGML.

shareware

Shareware is software made for profit that allows a trial period before purchase. Typically shareware can be freely downloaded, used for a period of weeks (or sometimes even months), and either purchased or discarded after it has been learned whether or not it will satisfy the user's needs.

shell

A CLI designed to simplify complex OS commands. Some OSes (like AmigaOS, the Hurd, and UNIX) have built-in support to make the concurrent use of multiple shells easy. Common shells include the Korn Shell (ksh), the Bourne Shell (sh or bsh), the Bourne-Again Shell, (bash or bsh), the C-Shell (csh), etc.

SIMM

A physical component used to add RAM to a computer. Similar to, but incompatible with, DIMMs.

Smalltalk

Smalltalk is an efficient language for writing computer programs. Historically it is one of the first object-oriented languages, and is not only used today in its pure form but shows its influence in other languages like Objective-C.

Solaris

Solaris is the commercial variant of UNIX currently produced by Sun. It is an industrial strength, nigh bulletproof, powerful multitasking OS that will run on SPARC, x86, and PowerPC based machines.

spam

Generally spam is unwanted, unrequested e-mail or Usenet news. It is typically sent out in bulk to huge address lists that were automatically generated by various robots endlessly searching the Internet and newsgroups for things that resemble e-mail addresses. The legality of spam is a topic of much debate; it is at best only borderline legal, and spammers have been successfully persecuted in some states.

SPARC

The SPARC is a RISC processor developed by Sun. The design was more or less released to the world, and it is currently produced by around a dozen different companies too numerous to even bother mentioning. It is worth noting that even computers made by Sun typically sport SPARCs made by other companies. A couple different OSes run on SPARC based machines, including Solaris, SunOS, and Linux. Some of the newer SPARC models are called UltraSPARCs.

sprite

The term sprite originally referred to a small MOB, usually implemented in hardware. Lately it is also being used to refer to a single image used piecemeal within a Web site in order to avoid incurring the time penalty of downloading multiple files.

SQL

SQL (pronounced **Sequel**) is an interpreted language specially designed for database access. It is supported by virtually every major modern database system.

Sugar

The window manager used by the OLPC XO. It is made to run on top of Linux.

SunOS

SunOS is the commercial variant of UNIX formerly produced (but still supported) by Sun.

SVG

Scalable Vector Graphics data is an XML file that is used to hold graphical data that can be resized without loss of quality. SVG data can be kept in its own file, or even embedded within a web page (although not all browsers are capable of displaying such data).

Tcl/Tk

The Tool Command Language is a portable interpreted computer language designed to be easy to use. Tk is a GUI toolkit for Tcl. Tcl is a fairly popular language for both integrating existing applications and for creating Web applets (note that applets written in Tcl are often called Tcklets). Tcl/Tk is available for free for most platforms, and plug-ins are available to enable many browsers to play Tcklets.

TCP/IP

TCP/IP is a protocol for computer networks. The Internet is largely built on top of TCP/IP (it is the more reliable of the two primary Internet Protocols -- TCP stands for Transmission Control Protocol).

terminator

A terminator is a dedicated device used to mark the end of a device chain (as is most typically found with SCSI devices). If such a chain is not properly terminated, weird results can occur.

TEX

TEX (pronounced "tek") is a freely available, industrial strength typesetting program that can be run on many different platforms. These qualities make it exceptionally popular in schools, and frequently software developed at a university will have its documentation in TEX format. TEX is not limited to educational use, though; many professional books were typeset with TEX. TEX's primary drawback is that it can be quite difficult to set up initially.

THz & terahertz

One terahertz is equivalent to 1000 gigahertz.

TrackBack

TrackBacks essentially provide a means whereby different web sites can post messages to one another not just to inform each other about citations, but also to alert one another of related resources. Typically, a blog may display quotations from another blog through the use of TrackBacks.

UDP/IP

UDP/IP is a protocol for computer networks. It is the faster of the two primary Internet Protocols. UDP stands for User Datagram Protocol.

Unicode

The Unicode character set is a superset of the ASCII character set with provisions made for handling international symbols and characters from other languages. Unicode is sixteen bit, so takes up roughly twice the space as simple ASCII, but is correspondingly more flexible.

UNIX

UNIX is a family of OSes, each being made by a different company or organization but all offering a very similar look and feel. It can not quite be considered non-proprietary, however, as the differences between different vendor's versions can be significant (it is still generally possible to switch from one vendor's UNIX to another without too much effort; today the differences between different UNIXes are similar to the differences between the different MS-Windows; historically there were two different UNIX camps, Berkeley / BSD and AT&T / System V, but the assorted vendors have worked together to minimalize the differences). The free variant Linux is one of the closest things to a current, non-proprietary OS; its development is controlled by a non-profit organization and its distribution is provided by several companies. UNIX is powerful; it is fully multitasking and can do pretty much anything that any OS can do (look to the Hurd if you need a more powerful OS). With power comes complexity, however, and

UNIX tends not to be overly friendly to beginners (although those who think UNIX is difficult or cryptic apparently have not used CP/M). Window managers are available for UNIX (running under X-Windows) and once properly configured common operations will be almost as simple on a UNIX machine as on a Mac. Out of all the OSes in current use, UNIX has the greatest range of hardware support. It will run on machines built around many different processors. Lightweight versions of UNIX have been made to run on PDAs, and in the other direction, full featured versions make full advantage of all the resources on large, multi-processor machines. Some different UNIX versions include Solaris, Linux, IRIX, AIX, SunOS, FreeBSD, Digital UNIX, HP-UX, NetBSD, OpenBSD, etc.

upload

To upload a file is to copy it from your computer to a remote computer. The opposite is download.

UPS

An **u**ninterrupted **p**ower **s**upply uses heavy duty batteries to help smooth out its input power source.

URI

A **U**niform **R**esource **I**dentifier is basically just a unique address for almost any type of resource. It is similar to but more general than a URL; in fact, it may also be a URN.

URL

A **U**niform **R**esource **L**ocator is basically just an address for a file that can be given to a browser. It starts with a protocol type (such as http, ftp, or gopher) and is followed by a colon, machine name, and file name in UNIX style. Optionally an octothorpe character "#" and and arguments will follow the file name; this can be used to further define position within a page and perform a few other tricks. Similar to but less general than a URI.

URN

A **U**niform **R**esource **N**ame is basically just a unique address for almost any type of resource unlike a URL it will probably not resolve with a browser.

USB

A really fast type of serial port that offers many of the best features of SCSI without the price. Faster than many types of parallel port, a single USB port is capable of chaining many devices without the need of a terminator. USB is much slower (but somewhat less expensive) than FireWire.

uucode

The point of uucode is to allow 8-bit binary data to be transferred through the more common 7-bit ASCII channels (most especially e-mail). The facilities for dealing with uucoded files exist for many different machine types, and the most common programs are called "uuencode" for encoding the original binary file into a 7-bit file and "uudecode" for restoring the original binary file from the encoded one. Sometimes different uuencode and uudecode programs will work in subtly different manners causing annoying compatibility problems. Bcode was invented to provide the same service as uucode but to maintain a tighter standard.

variable width

As applied to a font, variable width means that different characters will have different widths as appropriate. For example, an "i" will take up much less space than an "m". The opposite of variable width is fixed width. The terms "proportional width" and "proportionally spaced" mean the same thing as variable width. Some common variable width fonts include Times, Helvetica, and Bookman.

VAX

The VAX is a computer platform developed by Digital. Its plural is VAXen. VAXen are large expensive machines that were once quite popular in large businesses; today modern UNIX workstations have all the capability of VAXen but take up much less space. Their OS is called VMS.

vector

This term has two common meanings. The first is in the geometric sense: a vector defines a direction and magnitude. The second concerns the formatting of fonts and images. If a font is a vector font or an image is a vector image, it is defined as lines of relative size and direction rather than as collections of pixels (the method used in bitmapped fonts and images). This makes it easier to change the size of the font or image, but puts a bigger load on the device that has to display the font or image. The term "outline font" means the same thing as vector font.

Veronica & Veronica2

Although traditionally written as a proper name, Veronica is actually an acronym for "**v**ery **e**asy **r**odent-**o**riented **n**etwide **i**ndex to **c**omputerized **a**rchives", where the "rodent" refers to gopher. The acronym was obviously a little forced to go along with the pre-existing (and now largely unused) Archie, in order to have a little fun with a comic book reference. Regardless, Veronica (or these days more likely Veronica2) is essentially a search engine for gopher resources.

VIC-20

The Commodore VIC-20 computer sold millions of units and is generally considered to have been the first affordable home computer. It features a ROM-based BASIC and uses it as a default "OS". It is based on the 65xx family of processors. VIC (in case you are wondering) can stand for either **v**ideo **i**nterface **c** or **v**ideo **i**nterface **c**omputer. The VIC-20 is the precursor to the C64/128.

virtual machine

A virtual machine is a machine completely defined and implemented in software rather than hardware. It is often referred to as a "runtime environment"; code compiled for such a machine is typically called bytecode.

virtual memory

This is a scheme by which disk space is made to substitute for the more expensive RAM space. Using it will often enable a comptuer to do things it could not do without it, but it will also often result in an overall slowing down of the system. The concept of swap space is very similar.

virtual reality

Virtual reality (often called VR for short) is generally speaking an attempt to provide more natural, human interfaces to software. It can be as simple as a pseudo 3D interface or as elaborate as an isolated room in which the computer can control the user's senses of vision, hearing, and even smell and touch.

virus

A virus is a program that will seek to duplicate itself in memory and on disks, but in a subtle way that will not immediately be noticed. A computer on the same network as an infected computer or that uses an infected disk (even a floppy) or that downloads and runs an infected program can itself become infected. A virus can only spread to computers of the same platform. For example, on a network consisting of a WinTel box, a Mac, and a Linux box, if one machine acquires a virus the other two will probably still be safe. Note also that different platforms have different general levels of resistance; UNIX machines are almost immune, Win '95 / '98 / ME / XP is quite vulnerable, and most others lie somewhere in between.

VMS

The industrial strength OS that runs on VAXen.

VoIP

VoIP means "Voice over IP" and it is quite simply a way of utilizing the Internet (or even in some cases intranets) for telephone conversations. The primary motivations for doing so are cost and convenience as VoIP is significantly less expensive than typical telephone long distance packages, plus one high speed Internet connection can serve for multiple phone lines.

VRML

A **V**irtual **R**eality **M**odeling **L**anguage file is used to represent VR objects. It has essentially been superceded by X3D.

W3C

The World Wide Web Consortium (usually abbreviated W3C) is a non-profit, advisory body that makes suggestions on the future direction of the World Wide Web, HTML, CSS, and browsers.

Waba

An extremely lightweight subset of Java optimized for use on PDAs.

WebDAV

WebDAV stands for Web-based Distributed Authoring and Versioning, and is designed to provide a way of editing Web-based resources in place. It serves as a more modern (and often more secure) replacement for FTP in many cases.

WebTV

A WebTV box hooks up to an ordinary television set and displays web pages. It will not display them as well as a dedicated computer.

window manager

A window manager is a program that acts as a graphical go-between for a user and an OS. It provides a GUI for the OS. Some OSes incorporate the window manager into their own internal code, but many do not for reasons of efficiency. Some OSes partially make the division. Some common true window managers include CDE (Common Desktop Environment), GNOME, KDE, Aqua, OpenWindows, Motif, FVWM, Sugar, and Enlightenment. Some common hybrid window managers with OS extensions include Windows ME, Windows 98, Windows 95, Windows 3.1, OS/2 and GEOS.

Windows '95

Windows '95 is currently the second most popular variant of MS-Windows. It was designed to be the replacement Windows 3.1 but has not yet done so completely partly because of suspected security problems but even more because it is not as lightweight and will not work on all the machines that Windows 3.1 will. It is more capable than Windows 3.1 though and now has excellent driver support and more games available for it than any other platform. It is made to run on top of MS-DOS and will not do much of anything if MS-DOS is not on the system. It is thus not strictly an OS per se, but nor is it a true window manager either; rather the combination of MS-DOS and Windows '95 result in a full OS with GUI. It is partially multitasking but has a much greater chance of crashing than Windows NT does (or probably even Mac OS) if faced with a buggy program. Windows '95 runs only on x86 based machines. Currently Windows '95 has several Y2K issues, some of which have patches that can be downloaded for free, and some of which do not yet have fixes at all.

Windows '98

Windows '98 is quite possibly the second most popular form of MS-Windows, in spite of the fact that its official release is currently a point of legal debate with at least nineteen states, the federal government, and a handful of foreign countries as it has a few questionable features that might restrict the novice computer user and/or unfairly compete with other computer companies. It also has some specific issues with the version of Java that comes prepackaged with it that has never been adequately fixed, and it still has several Y2K issues, most of which have patches that can be downloaded for free (in fact, Microsoft guarantees that it will work properly through 2000 with the proper patches), but some of which do not yet have fixes at all (it won't work properly through 2001 at this point). In any case, it was designed to replace Windows '95.

Windows 2000

Windows 2000 was the intended replacement for Windows NT and in that capacity received relatively lukewarm support. Being based on Windows NT, it inherits some of its driver support problems. Originally it was also supposed to replace Windows '98, but Windows ME was made to do that instead, and the merger between Windows NT and Windows '98 was postponed until Windows XP.

Windows 3.1

Windows 3.1 remains a surprisingly popular variant of MS-Windows. It is lighter weight than either Windows '95 or Windows NT (but not lighter weight than GEOS) but less capable than the other two. It is made to run on top of MS-DOS and will not do much of anything if MS-DOS is not on the system. It is thus not strictly an OS per se, but nor is it a true window manager, either; rather the combination of MS-DOS and Windows 3.1 result in a full OS with GUI. Its driver support is good, but its game selection is limited. Windows 3.1 runs only on x86 based machines. It has some severe Y2K issues that may or may not be fixed.

Windows CE

Windows CE is the lightweight variant of MS-Windows. It offers the general look and feel of Windows '95 but is targetted primarily for hand-held devices, PDAs, NCs, and embedded devices. It does not have all the features of either Windows '95 or Windows NT and is very different from Windows 3.1. In particular, it will not run any software made for any of the other versions of MS-Windows. Special versions of each program must be made. Furthermore, there are actually a few slightly different variants of Windows CE, and no variant is guaranteed to be able to run software made specifically for another one. Driver support is also fairly poor for all types, and few games are made for it. Windows CE will run on a few different processor types, including the x86 and several different processors dedicated to PDAs, embedded systems, and hand-held devices.

Windows ME

Windows ME is yet another flavor of MS-Windows (specifically the planned replacement for Windows '98). Windows ME currently runs only on the x86 processor.

Windows NT

Windows NT is the industrial-strength variant of MS-Windows. Current revisions offer the look and feel of Windows '95 and older revisions offer the look and feel of Windows 3.1. It is the most robust flavor of MS-Windows and is fully multitasking. It is also by far the most expensive flavor of MS-Windows and has far less software available for it than Windows '95 or '98. In particular, do not expect to play many games on a Windows NT machine, and expect some difficulty in obtaining good drivers. Windows NT will run on a few different processor types, including the x86, the Alpha, and the PowerPC. Plans are in place to port Windows NT to the Merced when it becomes available.

Windows Vista

Windows Vista is the newest flavor of MS-Windows (specifically the planned replacement for Windows XP). Windows Vista (originally known as Longhorn) currently only runs on x86 processors.

Windows XP

Windows XP is yet another flavor of MS-Windows (specifically the planned replacement for both Windows ME and Windows 2000). Windows XP currently only runs on the x86 processors. Windows XP is currently the most popular form of MS-Windows.

WinTel

An x86 based system running some flavor of MS-Windows.

workstation

Depending upon whom you ask, a workstation is either an industrial strength desktop computer or its own category above the desktops. Workstations typically have some flavor of UNIX for their OS, but there has been a recent trend to call high-end Windows NT and Windows 2000 machines workstations, too.

WYSIWYG

What **y**ou **s**ee **is w**hat **y**ou **g**et; an adjective applied to a program that attempts to exactly represent printed output on the screen. Related to WYSIWYM but quite different.

WYSIWYM

What **y**ou **s**ee **is w**hat **y**ou **m**ean; an adjective applied to a program that does not attempt to exactly represent printed output on the screen, but rather defines how things are used and so will adapt to different paper sizes, etc. Related to WYSIWYG but quite different.

X-Face

X-Faces are small monochrome images embedded in headers for both provides a e-mail and news messages. Better mail and news applications will display them (sometimes automatically, sometimes only per request).

X-Windows

X-Windows provides a GUI for most UNIX systems, but can also be found as an add-on library for other computers. Numerous window managers run on top of it. It is often just called "X".

X3D

Extensible **3D** Graphics data is an XML file that is used to hold three-dimensional graphical data. It is the successor to VRML.

x86

The x86 series of processors includes the Pentium, Pentium Pro, Pentium II, Pentium III, Celeron, and Athlon as well as the 786, 686, 586, 486, 386, 286, 8086, 8088, etc. It is an exceptionally popular design (by far the most popular CISC series) in spite of the fact that even its fastest model is significantly slower than the assorted RISC processors. Many different OSes run on machines built around x86 processors, including MS-DOS, Windows 3.1, Windows '95, Windows '98, Windows ME, Windows NT, Windows 2000, Windows CE, Windows XP, GEOS, Linux, Solaris, OpenBSD, NetBSD, FreeBSD, Mac OS X, OS/2, BeOS, CP/M, etc. A couple different companies produce x86 processors, but the bulk of them are produced by Intel. It is expected that this processor will eventually be completely replaced by the Merced, but the Merced development schedule is somewhat behind. Also, it should be noted that the Pentium III processor has stirred some controversy by including a "fingerprint" that will enable individual computer usage of web pages etc. to be accurately tracked.

XBL

An XML Binding Language document is used to associate executable content with an XML tag. It is itself an XML file, and is used most frequently (although not exclusively) in conjunction with XUL.

XHTML

The Extensible **H**ypertext **M**ark-up **L**anguage is essentially a cleaner, stricter version of HTML. It is a proper subset of XML.

XML

The Extensible **M**ark-up **L**anguage is a subset of SGML and a superset of XHTML. It is used for numerous things including (among many others) RSS and RDF.

XML-RPC

XML-RPC provides a fairly lightweight means by which one computer can execute a program on a co-operating machine across a network like the Internet. It is based on XML and is used for everything from fetching stock quotes to checking weather forcasts.

XO

The energy-efficient, kid-friendly laptop produced by the OLPC project. It runs Sugar for its window manager and Linux for its OS. It sports numerous built-in features like wireless networking, a video camera & microphone, a few USB ports, and audio in/out jacks. It comes with several educational applications (which it refers to as "Activities"), most of which are written in Python.

XSL

The Extensible Stylesheet Language is like CSS for XML. It provides a means of describing how an XML resource should be displayed.

XSLT

XSL Transformations are used to transform one type of XML into another. It is a component of XSL that can be (and often is) used independently.

XUL

An XML User-Interface Language document is used to define a user interface for an application using XML to specify the individual controls as well as the overall layout.

Y2K

The general class of problems resulting from the wrapping of computers' internal date timers is given this label in honor of the most obvious occurrence -- when the year changes from 1999 to 2000 (abbreviated in some programs as 99 to 00 indicating a backwards time movement). Contrary to popular belief, these problems will not all manifest themselves on the first day of 2000, but will in fact happen over a range of dates extending out beyond 2075. A computer that does not have problems prior to the beginning of 2001 is considered "Y2K compliant", and a computer that does not have problems within the next ten years or so is considered for all practical purposes to be "Y2K clean". Whether or not a given computer is "clean" depends upon both its OS and its applications (and in some unfortunate cases, its hardware). The quick rundown on common home / small business machines (roughly from best to worst) is that:

   All Mac OS systems are okay until at least the year 2040. By that time a patch should be
      available.
   All BeOS systems are okay until the year 2040 (2038?). By that time a patch should be
      available.
   Most UNIX versions are either okay or currently have free fixes available (and typically would
      not have major problems until 2038 or later in any case).
   NewtonOS has a problem with the year 2010, but has a free fix available.
   Newer AmigaOS systems are okay; older ones have a problem with the year 2000 but have a
      free fix available. They also have a year 2077 problem that does not yet have a free fix.
   Some OS/2 systems have a year 2000 problem, but free fixes are available.
   All CP/M versions have a year 2000 problem, but free fixes are available.
   PC-DOS has a year 2000 problem, but a free fix is available.
   DR-DOS has a year 2000 problem, but a free fix is available.
   Different versions of GEOS have different problems ranging from minor year 2000 problems
      (with fixes in the works) to larger year 2080 problems (that do not have fixes yet). The
      only problem that may not have a fix in time is the year 2000 problem on the Apple][
      version of GEOS; not only was that version discontinued, unlike the other GEOS
      versions it no longer has a parent company to take care of it.
   All MS-Windows versions (except possibly Windows 2000 and Windows ME) have multiple
      problems with the year 2000 and/or 2001, most of which have free fixes but some of
      which still lack free fixes as of this writing. Even new machines off the shelf that are
      labelled "Y2K Compliant" usually are not unless additional software is purchased and
      installed. Basically WinNT and WinCE can be properly patched, Windows '98 can be
      patched to work properly through 2000 (possibly not 2001), Windows '95 can be at least
      partially patched for 2000 (but not 2001) but is not being guaranteed by Microsoft, and
      Windows 3.1 cannot be fully patched.
   MS-DOS has problems with at least the year 2000 (and probably more). None of its problems
      have been addressed as of this writing. Possible fixes are to change over to either PC-
      DOS or DR-DOS.

Results vary wildly for common applications, so it is better to be safe than sorry and check out the ones that you use. It should also be noted that some of the biggest expected Y2K problems will be at the two ends of the computer spectrum with older legacy mainframes (such as power some large banks) and some of the various tiny embedded computers (such as power most burgler alarms and many assorted appliances). Finally, it should also be mentioned that some older WinTel boxes and Amigas may have Y2K problems in their hardware requiring a card addition or replacement.

Z-Machine

A virtual machine optimized for running interactive fiction, interactive tutorials, and other interactive things of a primarily textual nature. Z-Machines have been ported to almost every platform in use today. Z-machine bytecode is usually called Z-code. The Glulx virtual machine is of the same idea but somewhat more modern in concept.

Z80

The Z80 series of processors is a CISC design and is not being used in too many new stand-alone computer systems, but can still be occasionally found in embedded systems. It is the most popular processor for CP/M machines.

Zaurus

The Zaurus is a brand of PDA. It is generally in between a Palm and a Newton in capability.

zip

There are three common zips in the computer world that are completely different from one another. One is a type of removable removable disk slightly larger (physically) and vastly larger (capacity) than a floppy. The second is a group of programs used for running interactive fiction. The third is a group of programs used for compression.

Zoomer

The Zoomer is a type of PDA. Zoomers all use GEOS for their OS and are / were produced by numerous different companies and are thus found under numerous different names. The "classic" Zoomers are known as the Z-7000, the Z-PDA, and the GRiDpad and were made by Casio, Tandy, and AST respectively. Newer Zoomers include HP's OmniGo models, Hyundai's Gulliver (which may not have actually been released to the general public), and Nokia's Communicator line of PDA / cell phone hybrids.

ANSWER SHEET

NO. _____ PART _____ TITLE OF POSITION _____

CE OF EXAMINATION _____ DATE _____

(CITY OR TOWN)　　　　　　　　　　(STATE)

RATING

USE THE SPECIAL PENCIL.　MAKE GLOSSY BLACK MARKS.

	A B C D E		A B C D E		A B C D E		A B C D E		A B C D E
1		26		51		76		101	
2		27		52		77		102	
3		28		53		78		103	
4		29		54		79		104	
5		30		55		80		105	
6		31		56		81		106	
7		32		57		82		107	
8		33		58		83		108	
9		34		59		84		109	
10		35		60		85		110	

Make only ONE mark for each answer.　Additional and stray marks may be
counted as mistakes.　In making corrections, erase errors COMPLETELY.

	A B C D E		A B C D E		A B C D E		A B C D E		A B C D E
11		36		61		86		111	
12		37		62		87		112	
13		38		63		88		113	
14		39		64		89		114	
15		40		65		90		115	
16		41		66		91		116	
17		42		67		92		117	
18		43		68		93		118	
19		44		69		94		119	
20		45		70		95		120	
21		46		71		96		121	
22		47		72		97		122	
23		48		73		98		123	
24		49		74		99		124	
25		50		75		100		125	

ANSWER SHEET

TEST NO. ____________ PART ______ TITLE OF POSITION ______________________________
(AS GIVEN IN EXAMINATION ANNOUNCEMENT - INCLUDE OPTION, IF ANY)

PLACE OF EXAMINATION ______________________________ ______________ DATE ______________
(CITY OR TOWN) (STATE)

RATING

USE THE SPECIAL PENCIL. MAKE GLOSSY BLACK MARKS.

1 A B C D E	26 A B C D E	51 A B C D E	76 A B C D E	101 A B C D E
2 A B C D E	27 A B C D E	52 A B C D E	77 A B C D E	102 A B C D E
3 A B C D E	28 A B C D E	53 A B C D E	78 A B C D E	103 A B C D E
4 A B C D E	29 A B C D E	54 A B C D E	79 A B C D E	104 A B C D E
5 A B C D E	30 A B C D E	55 A B C D E	80 A B C D E	105 A B C D E
6 A B C D E	31 A B C D E	56 A B C D E	81 A B C D E	106 A B C D E
7 A B C D E	32 A B C D E	57 A B C D E	82 A B C D E	107 A B C D E
8 A B C D E	33 A B C D E	58 A B C D E	83 A B C D E	108 A B C D E
9 A B C D E	34 A B C D E	59 A B C D E	84 A B C D E	109 A B C D E
10 A B C D E	35 A B C D E	60 A B C D E	85 A B C D E	110 A B C D E

Make only ONE mark for each answer. Additional and stray marks may be counted as mistakes. In making corrections, erase errors COMPLETELY.

11 A B C D E	36 A B C D E	61 A B C D E	86 A B C D E	111 A B C D E
12 A B C D E	37 A B C D E	62 A B C D E	87 A B C D E	112 A B C D E
13 A B C D E	38 A B C D E	63 A B C D E	88 A B C D E	113 A B C D E
14 A B C D E	39 A B C D E	64 A B C D E	89 A B C D E	114 A B C D E
15 A B C D E	40 A B C D E	65 A B C D E	90 A B C D E	115 A B C D E
16 A B C D E	41 A B C D E	66 A B C D E	91 A B C D E	116 A B C D E
17 A B C D E	42 A B C D E	67 A B C D E	92 A B C D E	117 A B C D E
18 A B C D E	43 A B C D E	68 A B C D E	93 A B C D E	118 A B C D E
19 A B C D E	44 A B C D E	69 A B C D E	94 A B C D E	119 A B C D E
20 A B C D E	45 A B C D E	70 A B C D E	95 A B C D E	120 A B C D E
21 A B C D E	46 A B C D E	71 A B C D E	96 A B C D E	121 A B C D E
22 A B C D E	47 A B C D E	72 A B C D E	97 A B C D E	122 A B C D E
23 A B C D E	48 A B C D E	73 A B C D E	98 A B C D E	123 A B C D E
24 A B C D E	49 A B C D E	74 A B C D E	99 A B C D E	124 A B C D E
25 A B C D E	50 A B C D E	75 A B C D E	100 A B C D E	125 A B C D E